NATURE CHICAGOLAND

MORE THAN 120 FANTASTIC NATURE DESTINATIONS THAT YOU MUST VISIT

BY ANDREW MORKES

Nature in Chicagoland Press LLC
Chicago, Illinois

Library of Congress Cataloging-in-Publication Data
Names: Morkes, Andrew, author.
Title: Nature in Chicagoland : more than 120 fantastic nature destinations that you must visit / by Andrew Morkes.
Description: Chicago, Illinois : College & Career Press LLC/Nature in Chicagoland Press LLC, [2022] | Includes bibliographical references and index. | Summary: "Nature in Chicagoland: More Than 120 Fantastic Nature Destinations That You Must Visit is a great resource for nature newbies, lifelong residents who are tired of visiting the same old nature spots, those looking for something to do during the pandemic, and tourists seeking some outdoor adventures. Destinations include forest preserves; nature centers; city, state, and national parks; beaches; tallgrass prairies; wetlands; scenic rivers; and much more in Chicagoland and the nearby states of Indiana, Michigan, and Wisconsin. In these places you'll get the chance to explore forests, wetlands, beaches, savanna, and other ecosystems. Nature in Chicagoland offers information on the following places and activities: Nature Centers; Hiking Trails; Day & Weekend Road Trips; Kids Activities; Camping Spots; Birdwatching Hotspots; Bicycling Trails; Kayaking/Canoeing/Boating; Picnicking Spots; Fishing; Spring Wildflower Viewing; Fall Colors Viewing; Running/Exercise; Winter Activities Such as Snowshoeing, Ice Skating, Cross-Country Skiing, Sledding, and Ice Fishing; Local History; Self-Enrichment Classes and Other Opportunities; and Geo650caching. Nature in Chicagoland also includes articles that provide advice on camping with kids, enjoying a successful snowshoeing adventure, and much more, as well as personal essays about gardening, enjoying nature with one's children, savoring the fall colors, and protecting the environment. Other resources include contact information for forest preserve districts, state departments of natural resources, and environmental and other nature-focused organizations"-- Provided by publisher.
Identifiers: LCCN 2021013847 | ISBN 9780982921050 (paperback)
Subjects: LCSH: Outdoor recreation--Illinois--Chicago Region--Guidebooks. | Ecotourism--Illinois--Chicago Region--Guidebooks. | Chicago Region (Ill.)--Guidebooks.
Classification: LCC GV191.42.I3 M67 2022 | DDC 796.50977311--dc23
LC record available at https://lccn.loc.gov/2021013847

Published and distributed by:
Nature in Chicagoland Press LLC (a subsidiary of College & Career Press, LLC)
PO Box 300484
Chicago, IL 60630
amorkes@chicagopa.com
www.ccpnewsletters.com

Copyright © 2022 College & Career Press, LLC
ISBN 13: 978-0-9829210-5-0
All rights reserved. No part of this publication may be reproduced, stored in an electronic retrieval system, or transmitted by any means, electronic, mechanical, photocopying, or otherwise, without the prior permission of the publisher.

Printed in the United States of America
21-06

© Amy McKenna

ABOUT THE AUTHOR

I have been a writer and editor for more than 25 years. I'm the founder of College & Career Press (2002); the editorial director of the *CAM Report* career newsletter and *College Spotlight* newsletter; the author and publisher of "The Morkes Report: College and Career Planning Trends" blog; and the author and publisher of *Hot Health Care Careers: 30 Occupations With Fast Growth and Many New Job Openings; Nontraditional Careers for Women and Men: More Than 30 Great Jobs for Women and Men With Apprenticeships Through PhDs; They Teach That in College!?: A Resource Guide to More Than 100 Interesting College Majors*, which was selected as one of the best books of the year by the library journal *Voice of Youth Advocates*; and other titles. *They Teach That in College!?* provides more information on environmental- and sustainability-related majors such as Ecotourism, Range Management, Renewable Energy, Sustainability and the Built Environment, Sustainability Studies, and Sustainable Agriculture/Organic Farming. I'm also a member of the parent advisory board at my son's school.

In addition to these publications, I've written more than 40 books about careers for other publishing and media companies including Infobase (such as the venerable *Encyclopedia of Careers & Vocational Guidance*, the *Vault Career Guide to Accounting*, and many volumes in the Careers in Focus, Discovering Careers, What Can I Do Now?!, and Career Skills Library series) and Mason Crest (including those in the Careers in the Building Trades, Cool Careers in Science, and Careers With Earnings Potential series).

My poetry has appeared in *Cadence, Wisconsin Review, Poetry Motel, Strong Coffee,* and *Mid-America Review.*

DEDICATION

This book is dedicated to my father (George Morkes) and mother (Marion Morkes). My dad, who died more than 20 years ago, taught me to appreciate nature and to love hiking and camping. This love of nature and outdoor activities has been like a special friend to me throughout my life. Hiking and camping have provided me with so many opportunities—to make new friends, escape the 9-to-5 world on solo trips, launch my *Nature in Chicagoland* blog (https://natureinchicago.wordpress.com), write this book, and discover amazing natural places. I've tried to pass this love on to my 11-year-old son. I've taken him camping since he was four, and hiking from the time he was a year old in our child carrier backpack. The outdoors is something my father and I shared, and now my son and I are doing the same—making memories and experiencing natural destinations in the Chicagoland area and beyond that most people never see. Thanks, dad, for helping to create a great family tradition that I hope my son passes on to his children. I wish I could share all of these adventures with you.

© Andrew Morkes

© Andrew Morkes

My mother is not a hiker, but she loves the outdoors. She is a magician when it comes to plants, flowers, and gardening, in general. She beautified her neighborhood of Beverly for more than 40 years with canna lilies, hostas, ornamental grasses, wildflowers, and much more—mostly at her own expense. At one time, my mom was doing the gardening for our local Metra station, grocery store, coffee shop, and cleaners, in addition to her own large yard. She even received an Honorable Mention in the City of Chicago`s Annual Garden & Block Contest in 1989. My mom has passed on her love of gardening, birds, and nature to me, and I am grateful for this and our continuing conversations about the natural world. Thanks, mom, for teaching me about nature and for always being there for me.

TABLE OF CONTENTS

This table of contents provides a "big picture" summary of the sections in *Nature in Chicagoland*. Visit pages 6 to 15 for detailed lists of the destinations in the book.

How to Use This Book 16
Introduction 18
Chicago Destinations 21
Chicagoland North Destinations 65
Chicagoland Northwest, West, and Beyond Destinations 81
Chicagoland South and Beyond Destinations 141
Indiana Destinations 223
Michigan Destinations 242
Wisconsin Destinations 267
Nature Essays 275
    8 Reasons Why I Love the Outdoors—and You Should, Too ...275
    18 Tips for Camping With Kids 278
    Nippersink Creek Provides a Great Kayaking or Canoeing Adventure Just an Hour From Chicago 283
    12 Tips for a Successful Winter Hike 287
    First-Time Snowshoer Tells All: 10 Tips for Success and My Son's Thank You 290
    On the Joys of Carrying My Son 293
Journals, Newsletters, and Books 295
Nature Organizations and Agencies 297
Index 299
Acknowledgments 304

CHICAGO MAP

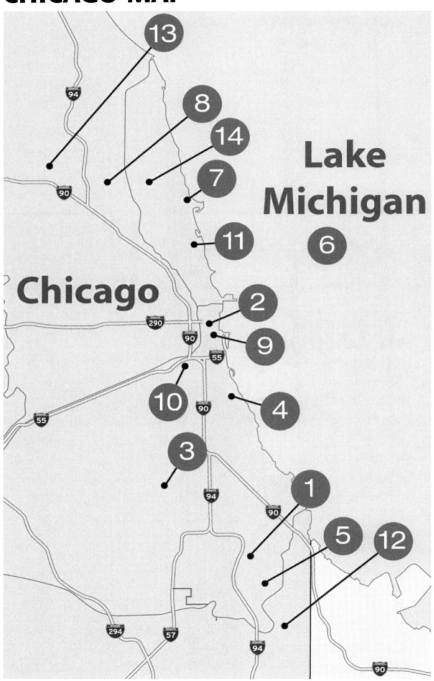

The quarry pond at Palmisano Park © Andrew Morkes

CHICAGO DESTINATIONS

Big Marsh Bike Park (#1 on map) 21
Chicago Riverwalk (#2 on map) 24
Dan Ryan Woods (#3 on map) 30
Garden of the Phoenix in Jackson Park (#4 on map) 34
Indian Ridge Marsh Park (#5 on map) 37
Lake Michigan (#6 on map) 41
Montrose Point Bird Sanctuary (#7 on map) 46
North Park Village Nature Center (#8 on map) 49
Outerbelt Trail (#9 on map) 51
Palmisano Park (#10 on map) 52
Peggy Notebaert Nature Museum (#11 on map) 56
Powderhorn Prairie, Marsh, and Lake (#12 on map) 58
Thaddeus S. "Ted" Lechowicz Woods (#13 on map) 61
West Ridge Nature Preserve (#14 on map) 63

CHICAGOLAND NORTH MAP

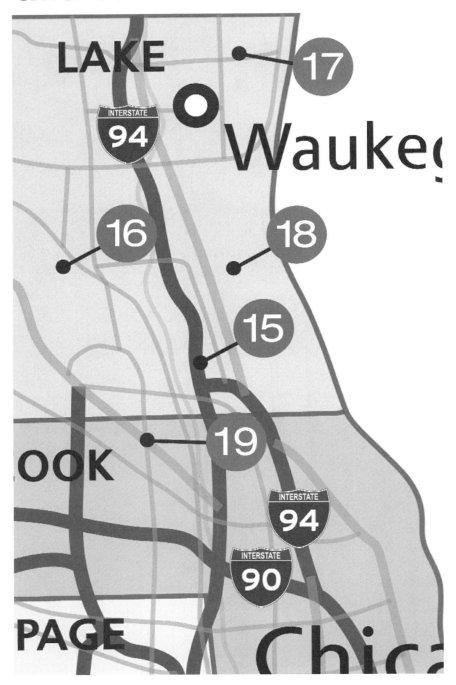

Edward L. Ryerson Woods © Andrew Morkes

CHICAGOLAND NORTH DESTINATIONS

Chicago Botanic Garden (#15 on map) 66
Edward L. Ryerson Woods (#16 on map) .70
Illinois Beach State Park (#17 on map) 73
Openlands Lakeshore Preserve (#18 on map) 75
River Trail Nature Center (#19 on map) 77

© Andrew Morkes

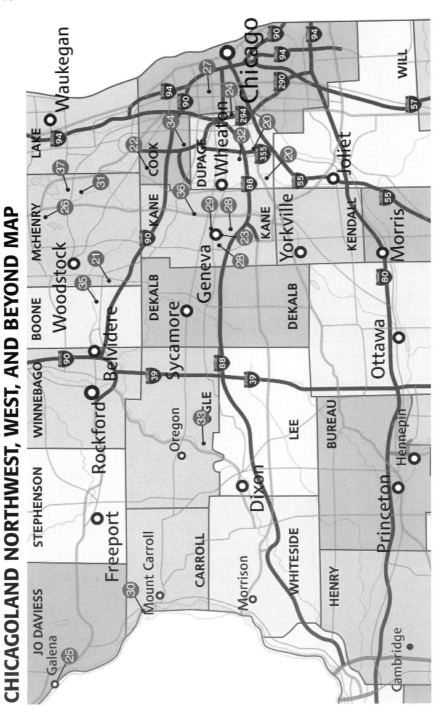

Wapello Land Reserve (in the Galena area) © Andrew Morkes

CHICAGOLAND NORTHWEST, WEST, AND BEYOND DESTINATIONS

Belmont Prairie (#20 on map) 81
Coral Woods Conservation Area (#21 on map) 85
Crabtree Nature Center (#22 on map) 87
Dick Young Forest Preserve (#23 on map) 90
Fullersburg Woods Nature Education Center (#24 on map) 94
Galena, Illinois (#25 on map) 97
Glacial Park (#26 on map) 104
Hal Tyrrell Trailside Museum of Natural History (#27 on map) ...107
Johnson's Mound Forest Preserve (#28 on map) 109
Leroy Oakes Forest Preserve (#29 on map) 112
Mississippi Palisades State Park (#30 on map) 115
Moraine Hills State Park (#31 on map) 117
Morton Arboretum (#32 on map) 120
Nachusa Grasslands (#33 on map) 125
Ned Brown Preserve (#34 on map) 131
Pleasant Valley Conservation Area (#35 on map) 133
Tekakwitha Woods Forest Preserve (#36 on map) 135
Volo Bog State Natural Area (#37 on map) 138

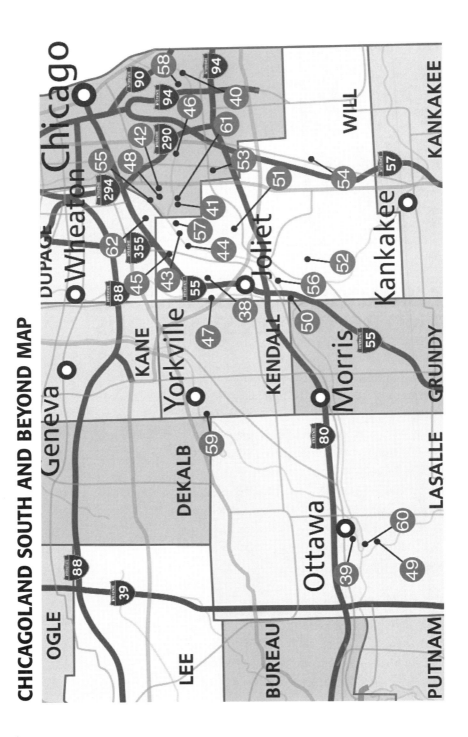

CHICAGOLAND SOUTH AND BEYOND DESTINATIONS

Black Partridge Woods (#38 on map) 141
Buffalo Rock State Park (#39 on map) 144
Burnham Prairie Nature Preserve (#40 on map) 147
Cap Sauer's Holding Nature Preserve (#41 on map) 149
Cranberry Slough Nature Preserve (#42 on map) 156
The Forge: Lemont Quarries (#43 on map) 158
Isle a la Cache Museum and Nature Preserve (#44 on map) 161
Keepataw Preserve (#45 on map) 164
Lake Katherine Nature Center and Botanic Gardens (#46 on map)
. 167
Lake Renwick Preserve and Heron Rookery Nature Preserve
(#47 on map) 170
Little Red Schoolhouse Nature Center (#48 on map) 175
Matthiessen State Park (#49 on map) 177
McKinley Woods (#50 on map) 181
Messenger Woods (#51 on map) 183
Midewin National Tallgrass Prairie (#52 on map) 187
Orland Grassland (#53 on map) 192
Raccoon Grove Nature Preserve (#54 on map) 195
Red Gate Woods (#55 on map) 197
Rock Run Rookery Preserve (#56 on map) 201
Sagawau Environmental Learning Center (#57 on map) 204
Sand Ridge Nature Center (#58 on map) 206
Silver Springs State Fish and Wildlife Area (#59 on map) 210
Starved Rock State Park (#60 on map) 212
Swallow Cliff Woods (#61 on map) 218
Waterfall Glen Forest Preserve (#62 on map) 220

INDIANA, MICHIGAN, AND WISCONSIN MAP

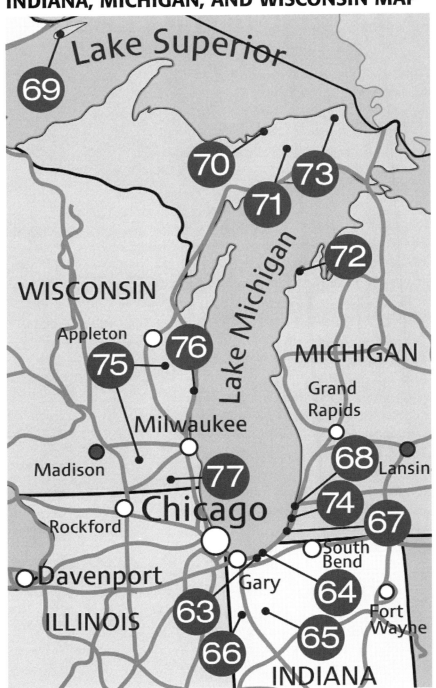

Miners Castle at Pictured Rocks National Lakeshore © Andrew Morkes

INDIANA, MICHIGAN, AND WISCONSIN DESTINATIONS

Indiana
Indiana Dunes National Park (#63 on map) 223
Indiana Dunes State Park (#64 on map) 227
Jasper-Pulaski Fish and Wildlife Area (#65 on map) 231
Kankakee Sands (#66 on map) 237
Michigan
Galien River County Park (#67 on map) 242
Grand Mere State Park (#68 on map) 244
Isle Royale National Park (#69 on map) 246
Pictured Rocks National Lakeshore (#70 on map) 250
Seney National Wildlife Refuge (#71 on map) 256
Sleeping Bear Dunes National Lakeshore (#72 on map) 259
Tahquamenon Falls State Park (#73 on map) 262
Warren Dunes State Park (#74 on map) 265
Wisconsin
Kettle Moraine State Forest (#75 on map) 267
Kohler-Andrae State Park (#76 on map) 270
Richard Bong State Recreation Area (#77 on map) 273

HOW TO USE THIS BOOK

Nature in Chicagoland has the following main sections.
Chicago Destinations
Chicagoland North Destinations
Chicagoland Northwest, West, and Beyond Destinations
Chicagoland South and Beyond Destinations
Indiana Destinations
Michigan Destinations
Wisconsin Destinations
Nature Essays

The regional and state sections list nature destinations that you can visit in that area. The essays provide advice on camping, hiking, and other topics, as well as share my experiences with my family in the natural world.

DESTINATION ARTICLE STRUCTURE

Opening Fact Box

Each destination article features an opening box that has the following format:

Where: The destination's address is listed. Mileage is provided for any destination that is more than 75 miles away from downtown Chicago.

Learn More: This section lists the name of the organization that manages the property, its telephone number (when available), and websites that you can visit to obtain more information.

Hours: This section lists the operating hours for the facility. Note that operating hours may vary by season, and there may be different operating hours for a destination's visitor center as compared to its grounds and hiking trails. Before your visit, be sure to check with the facility for its current operating hours.

Quick Review: This section provides a brief overview of what the destination has to offer, what type of natural environments (forest, beach, wetlands, etc.) you'll find there, and other facts. Most places in this book are free to visit, but I will tell you in this section if there is an admission fee or other user costs. People love bringing their dogs with them on their outdoor adventures, so I also note if your canine companions are allowed at the facility. At the end of this paragraph, the destination location number that is listed on the maps on pages 6-15 is listed.

What You Can Do There: In this section, I provide an alphabetical list of activities that you can do and facilities that you can visit at the destination. Here are the categories in this section: Archery Range, Backpacking, Beach Fun, Bicycling, Birdwatching, Bookstore, Camping, Canoeing/Kayaking/Boating, Cross-Country Skiing, Downhill Skiing, Dune Climbing, Educational and Self-Enrichment Opportunities and Classes, Fishing, General Store, Geocaching, Golf, Guided Tours, Hiking, Horseback Riding, Hot-Air Balloon Rides, Hunting, Ice

How to Use This Book 17

Skating, Lighthouse, Local History, Metal Detecting, Model Airplane Field, Model Train Exhibit, Museum, Orienteering Course, Photography, Picnicking, Restaurant, Running/Exercise, SCUBA Diving, Shipwrecks, Shops, Sledding, Snowmobiling, Snowshoeing, Swimming, Tram, Visitor Center.

MAIN ARTICLE

In the main article, I tell you about my experiences at the destination; discuss my favorite activities (hiking, camping, visitor center, etc.) and suggest activities that you might like; and provide other information that paints a picture of the nature spot and gives you the information that you need to know to plan your visit.

Each article concludes with a list of nearby places you can check out after completing your time at the destination(s) in the chapter. Most of these nearby destinations are within 10 miles of the primary destination but, in some instances, I include properties that are further away because they are "must visits" or because there are not many destinations within 10 miles of the original property.

Some articles feature sidebars that provide additional information about the history, flora or fauna, or non-nature destinations in the area.

COVID-19 AND THE GREAT OUTDOORS

The COVID-19 pandemic prompted many nature centers, state and national parks, forest preserves, and other organizations to reduce their hours, close some of their facilities, and incorporate physical distancing rules at facilities that remained open. Although we are hopefully on the tail end of the pandemic in the United States, some facilities remain closed or are operating with reduced hours. As a result, it's important that you check with the destination to determine its current operational status. You don't want to drive 30 miles to a state park only to realize that it has been closed due to the pandemic or other factors (e.g., flooding, storm damage, repairs/renovation). This should always be your approach—pandemic or no pandemic—because it never feels good to arrive to see a forest preserve parking lot chained shut or a closed sign in the window of a nature center that you expected to be open.

Disclaimer:

Every effort was made to make sure that the information presented in the book was accurate at the time of going to press. The author, Nature in Chicagoland Press LLC, and College & Career Press LLC do not assume and hereby disclaim any liability to anyone who reads this book who experiences damage, personal injury, or death caused by any errors and omissions in the book. All life activities (including those in the outdoors) involve some degree of risk, and readers must make every effort to reduce these risks by obtaining current information about destinations in the book, protecting their physical being and property when in nature areas, being extremely careful when hiking and participating in other outdoor activities (and visiting indoor nature facilities), and not undertaking nature-related activities that are beyond their skill and/or fitness level.

INTRODUCTION

I think about nature, hiking, wildlife, camping, and all things outdoors like some people think about their favorite sports team, discovering and trying new restaurants, or revisiting a favorite book or movie. OK, I love these things, too, but I have a special place in my heart for the natural world. Some of my first memories as a child were playing in the leaves and searching for bugs in my backyard in Beverly (a Chicago neighborhood) and hiking with my mom, dad, and brother in the Palos Forest Preserves in the southwest suburbs. As I got older, I began camping for a week or two each year with my dad and fellow Boy Scouts at Owasippe Scout Reservation in Michigan. Once, a few friends and I were lost in the Owasippe woods, but it seemed more fun than scary. By my twenties, I began hiking, camping, and exploring the United States with friends and sometimes as a solo traveler. I'd squeeze in a hike several times a week before work. And, several times a year, I'd ship a locker box of camping gear across the country and then fly to visit friends in New Mexico and Arizona.

I loved hiking and exploring the deserts, forests, grasslands, badlands, and lakeshores of America—often alone and unburdened by responsibilities. These explorations were a big part of my life before my now 11-year-old son came along. It was exhilarating to leave the crazy, bustling metropolis of Chicago and be alone in the wilderness without a soul around for miles and miles, surrounded by megafauna that could cause you grievous bodily harm if you did something stupid, had bad luck, or just weren't paying attention to the world around you.

But when lack of money or time constraints kept me from visiting these amazing places, I embraced the "wilds" of Chicagoland and learned there was considerable natural beauty and wonder in or near our big, sprawling city and suburbs. In my definition, "Chicagoland" consists of Chicago, its collar counties, and any natural destination that's within a day's drive of our great city (more on this later). No, you won't see bears, moose, or wolves near Chicagoland (except at the zoo), but you can glimpse deer, coyotes, bobcats, river otters, minks, muskrats, frogs, fish, and an amazing array of bird species—from eagles and hawks to migrating birds such as sandhill cranes, great blue herons, black-throated blue warblers, and indigo buntings that weeks before were wintering in the tropics. Would you believe that you can also see bison? They have been re-introduced to Midewin National Tallgrass Prairie in Wilmington, Illinois, and in nearly 10 other places in Chicagoland. Elk? Just visit Busse Woods in Elk Grove Village. (The elk were brought to our area from Yellowstone National Park in 1925.) The endangered piping plover? Head to Montrose Point Bird Sanctuary to see Monty and Rose, the first plovers to nest within the Chicago city limits since 1955. But be sure to enjoy them from afar with binoculars so that you don't disturb them. Mountain lions? Okay, just the one that ventured from the Black Hills in South Dakota to Roscoe Village (a Chicago neighborhood) back in 2008, but every time I hike, I keep an eye out for number two.

Introduction 19

In short, Chicagoland provides a plethora of awe-inspiring nature. There is Lake Michigan, our vast inland sea; the Chicago River, the Fox River, Des Plaines River, and other area rivers, which are gradually being restored from their criminal lack of stewardship to be healthy enough to host beavers, river otters, and a vast range of fish and other aquatic life, and be enjoyed by kayakers and people on boat tours; and the dense, sometimes hilly forest preserves of Cook County, the collar counties, and other counties, where, if you pick the right spot, you can walk all day without seeing another person. Would you be surprised to learn that Cook County is the most forested urban county in the United States? That there is only one canyon in Cook County? You'll find it at Sagawau Environmental Learning Center near Lemont. That the preserves are home to nearly 50 distinct plant communities, some of which are found only in the Chicago region? That our area boasts one of our nation's newest national parks (Indiana Dunes National Park)? I was. You can also find nature in our city parks, our backyards, and even our deck gardens. There's beauty and even a bit of semi-wilderness in many places if you look hard enough.

And let's not forget the amazing geological and archaeological history of the Chicago area. Chicago was once covered by a warm, shallow sea that teemed with tropical life—great cephalopods, which looked like octopuses; crinoids, which were cousins of starfish; trilobites, which were genetically linked to crabs; and probably primitive fish. When I was a boy in Beverly, I would dig up shells, crinoids, and fossilized coral that told me that my Chicago home below the Blue Island Ridge was much different millions of years ago. And during those same digs in my backyard, I would occasionally discover arrowheads left by the Native Americans who had inhabited this area for tens of thousands of years. Many don't realize that the remains of Potawatomi, Miami, and Illinois Native American villages lie below our gardens and streets, our elevated train lines and skyscrapers sit atop what were once Native American burial mounds (before many were removed to use as landfill…criminal), and our forest preserves still harbor centuries of French and Native American history just waiting to be discovered.

Chicagoland's weather is also noteworthy. Allow me to create an urban legend that just like the Inuit have a thousand words for snow, Chicagoans have a thousand words for weather—and only half of them are curse words! Snow. Driving rain and sleet. Hail. Sunshine…and that's just in one day. I'm fascinated by weather phenomena—whether it's supercell thunderstorms and tornadoes, sundogs and sun pillars, or just a beautiful rainbow or striking shelf cloud.

Which leads me to this book. *Nature in Chicagoland: More Than 120 Fantastic Nature Destinations That You Must Visit*, which features my favorite places to visit in the area. Some are child-friendly, while others are wild and wonderful. Some I've visited dozens of times, while others are new discoveries or places I've only had the opportunity to visit a handful of times but dream of returning to more frequently. Some of the destinations in this book have been profiled in some form at my blog *Nature in Chicagoland* (https://natureinchicago.wordpress.com) but have been expanded to feature sidebars or other new information. Many of the destination profiles are completely new for this book. The majority of the forest preserves, nature centers, state parks, conservation areas, and other destinations are within a 15-minute to an hour's drive from the city of Chicago (and some are located in Chicago). I've also included a few of my favorite places in the Upper and Lower Peninsulas of Michigan, Wisconsin, and Indiana that will take longer to travel to, but which will re-pay you in beauty, amazing wildlife viewing, and great memories.

Nature in Chicagoland also features personal essays about my time in nature with my son and wife, snowshoeing, camping, and other topics that are dear to my heart. The forests, lakes, streams, prairies, and other natural habitats of Chicagoland and beyond have been the setting for so many life experiences that are integral to who I am, and I hope that they have done the same for you. The book concludes with a bibliography of Midwest-focused nature books, journals, and newsletters and a list of local, state, and national nature organizations that you can contact for even more information.

Writing this book was a labor of love, and I'm both sad that the writing and research (i.e., visiting dozens of state parks, forest preserves, nature centers, and other destinations) have ended and excited to share these wonderful places with you. I hope to see you on the trails amidst nature in Chicagoland!

A FINAL NOTE

While I often mention specific hiking/walking trails by name, this book does not provide a comprehensive list of trails. You will learn about my favorite trails at many of these destinations, but there are just too many paths and not enough pages to cover every trail in detail. Most of the forest preserve districts and other outdoor recreation management agencies provide excellent digital maps and trail guides at their websites, and print versions at nature centers or trailheads. Visit their websites to obtain these maps or obtain hard copies on-site.

I list (and marvel at) a lot of birds in this book, but I am not an ornithologist. Every day, I try to learn something new about birds to better identify and appreciate them, but I am still just a hobbyist. The same goes for flowers and plants. I'm not a botanist, but I keep learning all the time—and you should, too. There are many useful nature guides that can help you build your knowledge and learn facts about our natural world. Check the Bibliography at the end of this book for some suggestions.

Although I spotlight—or at least mention—more than 250 nature destinations in Chicagoland, I could never possibly cover every beautiful place in Chicagoland in one book. The reality is that there are just too many amazing places to include in one book—but that's a good thing for Chicagoland residents and visitors. To identify new places, I will continue to explore our beautiful nature areas at my blog, Nature in Chicagoland, as well as hopefully in another book. I would love your help, too. Please send your favorites to me at andymorkes@gmail.com. I'd love to hear from you and what you love about nature in Chicagoland.

CHICAGO

One of the bike trails at Big Marsh Park © Andrew Morkes

BIG MARSH PARK
SPECTACULAR BIKE TRACKS, BOUNTIFUL BIRDING, AND MUCH MORE

"Big Marsh Has Big Plans." That's the newspaper headline I'd write if I were covering the ongoing environmental restoration and nature and recreational development efforts at Big Marsh Park on Chicago's far Southeast Side. This natural area is located on 297 acres of reclaimed industrial land on the eastern shore of Lake Calumet, which is the largest body of water *in* the city of Chicago. Until 2002, Acme Steel Co. operated a coke plant (which is the main source of carbon used in steelmaking) that overlooked Big Marsh. During its industrial era, some of the Great Marsh wetland "was filled with the steel industry's slag, reaching depths up to 15 feet and taking up 88 acres of the 300 acres in the area," according to the Great Lakes Phragmites Collaborative. The City of Chicago acquired the property in the early 2000s, and the Chicago Park District acquired Big Marsh (which is officially known as Park 564...that really rolls off the tongue) from the city in 2011. Environmental restoration and remediation (including the removal of invasive species) began in earnest, and the park opened to the public in 2016 with the first components of a bike

22 Nature in Chicagoland

> **Where:** 11555 S. Stony Island Avenue, Chicago, IL 60617
>
> **Learn More:** Chicago Park District, www.chicagoparkdistrict.com/parks-facilities/big-marsh-park-park-no-564
>
> **Hours:**
>
> Sunrise to sunset, Monday to Friday
>
> 8:00 a.m. to 7:00 p.m., Saturday and Sunday
>
> **Quick Review:** A fun and amazing bike park—"33,000 square feet of excitement for beginners and experts alike"; great birdwatching; enjoyable hiking trails along ponds, marshes, and other natural areas; and an environmental learning center. No dogs allowed. (#1 on the map on page 6)
>
> **What You Can Do There:** Bicycling, Birdwatching, Camping (coming soon), Hiking, Nature Center, Photography, Picnicking, Running/Exercise, Self-Enrichment and Educational Programs, Snowshoeing

park, access to nature trails, and plans for an environmental education center that will serve as a community focal point for nature education and exploration in Chicago's often overlooked Southland.

Flash forward to present day. Big Marsh Park has arrived in a big way. It's become a popular destination for biking, hiking, and nature appreciation (especially birding). Big Marsh Park is probably best known for its unique biking opportunities. There are a variety of options that are still being developed and expanded, including:

- ✔ a single-track that includes wooden rollers, ladder bridges, and other features;
- ✔ three jump lines for BMX and dirt jumping enthusiasts of all skill levels; and
- ✔ two world-class, asphalt pump tracks, which provide nearly 33,000 square feet of year-round fun for people of all ages and abilities.

These options are amazing, and I'm sure Big Marsh will become a biking recreation mecca that attracts people from throughout Chicagoland.

There is also great hiking at Big Marsh Park on a variety of formal and informal hiking trails that take you along its many ponds and marshes, and through its woods and other natural areas. Two of its main trails can be found to the left and right of a short pier that leads to the marsh overlook. If you face the marsh, the Beaver Tree Trail is located to your left. On this trail, you'll travel through hilly, wooded terrain and along marshland. The trail to the right of the pier is called Deer Bone Point Trail. This path takes you along the shores of Big Marsh and neighboring wetlands. You might see turtles, white-tailed deer, beavers, muskrats, and coyotes during your hike, and you'll see a variety of birds (including egrets, herons, eagles, gulls, kingfishers, cranes, and ducks). In fact, more than 240 bird species have been spotted at Big Marsh Park, and some call it Chicago's "Hidden Birding Mecca." The birding website eBird (https://ebird.org/hotspot/L152605) offers a complete list of birds sighted at Big Marsh Park.

The Ford Calumet Environmental Center (FCEC) is scheduled to open on-site in 2021. It will offer exhibits about the area's industrial and natural history, classroom spaces that will be open to school and community groups, and a bike rental outfitter, among other amenities. Other planned additions to Big Marsh Park include a primitive camping area with 12 tent pads, a wildlife observation platform, and a fully accessible, three-mile trail that will take visitors to previously unreachable areas of the park.

Big Marsh Park has so much promise, and it's already amazing. I'm excited about what the future holds for the park and environmental restoration and reclamation in Chicago's Southland. Get in on the fun and head to Big Marsh Park for a great day of biking, hiking, and birdwatching.

NEARBY NATURE DESTINATIONS

Beaubien Woods; Burnham Prairie Nature Preserve; Hegewisch Marsh; Indian Ridge Marsh Park; Lake Michigan; Powderhorn Lake, Marsh, and Prairie; Sand Ridge Nature Center; Wolf Lake Memorial Park

View of Big Marsh © Andrew Morkes

CHICAGO RIVERWALK

ICONIC ARCHITECTURE, BEAUTIFUL VIEWS OF THE RIVER AND ITS WILDLIFE, AND SOME URBAN FUN

Paddlers on the Chicago River
© Andrew Morkes

The Chicago Riverwalk is a fun and beautiful destination in downtown Chicago but, before we discuss this relatively new addition to the city, I want to tell you a little about the history of the Chicago River to show you how far the river has come since its most polluted days. The Chicago River has been through a lot in its existence. It was once a repository for human waste and pollution from tanneries, meat processing plants, and other industries, and this waste flowed into Lake Michigan—the city's source of drinking water. In 1885, a heavy rainstorm caused this dangerous pollution to be flushed past the clean water intakes in the lake. "The resulting typhoid, cholera, and dysentery epidemics killed an estimated 12 percent of Chicago's 750,000 residents and raised a public outcry to find a permanent solution to the city's water supply and sewage disposal cri-

---

Where: A 1.25-mile-long path along the Main Branch of the Chicago River

Learn More: City of Chicago, www.chicagoriverwalk.us

Hours: 6 a.m. to 11 p.m.

Quick Review: Great views of the river and Chicago skyline; access to kayak rental, boat trips, and restaurants and cafes, as well as Lake Michigan and Navy Pier. Dogs are allowed, but they must be leashed. Bikes must be walked in certain areas. (#2 on the map on page 6)

What You Can Do There: Bicycling, Birdwatching, Boat Tours, Canoeing/Kayaking/Boating, Fishing, Museums/Memorials, Photography, Picnicking, Restaurants/Bars, Running/Exercise, Water Taxi

sis," according to the American Public Works Association. Efforts began to clean up the river and protect the water in Lake Michigan. In 1900, the city—with the help of the U.S. Army Corps of Engineers—reversed the flow of the Chicago River so that it traveled away from Lake Michigan and toward the Mississippi River. This improved health conditions for Chicagoans but worsened them for those downriver. Although the number of Chicagoans who became ill or died declined, the river continued to be an open sewer system. In the 1930s more steps were taken to improve the water quality of the Chicago River and treat wastewater before it was sent downstream. Yet...the Chicago River remained so polluted that the city literally turned its back on it, with many buildings near it lacking any windows that faced the river. The first Mayor Daley (Richard J.) predicted in 1973 that "Loop workers by next year would be catching salmon, trout, and bass" if only Congress would allow for the increased flow of Lake Michigan water into the river to improve its water quality. Mayor Daley's heart was in the right place, but it was not that easy because the river was so polluted.

But the river became cleaner with each passing decade. The Clean Water Act of 1972, deindustrialization of the river corridor, and efforts by environmental groups (such as Friends of the Chicago River) to both educate the public about the importance of protecting the river and remove invasive plants and introduce native species helped the Chicago River to slowly bounce back. There were only 10 species in the river in 1974, according to the Metropolitan Water Reclamation District of Greater Chicago. That number jumped to 76 in 2017.

The Chicago Riverwalk © Page Light Studios, Shutterstock

The city began turning toward the river, rather than away from it. In the last four decades (but especially the last 20 years), commercial and residential development has boomed along the river. In 1999, **Ping Tom Memorial Park** (1700 S. Wentworth Avenue, Chicago, IL 60616, www.chicagoparkdistrict.com/parks-facilities/tom-ping-memorial-park) was opened on the former site of a Chicago and Western Indiana Railroad yard in Chicago's Chinatown neighborhood. This beautiful park attracted people to the river for a variety of activities (e.g, nature strolls, fishing, birdwatching, boat races), and the public began to advocate for a healthier waterway and more greenspace along the river. In 2016, the Chicago Riverwalk opened along the river's Main Branch (or Stem) in downtown.

I tell this history of the river because 1) I think it's interesting, and 2) it helps us all to understand that a polluted and forgotten place can be saved with a lot of love, hard work, stricter environmental laws, and some government and private funding. There are many other places in Chicagoland that need this kind of love, but let's take a moment to appreciate this victory.

THE S.S. *EASTLAND* DISASTER

The Chicago River cannot be discussed without mentioning the *Eastland* Disaster, in which 844 people (including 22 entire families) lost their lives on the S.S. *Eastland* on July 24, 1915, fewer than 20 feet from shore. They were amongst more than 2,500 passengers who were headed to a company picnic in Michigan City, Indiana. As the ship was about to depart, it rolled over, sending some passengers flying into the fetid water and trapping others below deck. It was one of the worst maritime disasters in American history. A memorial to the victims is located along the Chicago Riverwalk just west of the Clark Street Bridge. You can learn more about this senseless tragedy by visiting the Eastland Disaster Historical Society's website, www.eastlanddisaster.org/history/what-happened.

THE CHICAGO RIVERWALK

The Chicago Riverwalk begins at Lake Street at the confluence of the North, South, and Main branches of the Chicago River and travels 1.25 miles along the Main Branch of the river to Lake Michigan. It is a wonderful—although sometimes crowded—addition to downtown Chicago. Here are some things you can do on the Riverwalk. Use this map (www.chicagoriverwalk.us/map) to organize your visit.

Enjoy the great views of the busy river (pleasure boats, kayakers, wildlife, etc.) and the Chicago skyline. There are six "coves" along the Riverwalk that offer different experiences—from tree-shaded areas and floating wetland gardens, to one with a fountain that the kids can play in, to those filled with dock areas and restaurants and cafes.

Admire Chicago's beautiful buildings. Chicago is one of the world's greatest cities for architecture, and the Riverwalk provides an excellent chance to view some of its noteworthy buildings. Some of my favorites include 150 North Riverside Plaza (designed by Goettsch Partners), One Illinois Center (Mies van der Rohe), 333 West Wacker (Kohn Pedersen Fox), Marina City (Bertrand Goldberg), and the Wrigley Building (Graham, Anderson, Probst & White). The Chicago Architecture Center (in partnership with First Lady Cruises) and other private cruise companies offer architecture tours that travel up and down the various branches of the river as well as onto Lake Michigan. Another option is to ride the less-expensive Chicago Water Taxi to various stops (including beautiful Ping Tom Park, which has a children's play area, swimming pool, and other amenities) along the river like my son and I did awhile back. My wife works downtown in one of the historic buildings along the river—and I'm jealous of her views. One of my best memories of our day on the Riverwalk was looking up to see my wife waving from a window high above as our water taxi passed her building several times. My seven-year-old got the biggest kick out of it—and so did I. The water taxis travel to various destinations on the Main, North, and South Branches of the river.

Rent a boat and explore the river. You can rent a kayak (or take a tour on one), reserve a seat on a cycleboat (or reserve the entire boat for a group of family or friends), rent an electric boat or retroboat, or book a spot on a char-

Centennial Fountain © Andrew Morkes

ter party boat. You can even dock your own vessel along the river. Visit www-chicagoriverwalk.us/explore for more information about these opportunities.

Have a picnic. There are tiered steps and other spots in various areas of the Riverwalk where you can enjoy a picnic lunch and savor the sights and sounds of the city. There are a few rules for picnicking. You cannot bring your own alcoholic beverages to the picnic areas; they must be purchased from vendors. And you cannot bring your own food or drink into restaurants and cafes along the river.

Enjoy dinner and a drink at a variety of riverside restaurants and bars. Let's be honest. The Chicago Riverwalk is probably best known for its entertainment options, where downtown workers blow off steam after a hard day on the job and tourists take a break after jamming a gazillion activities into one day and slowly walking six abreast down bustling Michigan Avenue. There are approximately 10 restaurants, cafes, bars, and sweets stands along the Riverwalk to choose from.

Enjoy some birdwatching. You may see American coots, barn swallows, red-winged blackbirds, Caspian terns, mallards, ring-billed and herring gulls, rock pigeons, American robins, European starlings, peregrine falcons, and other birds along the river and near Lake Michigan. Audubon Great Lakes offers monthly guided walks along the river. Visit https://gl.audubon.org/birds/chicago-river-walk for more information about the walks and the birds that you might see.

Ride your bicycle. The Riverwalk can get very crowded during warm weather, so the best time to do this would be early morning or later in the evening. You'll be required to walk your bicycle in certain areas. You can ride your bike (or rent one from Divvy, Chicago's bike share program; see www.divvy bikes.com) to Lake Michigan and head north or south on the Lakefront Trail.

Visit museums and memorials, including the McCormack Bridgehouse and Chicago River Museum (www.bridgehousemuseum.org), Chicago Architecture Center (www.architecture.org), Vietnam Veteran's Memorial Plaza, and S.S. *Eastland* Memorial.

Go fishing. Drop a line and try to catch a largemouth bass, sunfish, channel catfish, or carp. Although health authorities say that it's safe to eat these fish in small quantities and/or those that are less than 12 inches in length (common carp), do your own research to determine the health risks of eating fish caught in the river. Regardless of whether you "catch and release" or "catch and eat," you'll need to obtain a fishing license from the Illinois Department of Natural Resources.

Enjoy some public art. There are permanent and rotating works of public art displayed along the Riverwalk. Look for *The Radiance of Being*, a mural by Kate Lynn Lewis that celebrates 100 years of art deco; Ellen Lanyon's *Riverwalk Gateway*, a 27-foot-long trellised walkway that links the river to Lake Michigan and depicts the history of Chicago and the river from explorations of Jacques Marquette and Louis Jolliet in 1673 to modern times; and Carolyn Ottmers' *Allium*, a 10-foot-tall aluminum flower. Finally, check out Art on theMART (https://artonthemart.com), the largest digital art projection in the world. It covers more than 2.5 acres of theMART's river-facing façade. Art on theMART is available for viewing on select evenings from March through December.

FINAL THOUGHTS

When people discuss the most scenic vistas of Chicago, they often tout views of its skyline from afar or the lakefront, but I believe the prettiest view of the Windy City is looking down the Chicago River (either east or west) from the Riverwalk on a breezy, summer evening, the skyscrapers looming over the river like concrete and metal cliffs, the colorful lights of the city reflected on the water, ducks and other waterfowl swimming in the waves, boats moving up and down the river, and people walking on or relaxing by the Riverwalk. This urban nature and entertainment trail is a great addition to downtown Chicago, and you should check it out this spring, summer, or fall.

NEARBY NATURE DESTINATIONS AND ATTRACTIONS

Garden of the Phoenix, Garfield Park Conservatory, Lake Michigan, Lake Shore East Park, Lincoln Park, Maggie Daley Park, Millennium Park, Palmisano Park, Peggy Notebaert Nature Museum, Shedd Aquarium

The Chicago River in the evening in all its glory. © karamysh, Shutterstock

DAN RYAN WOODS

URBAN OPPORTUNITIES FOR HIKING, BIKING, PICNICKING, FITNESS, AND WINTER FUN

Only a small percentage of Forest Preserves of Cook County land is located within the city limits of Chicago, and Dan Ryan Woods is one of these properties. For more than a century, it's been a popular place for city dwellers to picnic, hike, sled, and otherwise enjoy nature. Before this time, a portion of Dan Ryan Woods was a livestock farm, and pigs and a herd of cattle grazed on its glacial ridges. In 1902, the *Chicago Live Stock World* newspaper described the farm as the "largest within the city limits of Chicago." And long, long (i.e., 14,000 years ago) before cattle roamed the hills and people celebrated weddings and high school graduations in its picnic groves, the woods (which sit on some of the highest land in Chicago...not all of Chicago is flat!) were the tip of an island in ancient Lake Chicago. The highest ground in Dan Ryan Woods was surrounded by water, and nomadic groups of Paleo Indians hunted mastodons and other megafauna in the area. The highest areas of the Dan Ryan Woods comprise the northern-most tip of an interesting piece of Chicago topography known as the Blue Island Ridge. The glacial ridge runs nearly six miles from Dan Ryan Woods to the suburb of Blue Island.

Where: On the South Side of Chicago near the historic neighborhoods of Beverly Hills/Morgan Park. There are six entrances; the Visitor Center is located at Western Avenue & 87th Street, Chicago, 60620.

Learn More: Forest Preserves of Cook County, https://fpdcc.com/places/locations/dan-ryan-woods

Hours: Grounds: Sunrise to sunset, year-round

Visitor Center: Open Memorial Day to Labor Day, Tuesday & Thursday: 8:30 a.m. to 4:30 p.m.; Saturday: 9 a.m. to 2 p.m.

Quick Review: A 257-acre urban preserve with sledding and snowboarding hills, historic aqueducts, fitness stairs, picnic groves, and a mile-long paved loop that connects to the Major Taylor Trail (good for biking and walking). Dogs allowed (on leashes). The 91st Street Stop on the Metra Rock Island line takes visitors right to the southeast corner of the woods. (#3 on the map on page 6)

What You Can Do There: Bicycling, Birdwatching, Cross-Country Skiing, Educational and Self-Enrichment Opportunities and Classes, Hiking, Indoor Event Rentals (for birthday parties, showers, classes, and meetings), Photography, Picnicking, Running/Exercise (including fitness stairs), Sledding, Snowboarding, Snowshoeing, Visitor Center

Chicago Destinations 31

© Andrew Morkes

But let's return to the present. Although the grounds are old at Dan Ryan Woods, many new improvements have been made to this recreation stalwart. Recent additions include new exercise stairs near the sledding hill (that some say are as popular as those found at Swallow Cliff Woods, see page 218) and a multi-faceted nature play area, where children can climb, make music, or look out over the landscape in a treehouse. The exercise stairs, nature play area, and sledding and snowboarding hill are near the Visitor Center.

The best hiking areas are found south of 87th Street. Wood-chip trails wind through old bur and white and red oak woodlands, where you can see spring ephemerals such as wild geranium, Jack-in-the-pulpit, red trillium, thicket parsley, and Virginia waterleaf. You'll also pass historic limestone aqueducts, which were built by the Civilian Conservation Corps in the 1930s to prevent water from washing away soil on the steep ridges. The elevation gradually decreases as you head east from Western Avenue, and you'll eventually enter an area that was once covered by Lake Chicago. In the southeast corner of the woods, there are red oaks, swamp white oaks, and American basswood, as well as fringed loosestrife, pale-leaved sunflower, and sedges and manna grasses.

If you're interested in biking, the Major Taylor Trail (https://fpdcc com/places/trails/major-taylor-trail) begins at the northeastern edge of Dan Ryan Woods, travels two miles to its southeastern boundary, and then continues another seven miles or so to Whistler Woods on the banks of the Little Calumet

> **DID YOU KNOW?**
>
> ✔ Dan Ryan Sr. was a former board member of Forest Preserves of Cook County. In 1924, what was then named Beverly Hills Preserve was renamed to Dan Ryan Woods in his honor.
>
> ✔ Marshall "Major" Taylor was an African American bicycle racer and civil rights advocate. When he was young, he became known for his ability to perform amazing bicycle tricks, during which he wore a soldier's uniform (hence the nickname, "Major"). Taylor became a world champion racer. "From 1898 to 1904 he was indeed the fastest bicycle rider in the world," according to MajorTaylorChicago.com. Visit this website to learn more about Taylor, his racing prowess, and the racism that he had to overcome to become a champion.
>
> ✔ The Beverly Improvement Association sponsors an annual Bird Watch and Nature Walk at Dan Ryan Woods. Visit www.facebook.com/thebia1 for more information.

River in Riverdale, Illinois. The trail includes paved segments, off-street paved segments managed by the Chicago Park District, and on-street segments.

NEARBY NATURE DESTINATIONS AND ATTRACTIONS

Big Marsh Park, Garden of the Phoenix (Jackson Park), Indian Ridge Marsh Park, Lake Katherine Nature Center and Botanic Gardens, Lake Michigan, Marquette Park, Whistler Woods Forest Preserve

ENJOY AN AFTERNOON OR EVENING IN BEVERLY HILLS/MORGAN PARK

After you've visited Dan Ryan Woods, head to the nearby Chicago neighborhood of Beverly Hills, which is just south of the woods. (Morgan Park is Beverly's southern neighbor, but most people just lump the two neighborhoods together and call them Beverly, and I'll do the same for the purposes of this article.) My family has lived in this hilly, historical, and tree-lined "village in the city," as its nickname goes—since the 1960s, and I spent the first 30+ years of my life there. Beverly is famous for its annual St. Patrick's Day Parade and the Beverly Art Walk, but there are many other things to do and see in one of Chicago's oldest and most scenic neighborhoods, including:

Visiting the Irish Castle (10244 S. Longwood Drive, 60643, https://chicagosonlycastle.org) and checking out other architectural gems in the neighborhood. The castle, which was completed in 1887, has been recognized by the Chicago Landmarks Commission as part of the Longwood Drive Historic District. It's also part of the Ridge Historic District, which is listed in the National Register of Historic Places. The castle is also known as the Givins Castle. After viewing the cas-

Chicago Destinations 33

tle, take some time to appreciate the diverse architectural styles of the homes in the neighborhood. Beverly has an amazing array of architectural styles (Italianate, Queen Anne, Carpenter Gothic, Prairie School, and Renaissance Revival) and homes designed by famous architects such as Frank Lloyd Wright, Walter Burley Griffin, George W. Maher, Daniel Burnham, and Howard Van Doren Shaw. You can check out some of these homes via local tours and the Chicago Architecture Center's Open House Chicago program (https://openhousechicago.org).

Having lunch or dinner and a cocktail (or a mocktail). There are many great places in Beverly to relax at after your time at Dan Ryan Woods. One of my favorites is **Horse Thief Hollow Brewing Company** (10426 S. Western Avenue, Chicago, 60643, https://horsethiefbrewing.com), which offers tasty craft beer and food. Art adorns the walls, you can enjoy live music on certain days, and there's a wonderful vibe at this popular destination. **Open Outcry Brewing Company** (10934 S. Western Avenue, Chicago, 60643, 773/629-6055, www.openoutcrybrewing.com) is another must-visit spot for excellent beer, mouth-watering food, and a fantastic rooftop deck. Other top-notch establishments include **Cork & Kerry** (10614 S. Western Avenue, Chicago, 60643, 773/445-2675, https://corkandkerrybeverly.com), **Barney Callaghan's Pub** (10618 S. Western Avenue, Chicago, 60643), **Calabria Imports** (a combo deli and casual restaurant that's located at 1905 W. 103rd Street, 60643, 773/396-5800, www.calabria-imports.com), **Beverly Bakery & Cafe** (10528 S. Western Avenue, Chicago, 60643, 773/238-5580, www.beverlycoffeeroasters.com), and **Wild Blossom Meadery and Winery** (9030 S. Hermitage, Chicago, 60620, 773/840-4642, www.wildblossommeadery.com).

Checking out some of my other favorite neighborhood destinations including:

✔ **Original Rainbow Cone** (9233. S. Western Avenue, 60643, 773/238-9833, www.rainbowcone.com)

✔ **Ridge Historical Society** (10621 S. Seeley Avenue, 60643, 773/881-1675, https://ridgehistory.org)

✔ **Bookie's New and Used Books** (10324 S. Western Avenue, 60643, 773/239-1110, www.bookiesbookstores.com)

✔ **Beverly Arts Center** (2407 W. 111th Street, 60655, 773/445-3838, https://beverlyartcenter.org)

✔ **Heritage Gallery** (1907 W. 103rd Street, 60643, 773/233-0084, www.facebook.com/HeritageGalleryChicago)

Popular places that I've not visited include **Belle Up**, a women's apparel, accessories, and gift boutique (1915 W. 103rd Street, Chicago, 60643, www.belleup.com); **Ain't She Sweet Café** (9920 S. Western, Chicago, 60643, 773/840-3309, www.aintshesweetcafe.com), **Pizzeria Deepo** (1742 W. 99th Street, Chicago, 60643, www.pizzeriadeepo.com), **Two Mile Coffee Bar** (9907 S. Walden Parkway, Chicago, 60643, www.twomilecoffee.com), and **Cakewalk Chicago** (1741 W. 99th Street, Chicago, 60643, www.cakewalkchicago.com).

Garden of the Phoenix © Thomas Barrat, Shutterstock

GARDEN OF THE PHOENIX AT JACKSON PARK

A PEACEFUL JAPANESE GARDEN WITH STUNNING VIEWS

More than 2.7 million people call Chicago home. It's a busy place, where people always seem to be on the move. The city's highways and roads are often jammed with traffic, its Lakefront Trail and beaches packed with people on warm days, and its downtown streets filled with workers and tourists (at least before the pandemic). This energy is exhilarating to some and tiring to many. If you fall into the latter category, you'll want to visit the Garden of the Phoenix in Jackson Park. At this South Side destination, you'll experience an overwhelming feeling of peace and solitude as you walk its winding stone paths that reveal new natural panoramas with every turn. As you walk, you'll cross arched footbridges; hear the sounds of waterfowl and waterfalls; savor the sight of blossom-laden azalea shrubs, cherry trees, and Japanese maples; and simply enjoy nature and hopefully a bit of solitude (especially if you visit early in the morning or late in the day).

The garden—which is also known as the Japanese Garden and the Osaka Garden (to celebrate Chicago's Sister City relationship with Osaka, Japan)—

> **Where:** 6300 S. Cornell Avenue, Chicago, IL 60637
>
> **Learn More:** Chicago Park District, www.chicagoparkdistrict.com/parks-facilities/japanese-garden
>
> **Hours:** Sunrise to sunset, year-round
>
> **Quick Review:** A soothing garden on Wooded Island in a Chicago city park with lagoons, waterfalls, winding paths, rock gardens, a moon bridge, beautiful flowers and trees (including cherry trees that blossom in the spring), and views of the Museum of Science & Industry (the last building remaining from the World's Columbian Exposition of 1893). No dogs allowed. (#4 on the map on page 6)
>
> **What You Can Do There:** Birdwatching, Hiking, Local History, Photography

was first developed in 1893 when the Japanese government built the Phoenix Temple (based on a classical Buddhist temple) and a small garden on Wooded Island as its pavilion for the World's Columbian Exposition. After the fair ended, the Japanese government gifted the pavilion to the city of Chicago. In the 1930s, the Chicago Park District restored the pavilion and planted a more extensive Japanese Garden. A man named Shoji Osata and his wife, Frances Fitzpatrick, maintained the garden and operated a teahouse there from 1935 through 1941. The health of the garden served as a microcosm of Japanese-American relations. On December 8, 1941, the United States declared war on Japan in response to that country's surprise attack on Pearl Harbor the prior day. Osata was interned along with more than 120,000 other Japanese Americans, and the garden fell into disrepair. The pavilion and the teahouse were destroyed by arson in 1946. Decades passed and relations between the United States and Japan improved. The garden was finally restored in 1981, with Keneji Domoto, an architect and landscape architect, serving as a consultant. Restorations and improvements continued in the mid-1990s through more recent years. In 2016, the artist, musician, and peace activist Yoko Ono installed *Sky Landing* on the island as a symbol of peace. At the dedication ceremony, she described the artwork as the "place where the sky and earth meet and create a seed to learn about the past and come together to create a future of peace and harmony, with nature and each other". Today, the Garden of the Phoenix is a beautiful oasis in the city and serves as a symbol of the friendship between the United States and Japan. In recent years, two carved wooden transom panels and sliding door paintings that were part of the Phoenix Temple at the World's Columbian Exposition were discovered and restored and displayed by the Art Institute of Chicago. You can learn more about the history of Japanese-American relations and the garden by visiting www.gardenofthephoenix.org.

View of the Museum of Science & Industry from the Garden of the Phoenix
© Jonah Anderson, Shutterstock

Spring is one of the best times to visit the garden because you can view the stunning white and pink blossoms of its cherry trees. To the Japanese, cherry blossoms symbolize both renewal and rebirth, but also the fleeting nature of life (the flowers reach peak beauty for only one to two weeks). For more than a thousand years, the Japanese have celebrated the emergence of the cherry blossoms by picnicking and relaxing beneath the cherry trees. They call this custom *hanami*. Visitors can celebrate their own version of hanami by visiting the Garden of the Phoenix in the spring to view the cherry blossoms and celebrate the end of another long, cold winter. There are now even more cherry blossoms to see because 160 additional cherry trees that were planted in Jackson Park near the garden have begun to bloom. I hope that the cherry blossoms of the Garden of the Phoenix and greater Jackson Park will someday rival those in Washington, D.C.

NEARBY NATURE DESTINATIONS AND ATTRACTIONS

Adler Planetarium, Big Marsh Park, Field Museum, Grant Park, Lake Michigan, Maggie Daley Park, Millennium Park, Museum of Science & Industry, Northerly Island Park, Palmisano Park, Shedd Aquarium, South Shore Natural Area

INDIAN RIDGE MARSH PARK

A BIRD HAVEN AND A STORY OF ENVIRONMENTAL REBIRTH

Milkweed bugs
© Andrew Morkes

Surrounded by steel processing plants and busy railroad lines and roads lies a place of wild beauty and an oasis for migrating great egrets, double crested cormorants, and little blue herons, among many other birds. Park No. 565 is a Chicago city park that's nothing like the well-manicured, picnic-benched– and baseball-diamonded green spaces that Chicagoans are familiar with. And that's a great thing!

Indian Ridge Marsh Park, as it is better known, features 154 acres of native marsh and wet prairie habitat. When I visited on a late October day, I parked in its north section off Torrence Avenue. Semi-trailers roared by. A freight train chugged across the golden-red-brown landscape to the west on the Norfolk and Western railroad tracks—a landfill looming above it in the distance. And I heard the big clanks and warning bells of heavy machinery operating somewhere nearby. It was not a promising start to a hike, but once I walked for a few minutes on the wood-chip trails, I was transported into a beautiful and serene

Where: 11740 S. Torrence Avenue, Chicago, IL 60617

Learn More: Chicago Park District, www.chicagoparkdistrict.com/parks-facilities/indian-ridge-marsh

Hours: 6 a.m. to 11 p.m. year-round

Quick Review: Nearly 155 acres of native marsh and wet prairie habitat. The park has north and south sections; both have parking lots and easy and enjoyable walking trails. During my visit, I loved the views of the marsh ponds, prairies, wetlands and the migrating waterfowl and year-round Chicago avian residents (200 species in all). Wildflowers in the late spring, summer, and fall, and stunning fall colors. (#5 on the map on page 6)

What You Can Do There: Birdwatching, Cross-Country Skiing, Hiking, Photography, Picnicking, Running/Exercise, Snowshoeing

Nature's airport © Andrew Morkes

place. Indian Ridge Marsh is just one of many small—but important—marsh and wet prairie habitats in the Calumet Region. Amidst the south suburban industrial sprawl, this is a key area for wildlife, especially migrating birds. Not only egrets, cormorants, and herons as I mentioned earlier, but also pied-billed grebes, blackcrowned night herons, yellow warblers, ospreys, peregrine falcons, bald eagles, belted kingfishers, common moorhens, and yellow-headed blackbirds. In fact, Indian Ridge Marsh is home to 200 bird species. Many of these birds visit the area as they migrate along the Mississippi Flyway, the second-largest north-south route for migrating birds on the continent. During your visit, you might also see deer (I saw some prints as I hiked), coyotes, muskrats, frogs, turtles (including the state endangered Blanding's turtle), snakes, and dinosaurs (not!...just checking if you're still paying attention).

Wetlands and marshes once existed throughout southeast Chicagoland. But as manufacturing plants (especially those built by the steel industry) began to be established in areas adjoining or near Lake Michigan in Chicago's Southland, these vast green stretches shrunk to islands of biodiversity. Areas that were not protected became forgotten and polluted places in which slag from steelmaking operations and dredged materials from Calumet Harbor and River were dumped. Indian Ridge Marsh was once one of these despoiled places. But as the steel industry died (the last major steel manufacturer closed in 2001), visionary planners and environmentalists began to dream of restoring these areas and creating a connected patchwork of marshes, lakes, and wetlands that—once restored—could be home to migrating birds and their year-round friends, as well as other animals. The marshes also provide flood protection, cleanse pollutants, and offer other benefits. The restoration process is a story in itself, but too complex to cover in a short article. For those interested in learning more, I suggest checking out "Avian Oasis: Restoration at Indian Ridge Marsh has Turned a Wasteland Into an Important Home for Wildlife," by Sam Joyce.

© Andrew Morkes

Environmental restoration is ongoing at Indian Ridge Marsh and its neighbors Big Marsh (see page 21) and Burnham Marsh (see page 147), but this is a long process. You may see occasional slag (stone-like waste product created during the process of refining iron to steel) on the ground as you walk, and

WHILE YOU'RE IN THE NEIGHBORHOOD . . .

Check out **Pullman National Monument** (11141 S. Cottage Grove Avenue, Chicago, IL 60628, www.nps.gov/pull). At this National Park Service site, you won't find nature in abundance, but rather a wealth of history about the first model, planned industrial community in the United States; the Pullman Company; and George Pullman, the founder of the community. Another noteworthy site in the Pullman Historic District is the **A. Philip Randolph Pullman Porter Museum** (10406 S. Maryland Avenue, Chicago, IL 60628, https://aprpullmanportermuseum.org), which explores African American labor history. A. Philip Randolph was a labor and civil rights leader, and the founder of the Brotherhood of Sleeping Car Porters, a union that represented African-American railroad porters during contentious battles with the Pullman Company over worker rights.

A trail at Indian Ridge Marsh Park with a view of the Torrence Avenue Bridge (which crosses the Calumet River). © Andrew Morkes

there is still work to do to clean up the chemicals that were dumped in the area, but Indian Ridge Marsh is already a beautiful place and worth a visit. Since restoration (including the removal of invasive plants) has begun, bird populations have skyrocketed. It's inspiring to see some good come from bad.

FINAL THOUGHTS

I've spent a lot of time recently visiting nature spots on Chicago's South Side and in its south suburbs, and I've been impressed by the vast range of ecosystems and wildlife. Too often, people write off Chicago's Southland as industrial, crime-ridden, drive-by territory on the way to the harbor towns of Michigan—but that's a mistake. I encourage you to visit Chicago's Southland—my homeland—for some great nature adventures.

NEARBY NATURE DESTINATIONS

Beaubien Woods; Big Marsh Park; Burnham Prairie Nature Preserve; Hegewisch Marsh; Powderhorn Lake, Marsh, and Prairie; Sand Ridge Nature Center; Wolf Lake Memorial Park

LAKE MICHIGAN

OUR BEAUTIFUL INLAND SEA OFFERS OPPORTUNITIES FOR NATURE FUN IN ANY SEASON

Lake Michigan is the fifth-largest lake in the world. It provides water to more than 12 million people in the Midwest. The lake is a popular destination for recreational activities such as fishing, sailing, kayaking, and swimming; provides relief from the heat during the summer; and offers a place to de-stress from life in any season.

If you live in Chicagoland, Lake Michigan has probably played an integral role in your life. It has in mine. I remember building sandcastles and playing in the waves as a child with family friends at Rainbow Beach on Chicago's South Side. As a teenager, I received my first taste of freedom by being allowed to take a Metra Rock Island train with friends down to LaSalle Street Station, and then take a bus to near Oak Street Beach. Once we arrived at the beach, I was wowed by the fact that I was sitting in the soft sand, waves crashing, gulls flying above, and with a massive canyon of skyscrapers behind me. That wow turned to shock when the wind shifted, and the 75-degree early June day became a 60-degree "May" day in a matter of minutes due to Chicagoland's famous lake breeze. But the lake has always brought me more joy than pain. At the beginning of the school year when I was in college, I used to spend afternoons with my friend Vanessa at Columbia Beach in Rogers Park, dry off at 4:45 p.m., and then rush to my 5:00 p.m. creative writing class down the street at Loyola University Chicago. It was such a great feeling to sit in class discussing Raymond Carver,

Where: Located on the shores of Illinois, Indiana, Michigan, and Wisconsin

Learn More: Chicago Park District, ww.choosechicago.com/things-to-do/parks-outdoors, www.michigan.org/great-lakes/lake-michigan, https://wisconsinharbortowns.net

Hours: Varies by location

Quick Review: Approximately 1,640 miles of natural and urban coastline in Illinois, Indiana, Michigan, and Wisconsin. (#6 on the map on page 6)

What You Can Do There or Nearby: Beach Fun, Bicycling, Birdwatching, Boat Tours, Camping, Canoeing/Kayaking/Boating, Cross-Country Skiing, Dune Climbing, Educational and Self-Enrichment Opportunities and Classes, Fishing, Hiking, Horseback Riding, Lighthouse Viewing, Museums, Nature Centers, Photography, Picnicking, Running/Exercise, Snowshoeing, Swimming, Water Sports

42 Nature in Chicagoland

North Avenue Beach © f11photo, Shutterstock

Amiri Baraka, and Louise Erdrich knowing that I'd been swimming in the cool waters minutes earlier. And over the past few decades, I've walked along the shores of Lake Michigan (just like any other tourist), hiked along its sandy beaches and dunes at Indiana Dunes State and National Parks (see pages 223-230), and camped a five-minute walk from its crashing waves at Kohler-Andrae State Park (see page 270) in Wisconsin.

But you're here not to learn about my adventures at Lake Michigan, but to discover some great things to do at our vast, inland sea. Chicago has 26 miles of Lake Michigan shoreline—although some of this is industrial property where you'd never want to toss a Frisbee or relax on a beach blanket. Here are some things to do at or near Lake Michigan in Chicago.

Enjoy a lazy day at the beach. Summer is short in Chicagoland, so be sure to take some time to lounge at one of Chicago's 26 free beaches (visit www.chicagoparkdistrict.com/beaches for a list). If you're not the sitting and sunning type, take a long walk on one of these sandy beaches. Skip some stones. Listen to the sounds of gulls and other birds. Dip your feet in the water and feel the energy of the waves. Better yet, dive in and splash around. Jumping in the waves is not just a warm weather activity. During recent winters, people have begun to surf in the frigid waves, as well as plunge into the mid-30-degree Fahrenheit waters to fight the cold-weather blues.

Bike, walk, or run the Lakefront Trail. This approximately 18-mile path travels from Ardmore Avenue on the far north side of the city to 71st Street on its south side. Try all or some of this scenic trail for beautiful views of the lake, city parks, and the Chicago skyline. Visit www.chicagoparkdistrict.com/parks-facilities/lakefront-trail for more information.

Go birdwatching and hiking. You'll see beautiful birds all along the lakefront, but the best place to see birds—especially migrating ones—is at the Montrose Point Bird Sanctuary, often known as "The Magic Hedge," at **Montrose Beach** (4400 N. Simonds Drive, 60640, www.lakecookaudubon.org/birding-sites/montrose-point-bird-sanctuary). Birders have recorded more than 300 bird species, including the federally endangered Great Lakes piping plover. It's estimated that there are only 65 to 70 nesting pairs of piping plovers in the Great Lakes. In 2019, two piping plovers (who were named Monty and Rose) became the first to nest within the city limits of Chicago since 1955. There is even a short movie—*Monty and Rose*—about these two birds who caught the imagination of Chicagoans. While you're in the area, check out the **Bill Jarvis Migratory Bird Sanctuary** (3550 N. Lake Shore Drive, 60613), **Peggy Notebaert Nature Museum** (2430 N. Cannon Drive, 60614, https://naturemuseum.org), **Lincoln Park Zoo** (2001 N. Clark Street, 60614, www.lpzoo.org), and **Lincoln Park Conservatory** (2391 N. Stockton Drive, 60614, www.chicagoparkdistrict.com/parks-facilities/lincoln-park-conservatory). Other great birding sites along or near the lake include North Pond (in Lincoln

Gulls flocking to a fishing vessel on Lake Michigan.
© Katie Steiger-Meister, U.S. Fish & Wildlife Service

44 Nature in Chicagoland

Park), Grant Park, Jackson Park (especially Bobolink Meadow and the Wooded Island), Rainbow Beach, Washington Park, Steelworkers Park.

Northerly Island (1521 S. Linn White Drive, 60605, www.chicagoparkdistrict.com/parks-facilities/northerly-island) is another top birdwatching spot, as well as popular with walkers and runners. At this 91-acre park, you can view migratory birds and walk on a mile-long path that offers a stunning view of the Chicago skyline. Before you leave the area, don't forget to check out Chicago museum staples such as **The Field Museum** (1400 South Lake Shore Drive, 60605, www.fieldmuseum.org), **Shedd Aquarium** (1200 S. Lake Shore Drive, 60605, www.sheddaquarium.org), and the **Adler Planetarium** (1300 S. Lake Shore Drive, 60605, www.adlerplanetarium.org). **The McCormick Place Bird Sanctuary** (2301 S. Lake Shore Drive, 60616, www.choosechicago.com/listing/mccormick-bird-sanctuary) is also nearby.

LAKE MICHIGAN SHORELINE BY STATE

Michigan: 3,288 miles
Wisconsin: 407 miles
Illinois: 63 miles
Indiana: 45 miles

You can continue your nature explorations by heading south from downtown to check out **Promontory Point** (5491 S. Lake Shore Drive, 60615, www.chicagoparkdistrict.com/parks-facilities/promontory-point), the **Garden of the Phoenix in Jackson Park** (6300 S. Cornell Avenue, 60637; see page 34), and **Museum of Science & Industry** (5700 S. Lake Shore Drive, 60637, www.msichicago.org).

If you continue to travel south along the lakeshore, you'll reach the **South Shore Natural Area** (SSNA, 7059 S. South Shore Drive, 60649, www.chicagoparkdistrict.com/parks-facilities/south-shore-natural-area) at the historic South Shore Cultural Center (which is a pretty amazing place in itself). The SSNA features six acres of dunes, wetlands, a woodland, prairie, savanna, and shrubland habitats.

Participate in a variety of additional activities. Let's be honest. This chapter is much too short to cover the wide range of Lake Michigan–related activities that are available to you. These include fishing, boating (canoeing, kayaking, sailing, and boat tours), water sports (jet ski-

Promonotory Point   © Loro, Shutterstock

LAKE MICHIGAN AND POLLUTION

Many of us take the health of Lake Michigan for granted as we walk its beaches, swim in its cool depths, and, of course, drink its water. But underlying this beauty is the danger Lake Michigan, its entire ecosystem, and humans face because of ongoing pollution and environmental degradation. Human waste, microbeads used in cosmetics and other products that kill fish and other animals, algae from farm fertilizer runoff, invasive species, global warming, and toxic chemicals dumped by oil refineries and other manufacturers are just a few things that negatively affect the health of Lake Michigan. We all must work harder to understand the dangers that Lake Michigan faces if it continues to be misused and polluted. Many local and national environmental organizations are working hard to protect one of our area's most vital resources. Contact the following organizations to learn more about Lake Michigan and the other Great Lakes and what you can do to preserve them for future generations: Alliance for the Great Lakes (https://greatlakes.org), Center for Great Lakes Literacy (www.cgll.org), Freshwater Future (https://freshwaterfuture.org), and Sierra Club-Illinois Chapter (www.sierraclub.org/illinois).

ing, paddle boarding, etc.), and camping (including family camping at beautiful Northerly Island). Don't forget that Lake Michigan is a great destination in all seasons—even in the winter. And that it provides recreational opportunities to people in Illinois, Indiana, Wisconsin, and Michigan. During Chicago winters, you can snowshoe along the lake and cross-country ski and snowshoe at Northerly Island, ice skate at nearby **Maggie Daley Park** (337 E. Randolph Street, 60601, https://maggiedaleypark.com) and **Millennium Park** (201 E. Randolph Street, 60601, www.chicago.gov), and go sledding at the **Soldier Field Sledding Hill** (1410 S. Museum Campus Drive, 60605).

NEARBY NATURE DESTINATIONS

Hundreds, if not thousands, of parks and other recreational properties are found along or near Lake Michigan's coastline.

View of the Chicago skyline from Montrose Point © James Andrews1, Shutterstock

MONTROSE POINT BIRD SANCTUARY

A BEAUTIFUL BIRDING SPOT IN CHICAGO

When people think of Chicago's beaches, they conjure up images of sunbathers, volleyball players, runners, walkers, and cyclists all vying for space on the beaches and the Lakefront Trail. You can do all these activities on Chicago's beautiful lakeshore, but did you know that there is great birdwatching along the lake at Montrose Point Bird Sanctuary? Birders have recorded more than 300 bird species—including the federally endangered Great Lakes piping plover and only the second inland recording of the black-tailed gull in the United States—at this nearly 16-acre site. Migratory birds flock to this area due to "The Magic Hedge," a collection of shrubs, bushes, and small trees that provide cover and a food source as they refuel on their journey to the north or south. A nearby fishing pier (that is a good place to see waterfowl), a large butterfly meadow, dunes (known as the Montrose Beach Dunes Natural Area), and sandy beaches, among other factors, also play a role in making this area attractive to birds. And there is good news. The Chicago Park District plans to add three acres to the sanctuary to increase the nesting area for piping plovers and other birds.

During your visit you might see Le Conte's, white-crowned, Lincoln's, and fox sparrows and other birds in the meadow, and migrating songbirds in the

Where: 4400 N. Simonds Drive, Chicago, IL 60640
Learn More: www.lakecookaudubon.org/birding-sites/montrose-point-bird-sanctuary, www.chicagoparkdistrict.com/parks-facilities/lincoln-park-montrose-point-bird-sanctuary, http://theorniphile.info/birding-montrose-point/montrose-frequently-asked-questions.html
Hours: Dawn to dusk daily
Quick Review: This 15.6-acre nature area attracts tens of thousands of migratory birds each spring and fall and offers great views of the Chicago skyline. Dogs are only allowed in the canine area at the west end of Montrose Beach. (#7 on the map on page 6)
What You Can Do There: Birdwatching, Hiking, Photography
What You Can Do Nearby: Beach Fun, Bicycling, Boating, Fishing, Picnicking, Running/Exercise, Swimming

trees and brush nearby. The Lake-Cook Audubon Chapter of the Illinois Audubon Society says that you might see black-bellied plovers, American golden plovers, dunlins, least and semipalmated sandpipers, scoters, long-tailed ducks, red-throated loons, and peregrine falcons near the pier and in open water and in the sky. In the dunes, look for Nelson's, lark, and vesper sparrows, as well as snow buntings, snowy owls, short-eared owls, and Lapland longspurs in the winter. You can learn more about the variety of birds that visit Montrose Point Bird Sanctuary at http://theorniphile.info/birding-montrose-point. Additionally, Robert D. Hughes writes *The Montrose Birding Blog* (www.theorniphile.info/wordpress), which serves as a great place to learn about birds that have been seen recently at the sanctuary and conditions on-site. It also features a glossary of commonly used terms that pertain to the sanctuary and surrounding areas. The writer and filmmaker Bob Dolgan publishes an interesting, weekly e-newsletter called *This Week in Birding*, www.twibchicago.com. See page 50 for more information on piping plovers.

NEARBY NATURE DESTINATIONS AND ATTRACTIONS

Bill Jarvis Migratory Bird Sanctuary, Chicago Riverwalk, Lake Shore East Park, Lincoln Park, Lincoln Park Conservatory, Lincoln Park Zoo, Maggie Daley Park, McCormick Place Bird Sanctuary, Millennium Park, Northerly Island, Peggy Notebaert Nature Museum, Shedd Aquarium

10 GREAT PLACES TO VIEW BUTTERFLIES IN CHICAGO

The butterfly meadow at Montrose Point Bird Sanctuary is an excellent place to see butterflies. But there are many other spots you can glimpse giant swallowtail, monarch, orange sulphur, common buckeye, and other species of butterflies

MORE ABOUT PIPING PLOVERS

Piping plovers are a small plover species that have short bills. They feed on insects (small beetles, shore flies, water boatmen, midges), marine worms, and small crustaceans. In North America, piping plovers breed only in three geographic regions: the Atlantic Coast, the Northern Great Plains, and the Great Lakes. The U.S. Fish & Wildlife Service reports that Great Lakes piping plovers "breed on sparsely vegetated beaches, cobble pans, or sand spits of sand dune ecosystems along the Great Lakes shorelines." It's estimated that there are only 65 to 70 nesting pairs of piping plovers in the Great Lakes. In 2019, two piping plovers (who were named Monty and Rose) became the first to nest within the city limits of Chicago since 1955. The writer Bob Dolgan even created a short movie—*Monty and Rose*—about these two birds who caught the imagination of Chicagoans. Visit www.montyandrose.net to see the movie. Piping plovers winter along South Atlantic, Gulf Coast, and Caribbean beaches and barrier islands. Visit www.audubon.org/field-guide/bird/piping-plover to learn more about piping plovers.

A piping plover © U.S. Fish & Wildlife Service

(Illinois has about 150 species of these winged wonders). Top spots in Chicago include Humboldt Park Bird and Butterfly Sanctuary, Lincoln Park Zoo (Nature Boardwalk), North Park Village Nature Center (see page 49), Powderhorn Marsh and Prairie (see page 58), Peggy Notebaert Nature Museum (see page 56), and Rainbow Beach.

NORTH PARK VILLAGE NATURE CENTER

THE PERFECT PLACE TO SPEND A FEW HOURS HIKING, PICNICKING, AND LEARNING ABOUT NATURE

The boardwalk at the nature center
© Andrew Morkes

Do you have young children who are going stir crazy at home? Older kids who want to learn about nature and geology? No kids, but looking for an easy hike amidst nature—all within Chicago's city limits? Interested in taking a class on yoga, writing about nature, or other self-improvement topics? If so, the North Park Village Nature Center is a good destination. It's the only nature center in Chicago, and it features 46 acres of oak savannah, prairie, pond, and wetland surrounded by busy roads and hidden in the summer and fall by dense stands of trees and foliage.

The nature center is a popular destination for our family. It served as an excellent way to introduce our now six-year-old son to wildlife and nature.

Where: 5801 North Pulaski Road, Chicago, IL 60646

Learn More: Chicago Park District, 312/744-5472, www.chicagoparkdistrict.com/parks/North-Park-Village-Nature-Center, www.facebook.com/NorthParkVillageNatureCenter

Open: 10:00 a.m. to 4:00 p.m., daily (except closed on Thanksgiving, Christmas, New Year's Eve, and News Year's Day)

Quick Review: A nature preserve and educational facility that offers easy walking trails through woodlands, wetlands, prairie, and savanna; a hands-on exploratory room of natural objects (antlers, shells, pine cones, fossils, etc.); a children's play area that includes a small library; and public programs for preschoolers, school age children, families, and adults. (#8 on the map on page 6)

What You Can Do There: Birdwatching, Educational and Self-Enrichment Opportunities and Classes, Hiking, Nature Center, Photography, Picnicking, Snowshoeing

The pond at North Park Village Nature Center © Andrew Morkes

Wildflowers and wildlife abound in the late spring, summer, and fall. On a visit last summer, we saw fish, water spiders, frogs, turtles, chipmunks, raccoons, squirrels, and even a young buck, who came around a bend suddenly by the wetland boardwalk and walked toward us nonchalantly as if we were just three other deer. My son loved exploring the trails (which provide an easy hike except for one optional big hill that's fun to climb), laying down on the boardwalk to investigate the inhabitants of the wetland, and looking under logs for worms and bugs.

It may not seem like winter is the best time to visit a nature center, but I highly recommend a winter visit—especially after a heavy snowfall. The nature center will most likely be your own for a peaceful walk as the wind blows through the barren tree branches, snow coats the ground like a comfy blanket, and all types of wildlife slumber underfoot and deep beneath the ice-covered pond.

The nature center itself is pretty cool (if I may use a sophisticated word)—filled with "you can touch" specimens such as antlers, giant pinecones, bones, and rocks. You can also view a real "beehive" in a window at the center. There's a kid's activity room with nature books and animal puppets. The center offers many programs and special events such as the Maple Syrup Festival, Harvest Festival, Winter Solstice Celebration, and City Wilds Fest. Finally, be sure to pack a picnic lunch. Several picnic tables are available as you enter the woods.

NEARBY NATURE DESTINATIONS

Bunker Hill Woods, Caldwell Woods, Catherine Chevalier Woods, LaBagh Woods, Lake Michigan, Schiller Woods, Sidney Yates Flatwoods, Thaddeus S. "Ted" Lechowicz Woods, West Ridge Nature Preserve

THE OUTERBELT TRAIL

AN EPIC URBAN-SUBURBAN HIKE

The Outerbelt Trail is a 210-mile hike through and around Chicago that winds its way through a variety of natural spaces (areas in the Forest Preserves of Cook County, Chicago Park District, and Lake County Forest Preserves) and pedestrian or bike-walk infrastructure. You'll travel through areas of wilderness and swear you're in the wilds of northern Wisconsin or Michigan, and you'll also journey along Chicago's lakefront and through urban and suburban landscapes that mix nature and development. You will pass Chicago landmarks such as Lincoln Park Zoo, Brookfield Zoo, and Chicago Botanic Garden, as well as trek through forests, grasslands, bogs, marshes, prairies, and other ecosystems. Through-hikers can stay in forest preserve campgrounds or in hotels in areas where there are no camping options. The key to enjoying the Outerbelt Trail is to realize that you don't have to hike all 210 miles to get the Outerbelt experience, just a portion here or there until you've completed a majority or all of the trail. Or just complete a few miles and be done.

© Andrew Morkes

The first hikers completed the trail in spring 2018, staying at forest preserve campsites along the way. I've not hiked the Outerbelt Trail in its entirety, but I have traversed various legs of it during my 40 or more years of hiking in Chicagoland.

There are plenty of other hiking trails in Chicagoland (usually in the 10- to 25-mile range), but the Outerbelt Trail is unique because of its length and the wide variety of natural and built environments it traverses. Perhaps someday the Outerbelt Trail will become as famous as some of our nation's renowned through-trails. The Outerbelt Trail is in its infancy, and detailed maps and perhaps even a guidebook are coming in the future.

The Outerbelt Alliance NFP is an organization that promotes the use of the Outerbelt Trail. Visit its website, https://outerbelt.org, for more information. The Hiking Project, a crowd-sourced hiking guide, offers a continually revised map of the trail, as well as a suggested 12-day trail route, at www.hikingproject.com/trail/7066013/the-chicago-outerbelt-route.

PALMISANO PARK

40-FOOT LIMESTONE CLIFFS, GREAT VIEWS, FISHING, AND SLEDDING—ALL IN A CHICAGO NEIGHBORHOOD

Trail to the quarry © Andrew Morkes

You don't expect to find 40-foot limestone cliffs, a stream, beautiful waterfalls, and a pond in the middle of Chicago. But at Palmisano Park, that's just the case. This beautiful urban oasis is an attractive destination for hikers, runners, fishers, wanderers, dog walkers, kite-fliers, urban nature philosophers, and anyone else who loves the outdoors. And don't be misled by the term "park." This is no typical flat city park with freshly-mowed grass, dusty baseball diamonds, and a few beat-up picnic tables.

Palmisano Park is the site of an ancient coral reef that existed 400 million years ago. Dolomite limestone formed from the remains of the reef. In the late 1830s, limestone quarrying operations began at this site and continued till 1970. In the ensuing years, the quarry was used for construction waste. But city planners had another idea for the quarry—turn it into a park to provide the neighborhood with much-needed green space. More than 40,000 square feet of clean topsoil was brought to the site, and, in 2009, Palmisano Park opened to the public.

When I entered Palmisano Park (formerly known as Stearns Quarry) at its north entrance, I was struck by how quickly the sounds of city life dissolved. Blaring car horns and the whoosh of cars on the highways were replaced by

---

Where: 2700 S. Halsted Street, Chicago, IL 60608

Learn More: Chicago Park District, www.chicagoparkdistrict.com/parks-facilities/palmisano-henry-park

Hours: 6 a.m. to 11:00 p.m. every day of the year

Quick Review: A hidden gem in Chicago's Bridgeport neighborhood. Nice nature strolls (1.7 miles in all), interesting terrain, sledding, and great views of the Chicago skyline. Dogs allowed (but they must be leashed). (#10 on the map on page 6)

What You Can Do There: Birdwatching, Fishing, Hiking, Kite Flying, Photography, Picnicking, Running/Exercise, Sledding, Snowshoeing

cricket and birdsong and the sounds of the wind through the native prairie grasses and trees and cascading water (thanks to a beautiful water sculpture and other aquatic features). The landscape architect Ernest Wong designed the sculpture and the entire park, as well as Ping Tom Memorial Park in Chinatown.

At this entrance, visitors have the option to either hike trails that take them to the top of a hill or down to the quarry. I chose the latter. I hiked past late-blooming fall flowers and large boulders that were pulled from the quarry, enjoying the wetlands and prairie habitats as I gradually descended about 30 feet from street level.

PALMISANO PARK: THE MOVIE!

If Palmisano Park was a movie, one of its star actors would be the sky. The design of the hills and trails draw visitors' eyes to the vast sky. It was an Academy Award–winning view when I visited—the day was sunny and the sky was ocean blue and only blemished by a few wispy clouds. The juxtaposition of the prairie grass and oak and other trees against the backdrop of the blue sky reminded me of walking some of the trails at Indiana Dunes National Park (see page 223), or even hiking in the mountains in the western United States.

There are 1.7 miles of trails—metal walkways, recycled timber boardwalks, a crushed stone running path, and other surfaces. The gray metal walkways zig and zag down to the quarry bottom, and they're beautiful in their own right. One of the

The fishing pond at Palmisano Park © Andrew Morkes

© Andrew Morkes

best aspects of this park are the constantly changing views. It's been designed so that you see something different and unique every time you walk further along the trails.

And after some zigging and zagging, I arrived at the quarry fishing pond, which is stocked with bluegill, largemouth bass, and channel catfish, and features a fishing pier that works just as well for nature-watching. The park has a self-sustaining water system that collects rainwater, which is then channeled through wetland terraces throughout the park. Down at the fishing pond, surrounded by 40-foot limestone cliffs on several sides, you'll feel like you're not in the city anymore. You'll forget that thousands of cars are zooming by on Interstates 55 and 90/94 just to the north and east, respectively; forget that 2.7 million people live in this packed city (which boasted only about 4,000 people when it became incorporated in 1837); and forget that you're surrounded by bungalows, auto collision repair stores, fast food joints, and factories just beyond the park.

At the pond, I took some time for reflection and contemplation, and then moved on. The world seemed to come to a standstill at the fishing pond, but real-life responsibilities beckoned from outside this 27-acre gem.

I hiked along the base of the hill, and continued to marvel at the creativity and vision of Ernest Wong and others who created this beautiful addition to Chicago's park system.

Then it was time for the grand finale. I climbed the stone steps to the top of the hill (which local residents have dubbed "Mount Bridgeport"). I passed a few flowers valiantly hanging on amidst the recent freezing Chicago nights and then walked through an area of tall prairie grass. I caught a glimpse of something that surprised me. Through the tall grass I saw first Willis Tower and then the rest of

Chicago's skyline. I've lived in Chicago my entire life and viewed its stunning skyline thousands of times, but I was overcome by wonder because I'd never seen it from a prairie. These massive monoliths of modern life were obscured by the golden grass, which waved vigorously in the strong wind. They seemed small and insignificant partly hidden behind the grass.

I reached the top of the hill. There it was! My city—a captivating, yet befuddling, mix of beauty and violence, poverty and prosperity, miles of miles of concrete and asphalt, 110+ skyscrapers, and islands of nature (including Palmisano Park) hanging on for dear life. I felt like an explorer discovering something new, or at least seeing something in a new way.

I marveled at the view, but I knew I couldn't linger. In a few minutes I'd be back in my car on Halsted, and then merging onto Interstate 94 heading south to my childhood neighborhood of Beverly (see page 32). In a few moments, my solitary time at Palmisano Park would just be another memory as I joined the thousands of other human busy bees making their way through the city. I hoped that I would take something of what I felt and learned at Palmisano Park back into the real world.

TIPS AND INFO

✔ The park is named after Henry Palmisano, a fishing advocate and the proprietor of a neighborhood bait shop. He passed away during its construction.

✔ The park is not just a warm-weather destination. Mount Bridgeport has become a popular sledding destination in the winter.

✔ Birdwatching is another enjoyable activity at the park. During your hike, you might see downy woodpeckers, blue jays, finches, sparrows, and crows, among other types of birds.

✔ The meadow atop the hill is a popular spot for kite-flying.

✔ Palmisano Park is accessible by car (street parking is available on Halsted), but also by bus and the Orange Line. Visit www.transitchicago.com to access directions via public transportation.

✔ Washrooms are available at McGuane Park, which is just south of Palmisano Park. McGuane also has an indoor swimming pool, two gymnasiums, and an assembly hall.

NEARBY NATURE DESTINATIONS AND ATTRACTIONS

Garfield Park Conservatory, Jackson Park, Lake Michigan, Lincoln Park, Peggy Notebaert Nature Museum, Shedd Aquarium, South Shore Nature Sanctuary

PEGGY NOTEBAERT NATURE MUSEUM

LEARN ABOUT NATURE AND VIEW BUTTERFLIES, TURTLES, FISH, AND OTHER CREATURES

The Chicago Academy of Sciences opened the Peggy Notebaert Nature Museum in 1999 to offer hands-on educational experiences to visitors and conduct conservation research. Since then, it has become one of the most popular museums in Chicago. Here are a few things to do at the museum.

Visit the Judy Istock Butterfly Haven. This 2,700-square-foot greenhouse has more than 1,000 free-flying butterflies (40 species) and birds, and it is one of my favorite places at the museum. On freezing winter days, it's relaxing to visit the warm greenhouse filled with butterflies, tropical trees and plants, and soothing pools of water.

Great yellow Mormon butterfly
© meunierd, Shutterstock

Check out the Istock Family Look-in Lab to see scientists and volunteers care for and study the animals that are part of its living collection. It's neat to see all that it takes to keep them healthy and the steps scientists take to conduct research.

View live animals. In addition to butterflies and birds, the museum has box turtles, frogs, fish (dace, minnows, and darters), and other creatures.

Where: 2430 N. Cannon Drive, Chicago, IL 60614

Learn More: Chicago Academy of Sciences, 773/755-5100, https://naturemuseum.org

Hours: Contact the museum for the latest information.

Quick Review: A nature museum that features live animals (including a butterfly greenhouse), nature-oriented art exhibits, a short nature trail, and educational exhibits that help visitors learn more about conservation and the natural world. Admission fee required. (#11 on the map on page 6)

What You Can Do There: Birdwatching, Educational and Self-Enrichment Opportunities and Classes, Nature Center, Photography, Picnicking

BUTTERFLIES AND BIRDS

Here are just a few of the butterflies and birds you can see at the Judy Istock Butterfly Haven and the name of their home continent, region, or country.

Butterflies
Ruby-spotted swallowtail (Southern United States through South America)
Leopard lacewing (Asia)
Forest queen (Africa)
Common postman (Central and South America)
Great orange-tip (Asia)
Malachite (North through South America)

Birds
Gold-breasted waxbill (Sub-Saharan Africa)
Orange-cheeked waxbill (Sub-Saharan Africa)
Yellow-legged honeycreeper (South America)
Button quail (Australia and Asia)
Violaceous euphonia (South America)
Diamond dove (Australia)

Take your kids to splash in the RiverWorks exhibit. Children can learn about natural and human-changed waterways by reversing the flow of a "river," turning a river into a lake, building their own dam, and participating in other activities.

View other exhibits such as Mysteries of the Marsh (which explores seven types of marshland in Chicagoland), Birds of Chicago (that features specimens of more than 115 types of birds that live in Chicago), and Wilderness Walk (where you can trek through a re-creation of a prairie, savanna, and dune).

Participate in a wide range of activities, programs, and events at the museum, including a summer camp for kids ages five to eight, guided nature walks through the museum's outdoor exhibits, and nature art classes. Volunteer opportunities are also available.

Finally, consider becoming a member of the museum. Membership perks include free, daily general admission; reciprocal free admission to more than 300 museums around the world (including the Museum of Science and Industry, Field Museum, and the Adler Planetarium in Chicago, and the Burpee Museum of Natural History in Rockford, Illinois); a subscription to the *Nature Museum* e-newsletter; discounts on paid programs and events and at the museum's store and café; and other benefits.

NEARBY NATURE DESTINATIONS AND ATTRACTIONS

Chicago Riverwalk, Garfield Park Conservatory, Lake Michigan, Lake Shore East Park, Lincoln Park, Maggie Daley Park, Millennium Park, Montrose Point Bird Sanctuary, Palmisano Park, Shedd Aquarium

POWDERHORN PRAIRIE, MARSH, AND LAKE

A UNIQUE DUNE AND SWALE LANDSCAPE, FISHING, AND AN EXCITING RESTORATION PROJECT

Powderhorn Prairie, Marsh, and Lake is a nature gem tucked amongst rail yards, industry, and city and suburban neighborhoods on the far South Side of Chicago. There are two main Powderhorn properties: a 48-acre human-made lake with 7,000 feet of shoreline (which is located in Burnham, Illinois) and Powderhorn Prairie and Marsh Nature Preserve, which is the only state-dedicated nature preserve within Chicago city limits. The preserve protects a rare dune and swale landscape (parallel sandy ridges alternating with low wetlands that were formed by the retreat of glaciers and other processes 10,000 to 15,000 years ago; they often contain rare plants and animals).

I visited Powderhorn Prairie, Marsh, and Lake on a windy, summer-like day in October and was not disappointed. Although this area is not large, here are a few things you can do during your visit:

✔ **Hike the trail that meanders through the Powderhorn Prairie and Marsh Nature Preserve** (the path begins at the back of the parking lot). There are numerous sub trails, so be prepared to wander a bit or simply check out things that catch your fancy.

✔ **Enjoy the ecological diversity.** The preserve is home to approximately 250 plant species, 2,500 insect species, and 40 to 100 bird species. Two state-endangered species—Franklin's ground squirrel and Blanding's turtle—have been sighted at the preserve. According to Forest Preserves of Cook County, trees in this beautiful nature area include black oak, white oak, pin oak, sas-

---

Where: Enter from South Brainard Avenue, east of South Burnham Avenue/south of Avenue O, Burnham, IL 60633; a portion is in Chicago

Learn More: Forest Preserves of Cook County, https://fpdcc.com/places/locations/powderhorn-lake

Hours: Sunrise to sunset, year-round

Quick Review: A pretty lake and a dune and swale landscape that is home to about 250 plant species, 2,500 insect species, and up to 100 bird species. Portions of this area have been declared an Illinois Nature Preserve. (#12 on the map on page 6)

What You Can Do There: Bicycling, Birdwatching, Canoeing/Kayaking/Boating, Fishing/Ice Fishing, Hiking, Photography, Picnicking, Running/Exercise, Snowshoeing

Powderhorn Lake © Andrew Morkes

safras, among others. There are also woody plants such as hazelnut, elderberry, and buttonbush and lower-growing plants such as prickly pear cactus, nodding wild onion, Indian hemp, partridge pea, purple love grass, cinnamon willow-herb, rough blazingstar, Turk's cap lily, and slender false foxglove.

✔ **Look for the aforementioned prickly pear cacti.** It might surprise you to learn that prickly pear cactus can be found in the Chicago area, but areas near the lake used to be covered with cacti before the area was developed. I searched for the cacti during my hike, but did not find any. It was still fun to go on a prickly pear cacti quest. Note: You can also see prickly pear cactus at Kankakee Sands (see page 237).

✔ **Fish for largemouth bass, bluegill, northern pike, bullhead, perch, crappie, sunfish, and channel catfish.** Ice fishing is also popular in the winter.

✔ **Try kayaking, canoeing, or otherwise ply the waters.**

✔ **Picnic along the pretty shore of Powderhorn Lake.**

Powderhorn Prairie, Marsh, and Lake is a beautiful property, but like many nature areas in our highly industrialized society, it is out of whack ecologically if I may use complex scientific terminology. Powderhorn Lake (which was once a large marshland) and nearby Wolf Lake (which connects to Lake Michigan through the Indian Creek pathway to Calumet River) are currently isolated from one other, but historically were connected as part of a massive wetland complex in the Calumet Region. When the areas were linked, they served as a vital marsh ecosystem that hosted least bittern, common gallinule, pied-billed grebe, and other birds, as well as fish, amphibians, mammals, and other creatures. In recent years, water levels at the lake have been high, which have caused damaging water flows into the swales of the nature preserve, flooding in nearby neighborhoods, and too-high water levels at the lake's northern end, which, according to Forest Preserves of Cook County, "is no longer shallow enough to provide an effective fish nursery, impacting the stock of species like northern pike, largemouth bass, yellow perch, and American grass pickerel."

© Andrew Morkes

But there's good news. Big things will be happening at Powderhorn Prairie, Marsh, and Lake in the next three years. Audubon Great Lakes, Forest Preserves of Cook County, the National Oceanic and Atmospheric Administration, and the Great Lakes Commission have launched a project to restore more than 100 acres of wetlands at Powderhorn. The project will install a water control structure to control water levels, re-establish the fish hatchery at Powderhorn Lake, re-link the Powderhorn and Wolf Lake ecosystems, and hopefully reduce flooding in adjacent neighborhoods. "This project builds on a large partnership in the Calumet region of Illinois to restore marshes to their former glory, providing refuge for threatened and common wildlife and improving resilience to heavy storms and lake level fluctuations," said Chip O'Leary, deputy director for resource management at Forest Preserves of Cook County, in a news story at Audubon.com.

The restoration project is great news for an area of Chicagoland that has often received short shrift when it comes to environmental protection. I look forward to revisiting Powderhorn Prairie, Marsh, and Lake to follow the progress of the restoration project. Kudos to all of the organizations and environmental professionals that are making this restoration dream a reality.

NEARBY NATURE DESTINATIONS

Powderhorn Prairie, Marsh, and Lake is a relatively small area that you will probably spend no more than an hour or two visiting. But check out the following destinations to add to your itinerary to make a day of it: Beaubien Woods, Big Marsh Park, Burnham Prairie Nature Preserve, Hegewisch Marsh, Indian Ridge Marsh Park, Sand Ridge Nature Center, Wolf Lake Memorial Park.

THADDEUS S. "TED" LECHOWICZ WOODS

SHOWING SOME LOVE TO A LOCAL NEIGHBORHOOD PRESERVE

My son and I first visited "The Ted, which is officially named Thaddeus S. "Ted" Lechowicz Woods, in response to the reduced opportunities for recreation during the early days of the COVID-19 pandemic. With many of our area forest preserves closed to limit overcrowding, I looked for a place close to our home that we could go to hike and otherwise enjoy nature. We found The Ted, another example of a remnant ecosystem that's hanging on for life in the asphalt jungle that makes up much of Chicagoland. While humble in size, it's a pretty place that features some interesting topography. When we visited, the forest and hills near the river were covered in exuberant gatherings of Virginia bluebells and lesser celandine (which is a beautiful, but very damaging, invasive species—more on lesser celandine later in this story). For two people who had been largely sheltering-in-place for six weeks at that point, seeing the forest filled with flowers made us feel like Dorothy after her world turned from black and white to the bright colors of the fields and hills of Oz in *The Wizard of Oz*.

The Ted is not a wild place like Red Gate Woods (see page 197), Kankakee Sands (see page 237), or Nachusa Grassland (see page 125) that I usually like to visit, but I was happy to be outdoors enjoying nature with my son. There were plenty of runners, bikers, and strollers, but we largely left them behind as we ventured into the woods. We spotted ducks, and minnows, and water bugs. We heard steady birdsong. We marveled at old trees or those that had uniquely shaped branches and the blanket of yellow and blue flowers. We imagined taking our kayak down the river.

Through the trees, we admired the pretty bridge over the river. Cars whizzed by on Central Avenue. We heard a train to the east. Lechowicz Woods is remnant city

---

Where: The entrance is just off Central Avenue and just north of Elston Avenue on Chicago's Northwest Side.

Learn More: Forest Preserves of Cook County, https://fpdcc.com/places/locations/thaddeus-s-ted-lechowicz-woods

Hours: Sunrise to sunset, year-round

Quick Review: While humble in size, this pretty place features some interesting topography along the North Branch of the Chicago River; spring wildflowers; and opportunities for outdoor fun. Dogs allowed (but they must be leashed). (#13 on the map on page 6)

What You Can Do There: Bicycling, Birdwatching, Cross-Country Skiing, Hiking, Photography, Picnicking, Running/Exercise, Sledding, Snowshoeing

LESSER CELANDINE

What is something that is beautiful and soothing (especially after largely sheltering-in-place for six weeks), but extremely destructive to our local ecosystems and the scourge of botanists and environmental restoration workers everywhere? If you answered, lesser celandine, you're correct. (Lesser celandine is also known as fig buttercup, pilewort, small celandine, lesser crowfoot, buttercup, and dusky maiden.) This plant was native to Europe, northern Africa, Siberia, and western Asia, but was brought to the United States as an ornamental plant and quickly got out of control. The Urban Ecology Center says that lesser celandine is "so aggressive that many native plants that are very important for wildlife just can't compete. And lesser celandine emerges so early that it has already established itself by the time our native spring ephemerals are just starting to emerge." You can learn more about lesser celandine, other invasive species, and what you can do to stop these invasives from ruining the diversity of forests, grasslands, prairies, and wetlands at the center's website, https://urbanecologycenter.org. After visiting the Lechowicz Woods Facebook page (www.facebook.com/pages/Thaddeus-S-Ted-Lechowicz-Woods/1543786289203563), I learned that volunteers have been working hard to restore this beautiful area and improve its biological diversity.

nature for sure (with a serious problem with invasive species), but still wonderful in its own way. We walked. We explored. It was enough in the time of COVID-19.

I bet Lechowicz Woods is a beautiful and serene place just after sunrise when the woods open, or right before sunset. Give it a try if you're looking for some exercise and peace when life gets challenging. Go early or late in the day to avoid the crowds.

I must admit that The Ted is not a "bucket list" kind of place—like the rest of the destinations in this book. Rather, it's an example of Chicagoland nature that has managed to survive the rapid development of Chicagoland in the last 100 years. There is a Ted in your neighborhood that is small and a bit flawed, but still very beautiful. These remnants bring joy and peace to those who can't travel far from their homes or who just want to enjoy the sights and sounds of a forest, river, prairie or grassland for a short time amidst a pandemic or during their lunch break. I hope that you'll find your own Ted in your area and savor it. Finally, Lechowicz Woods links up with several other preserves and the North Branch Trail System. (You can actually walk or bike the trail all the way to the Chicago Botanic Garden, see page 66). Visit https://fpdcc.com/downloads/maps/trails/english/FPCC-North-Branch-Trail-Map-022020.pdf for a map to learn more.

NEARBY NATURE DESTINATIONS

Bunker Hill, Caldwell Woods, Catherine Chevalier Woods, LaBagh Woods, Lake Michigan, North Park Village Nature Center, Schiller Woods, Sidney Yates Flatwoods, West Ridge Nature Preserve

WEST RIDGE NATURE PRESERVE

AN OASIS NEXT TO A SPEEDWAY

Tree Towers © Andrew Morkes

Western Avenue between Peterson and Bryn Mawr Avenues is an urban speedway. Cars race through this densely packed neighborhood as if there's a pot of gold waiting at road's end in each direction. (Western, by the way, is the longest road—24 miles—in Chicago.) These thoughts passed through my mind as my nine-year-old son and I exited our car after parking on Western.

But within a few seconds after entering West Ridge Nature Preserve, we were in a different state of mind. It is a place of dense green woods, wildflowers, birdsong, and soothing waters. A place of peace and contemplation just steps away from the Chicago pot-of-gold speedway.

Until 2015, what is now known as West Ridge Nature Preserve was an undeveloped part of the historic Rosehill Cemetery (founded in 1859) that had never been used for burials. Its fetid pond and dense woods served as a dumping ground for excess dirt and debris from the cemetery. Then, after a strong push

Where: 5601 N. Western Avenue (intersection of Ardmore Avenue & Western), Chicago, IL 60659

Learn More: Chicago Park District, www.chicagoparkdistrict.com/parks-facilities/west-ridge-nature-park, www.facebook.com/groups/park568

Hours: Dawn to dusk, year-round

Quick Review: Nearly 22 acres of restored woodlands, wetlands, and a pond. A perfect place for a short hike or contemplation. Beautiful hiking trails, fishing access points, a kids' outdoor play area, and much more. There is no ice skating on the pond and no dogs allowed within the grounds. (#14 on the map on page 6)

What You Can Do There: Birdwatching, Educational and Self-Enrichment Opportunities and Classes, Fishing, Hiking, Kids Play Area, Photography, Picnicking, Running/Exercise, Snowshoeing

by community activists, the area was purchased by the Chicago Park District and reimagined as an urban oasis. Invasive plants were removed and replaced with more than 500 native trees and shrubs, a boardwalk and other trails were built, the pond was dredged and otherwise restored, and pleasant overlooks and fishing access points were created. The area is still a work in progress, but what exists now is beautiful, serene, and special—especially in a big city that is always in need of more green space.

My son and I had a wonderful time walking the trail that winds around the pond on a June day that was more like early-May with its cool temperature and chalky cloud cover. Here are some things you can do when you visit West Ridge Nature Preserve:

✔ **Enjoy strolling the boardwalk and other trails that circle the pond, streams, and travel through the woods.**

✔ **Go for a run.**

✔ **Cast your line to try to catch a bluegill or sunfish.**

✔ **Have a picnic along the shore of the pond.**

✔ **Go birdwatching.** Some of the birds spotted at the preserve include ring-billed gulls, great blue herons, northern flickers, American goldfinches, song sparrows, red-winged blackbirds, herring gulls, eastern kingbirds, red-eyed vireos, black-capped chickadees, yellow warblers, cedar waxwings, double-crested cormorants, blue gray gnatcatchers, ruby-throated hummingbirds, spotted sandpipers, and scarlet tanagers.

✔ **See other wildlife such as deer, turtles, coyotes, frogs, and toads.**

✔ **Take your kids to (or act like a kid again) at the Nature Play Space.**

✔ **Participate in a variety of activities,** such as kids' fishing clinics, toddler meet-ups (I assume parents can come along, too), bird and nature walks, and frog surveys. Visit www.westridgenaturepreserve.org/activities for a list of upcoming activities.

✔ **Close your eyes, dream, listed to the sounds of birdsong, and recharge your city-zapped batteries.**

West Ridge Nature Preserve is a special place that I hope you'll visit soon. I look forward to seeing the Chicago Park District's and volunteers' continuing efforts to revitalize this former dumping ground turned stunning urban oasis.

NEARBY NATURE DESTINATIONS AND ATTRACTIONS

Bunker Hill, Caldwell Woods, Catherine Chevalier Woods, LaBagh Woods, Lake Michigan, North Park Village Nature Center, Peggy Notebaert Nature Museum, Shedd Aquarium, Sidney Yates Flatwoods, Thaddeus S. "Ted" Lechowicz Woods

CHICAGOLAND NORTH

The Bell Tower Carillon at The Chicago Botanic Garden © Andrew Morkes

CHICAGO BOTANIC GARDEN

BREATHTAKING GARDENS, MODEL TRAINS, GREENHOUSES, AND FUN IN ANY SEASON

A moment of wonder © Andrew Morkes

The Chicago Botanic Garden (CBG) is a popular destination in any season—but especially during the warmer months. If you love nature and hikes and strolls through flower-filled meadows, English and Japanese gardens, forests, and much more, you could easily spend an entire day touring its 27 gardens and four natural areas. If you love plants, this place will take you to nature nirvana. There are 2,587,596 plants representing 9,694 plant varieties of 232 plant families onsite, according to the CBG website. Using the GardenGuide App 2.0 (www.chicagobotanic.org/app) is a great way to learn more about the Chicago Botanic Garden and navigate its vast expanses. Its features will be especially useful in warmer weather, when

Where: 1000 Lake Cook Road, Glencoe, IL 60022

Learn More: Forest Preserves of Cook County, 847/835-6801, www.chicagobotanic.org

Hours: Open every day of the year; hours change seasonally

Quick Review: A nature hotspot with something fun or beautiful for people of any age. There are 27 gardens and four natural areas (including a forest), which are situated on 385 acres on and around nine islands, with six miles of lake shoreline. Nature classes, many fun events, and other activities are available. No pets, skateboards, or rollerblades are allowed. Admission is free, but there is a charge for parking. (#15 on the map on page 8)

What You Can Do There: Bicycling (in certain areas), Birdwatching, Educational and Self-Enrichment Opportunities and Classes, Gift Shop, Hiking, Model Train Exhibit, Nature Center, Photography, Picnicking, Restaurant, Shopping, Tram

you can use its Walking Tours, What's in Bloom, and Plant Guide features. Maps and interpretive guides are also available at the garden.

There are three long, multiuse trails that travel through or near the Chicago Botanic Garden. They include the Green Bay Trail (www.traillink.com/trail/green-bay-trail), Skokie Valley Bikeway (www.traillink.com), and the North Branch Trail (https://fpdcc.com/places/trails/north-branch-trail-system), which brings you into the grounds of the garden).

Don't forget about visiting the CBG in the winter. Although the flowers are gone (except in the greenhouses), the trees are bare, and the lake and waterways may be frozen at times, there's plenty to do at the CBG in winter, including:

✔ Checking out the garden's popular Wonderland Express exhibit. It's an annual holiday extravaganza that features model trains journeying around and above dozens of Chicagoland's major landmarks—from Wrigley Field and the Baha'i Temple to Sears Tower and The Bean—all lovingly created with the use of leaves, wood, and other natural products. There are also water features, snowflakes occasionally falling from the indoor "sky," and holiday music.

✔ Having a relaxing meal or cup of coffee at the Garden View Café and watching nature through the windows. The food is great.

✔ Checking out the garden's large gift shop filled with ideas for holiday presents including books, live plants, kids' toys, clothing, and holiday ornaments.

Wonderland Express © Andrew Morkes

✔ Braving the cold and hiking the grounds (including McDonald's Woods) in solitude or near solitude.

✔ Walking the grounds to enjoy the holiday lights.

✔ Visiting the garden's three amazing greenhouses—two filled with exotic tropical plants (pruned in the summer so that they bloom in the winter to wow us sun-deprived, shivering Chicagoans) and another arrayed with an amazing medley of cacti and succulents (some more than 10-feet tall). Once you enter the greenhouses on a cold winter day, you'll never want to leave.

A wide range of cacti and other succulents are on display at the Chicago Botanic Garden.
© Andrew Morkes

✔ Listening to holiday music at the Christmas Brass Concert with the Chicago Brass Band or enjoying its Hanukkah Concert.

✔ Watching a holiday movie with the kids on select days in December.

✔ Seeing sculptors wield chainsaws and carving tools to create amazing ice art.

In any season, there are literally hundreds of events, classes, and other activities scheduled at the garden. According to its website, the CBG offers "1,500 classes, workshops, programs, and events on everything from the life cycle of plants to painting and photography, butterflies to bonsai, and wilderness survival to yoga workouts, in one of the largest blended indoor/outdoor learning environments in the area." Visit www.chicagobotanic.org/calendar for more info.

Finally, consider becoming a member of the Chicago Botanic Garden. Membership benefits include free parking, a quarterly magazine, and discounts at the café and Garden Shop, as well as discounts on events such as Butterflies & Blooms, Model Railroad Garden (a great summer option), and tram tour tickets. If you make several trips to the CBG, your membership will pay for itself.

Chicagoland North Destinations 69

BIRDING AT THE CHICAGO BOTANIC GARDEN

Although many people visit the CBG for its stunning plants, trees, and flowers, it's also a popular birdwatching destination. Hundreds of bird species have been sighted at the garden. The CBG says that the following bird species are common sights:

Spring: Baltimore oriole, killdeer, red-winged blackbird, rose-breasted grosbeak

Summer: great blue heron, indigo bunting, orchard oriole, purple martin

Fall: American robin, cedar waxwing, golden-crowned kinglet, white-throated sparrow

Winter: American tree sparrow, Cooper's hawk, dark-eyed junco, pine siskin

Year-round: American goldfinch, black-capped chickadee, blue jay, northern cardinal

NEARBY NATURE DESTINATIONS

Captain Daniel Wright Woods Forest Preserve, Edward L. Ryerson Conservation Area, Fort Sheridan Forest Preserve, Harms Woods, Mellody Farm Nature Preserve, Openlands Lakeshore Preserve, Potawatomi Woods, River Trail Nature Center, Skokie Lagoons, Somme Woods

ALL ABOUT MCDONALD'S WOODS

McDonald's Woods, a 100-acre oak woodland at the Chicago Botanic Garden, may be small, but it is home to an amazing range of plants and animals. In fact, garden staff and volunteers have tallied more than 350 species of native plants (including red trillium, Short's aster, purple spring cross, and tall thistle). At least seven state-listed threatened or endangered plant species grow in the woods. They include northern cranesbill, forked aster, dwarf raspberry, bent-seeded hop sedge, brome hummock sedge, small sundrops, and dog violet. Nearly 120 species of birds (such as red-eyed vireo, downy woodpecker, and white-breasted nuthatch) have been sighted at McDonald's Woods, which features red, swamp white, and white oaks. Twenty species of mammals live there. There are two trails: a 0.38-mile North Trail Loop and a 0.22-mile South Trail Loop. Visit the woods on your next trip to the botanic garden for a peaceful and refreshing experience.

EDWARD L. RYERSON CONSERVATION AREA

A HIKERS' HEAVEN, A BIODIVERSITY HOTSPOT, AND OPPORTUNITIES TO LEARN ABOUT LOCAL HISTORY

In the 1920s, a small number of wealthy families—including the Ryerson, Fisher, and Borland clans—bought land at what is now Ryerson Woods and built log cabins as weekend retreats from city life. In 1942, Edward L. Ryerson, a steel magnate and civic leader, built Brushwood as a summer estate. For decades, the property served as his family's summer home. In 1966, Edward and his wife Nora donated Brushwood and 257 acres to Lake County Forest Preserves. The other families also donated their land to help the Edward L. Ryerson Conservation Area to grow to its current 565 acres.

Where do I start when trying to tell you about all the great things you can do at this beautiful nature preserve? It's hard to decide because Ryerson Conservation Area (which is also known as Ryerson Woods) is both an Illinois Nature Preserve (one of nearly 400 such preserves that collectively protect the highest-quality areas in the Prairie State) and is listed on the National Register of Historic Places.

Let's start with the nature-oriented aspects of Ryerson, which my wife, my 10-year-old son, and I visited on an unseasonably warm day in early April. At Ryerson, you can find two rare ecosystems. There are flatwoods (a northern Illinois landscape where you can view pretty marsh and meadow plants such as great blue lobelia, gen-

---

Where: 21950 North Riverwoods Road, Riverwoods, IL 60015

Learn More: Lake County Forest Preserves, www.lcfpd.org/ryerson

Hours: Grounds: 6:30 a.m. to sunset

Welcome Center: 9 a.m. to 5 p.m., Tuesday to Saturday; 11 a.m. to 4 p.m., Sundays; on Mondays, the restrooms are only open. The center is closed on select holidays.

Quick Review: More than 6.5 miles of scenic trails along the Des Plaines River and in nearby woods. This is a place of peace, open land, and beauty. Visit Ryerson for stunning spring wildflowers, vivid fall colors, and all the beautiful moments in between. No bicycles, snowmobiles, horses, or dogs and other pets are allowed. (#16 on the map on page 8)

What You Can Do There: Birdwatching, Cross-Country Skiing, Educational and Self-Enrichment Programs, Farm, Hiking, Local History, Nature Center, Photography, Picnicking, Running/Exercise, Snowshoeing

Boardwalk along the Des Plaines River © urbs in horto, Shutterstock

tian, and cardinal flower) and a floodplain forest (which features silver maple and bur oak). While walking in the floodplain forest and other areas, look for blue-spotted salamanders. They are only found in the northeastern part of Illinois but are common in the Great Lakes region. Ryerson is a biodiversity hotspot, with nearly 600 species of flowering plants and more than 150 bird species.

There are more than 6.5 miles of wide, well-managed hiking/walking trails at Ryerson Woods. Some trails travel along the Des Plaines River, while others allow hikers to trek through prairies and forests.

We parked at the Welcome Center (https://www.lcfpd.org/ryerson/welcome-center) parking lot and first took the 0.4-mile loop trail, which traverses a portion of the river and travels through woodlands on dirt and boardwalk trails. The trees were still bare, but we spotted the first sprouts of spring (trillium, wild leek, false rue anemone, and spring beauty) and a few flowers. By late April/early May, visitors will get the chance to see Dutchman's breeches, bloodroot, sharplobed hepatica, white trout lily, mayapple, cutleaf toothwort, spring cress, and marsh marigold. If you visit in late spring, you can see wild geranium, wild ginger, shooting star, swamp buttercup, Jack-in-the-pulpit, woodland phlox, and other plants.

We next hiked a loop trail that began at the Welcome Center and traveled south along the Des Plaines River for the first half-mile or so. We saw several ducks, as well as two turtles that were as big as serving platters on an episode of *Downton Abbey*. The loop trail then headed east into the woods, where there were many more flowers than we'd seen on the earlier trail. The trails are situated in such a way that you can tailor them to your preferences (i.e., short loop trail to wander with your young children, medium-length routes that allow you

Cabin at Ryerson Woods
© Andrew Morkes

to experience Ryerson's various ecosystems, and longer trails that will allow you to walk for miles and miles in peaceful solitude).

Aside from the nature-oriented aspects, there is plenty more to do at Ryerson Woods in normal times (i.e., post-COVID-19). There is the aforementioned Welcome Center' a small farm area, where you might see sheep, chickens, and goats; and historic cabins, where you can learn about the early history of the area as well as about Illinois nature history and the Des Plaines River. Additionally, Ryerson Woods hosts popular annual events such as Halloween Hikes and Maple Syrup Hikes.

Be sure to check out Brushwood, the former summer mansion of Edward and Nora Ryerson. It is listed on the National Register of Historic Places. You can tour the home and enjoy concerts and art exhibits, take classes, and participate in other cultural activities. Visit www.brushwoodcenter.org/events.html for a list of scheduled events. There is a parking lot at Brushwood, which can serve as a starting point for many of the hikes in the central and southern portions of the conservation area.

In our two hours at Ryerson Woods, we barely scratched the surface of what there is to do at this Lake County gem. I look forward to hiking more of its trails and visiting the Welcome Center, Brushwood, the farm, and the historic cabins.

NEARBY NATURE DESTINATIONS

Buffalo Creek Forest Preserve, Captain Daniel Wright Woods Forest Preserve, Chicago Botanic Garden, Fort Sheridan Forest Preserve, Mellody Farm Nature Preserve, Potawatomi Woods, River Trail Nature Center, Somme Woods

RIVER TRAIL

The Des Plaines River Trail, a crushed-limestone multi-use path, is located across the river from Ryerson Woods. The trail travels for 31.4 miles (nearly the entire length of Lake County) as it winds through 12 forest preserves. It is open for hiking, bicycling, horseback riding, cross-country skiing, and snowmobiling (between Russell Road and Wadsworth Road only). Visit www.lcfpd.org/dprt to learn more.

ILLINOIS BEACH PARK

BEAUTIFUL DUNE AND LAKE VIEWS AND HIKING AND OTHER OUTDOOR RECREATIONAL ACTIVITIES

Illinois only has 63 miles of Lake Michigan shoreline and much of this land has been developed as part of city lakefronts, heavy industry, and private beachfront property. That's why Illinois Beach State Park is so important—and wonderful. It's the last remaining large swath of undeveloped Lake Michigan shoreline in the state. It's a place where you can still have a natural experience at the lakeshore—especially if you get away from the popular beaches and picnic areas.

There are many things to do and see at Illinois Beach State Park (IBSP), but first let me give you an overview of the park. The 4,160-acre park consists of two separate areas: a North Unit and a South Unit. The North Unit features the North Dunes Nature Preserve and opportunities for hiking, biking, fishing, cross-country skiing, picnicking, swimming, and birdwatching (you might see Henslow's sparrows, American bitterns, ospreys, great blue herons, egrets, belted kingfishers, and other birds during your visit). The North Point Marina—a full-service marina with 1,500 slips, a boat service center, and food concession—is located just north of the park. Note: The North Unit was formerly the site of an Illinois National Guard rifle range, so some locals still call it "Camp Logan." At the South Unit, you'll find the Visitor Center, Illinois Beach Resort and Conference Center, and the park's campsite, as well as opportunities to hike, bike, swim, fish, picnic (including a picnic area for those with disabilities), and

Where: 1 Lake Front Drive, Zion, IL 60099

Learn More: Illinois Department of Natural Resources, 847/662-4811, www2.illinois.gov/dnr/Parks/Pages/AdelineJayGeo-KarisIllinoisBeach.aspx

Hours: Sunrise to Sunset, year-round

Quick Review: Nearly 6.5 miles of beach, dunes, marshes, and forestland along Lake Michigan. Excellent hiking trails, enjoyable birdwatching, opportunities for beach fun, and much more. Campsites and lodging at the Illinois Beach Resort and Conference Center are available. Dogs (on leashes) are allowed in all areas except the beach and nature preserves. (#17 on the map on page 8)

What You Can Do There: Beach Fun, Bicycling, Birdwatching, Camping/Hotel, Canoeing/Kayaking/Boating, Cross-Country Skiing, Dune Climbing, Educational and Self-Enrichment Opportunities and Classes, Fishing, Geocaching, Hiking, Nature Center, Photography, Picnicking, Running/Exercise, SCUBA Diving, Snowshoeing

View of Lake Michigan from Illinois Beach State Park © Donna Ochoa, Shutterstock

do other activities such as birdwatching (at the lakeshore and at the Illinois Beach Nature Preserve). Here are some things to do at IBSP:

Take a hike. There are 5 miles of trails in the South Unit, including the 2.2-mile Dead River Loop Trail. In the North Unit, you can hike or cross-country ski on the Camp Logan Trail, a 1.8-mile multi-use loop path.

Stay overnight. The campground has 241 Class A Premium sites with electricity and access to showers and sanitary facilities. You can reserve a site at https://camp.exploremoreil.com. Some campsites are available on a first-come, first-served basis, but the campground fills up quickly on summer weekends. There are also three campsites for people with disabilities. The campground is open from April 1 through December 30. The Illinois Beach Resort and Conference Center is the only hotel in Illinois that's located directly on the shore of Lake Michigan. There are 96 rooms—all with lake views. Reservations can be made by visiting https://ilresorts.com or calling 847/625-7300.

Enjoy wildflowers and wildlife viewing. More than 650 plant species have been recorded in the dunes area alone. The Dead River—which meanders through marshland and is blocked by sandbars much of the year—actually features a variety of fish, amphibians, aquatic plants, and birds (such as sandhill cranes and great egrets). You'll also see Caspian terns and ring-billed gulls at the beach. You can see a long list of birds that have been sighted at IBSP by visiting https://ebird.org.

NEARBY NATURE DESTINATIONS AND OTHER ATTRACTIONS

Greenbelt Forest Preserve, Kenosha Sand Dunes, Lyons Woods Forest Preserve, Six Flags Great America

OPENLANDS LAKESHORE PRESERVE

BREATHTAKING VIEWS OF LAKE MICHIGAN, A RARE RAVINE AND BLUFF ECOSYSTEM, AND GREAT HIKING TRAILS

The land that makes up Openlands Lakeshore Preserve was once part of the historic Fort Sheridan military base. In the 1990s the base closed, and the land was gradually sold. In 2004, Openlands (a nonprofit conservation and open space advocacy organization that was founded in 1963) acquired 77 acres to create the preserve. Openlands faced many challenges as it worked to return this largely derelict land to a natural state. The three ravines in the preserve had been damaged from water runoff from the streets and homes above. The high volume of water caused erosion in the ravines and brought the seeds of invasive species (e.g., buckthorn, Norway maple, black locust, and honeysuckle) into the preserve—causing native plants to suffer. The Army had also dumped its trash in one of the ravines. Openlands staff and volunteers removed debris and invasive species, planted native seed mixes, repaired an old sewer system, conducted prescribed burns, and addressed some of the worst areas of erosion to turn the preserve into a healthy, natural environment. Restoration and improvement efforts are ongoing, but the work Openlands staff and volunteers did prompted the Illinois Nature Preserves Commission to designate the Openlands Lakeshore Preserve as an Illinois Nature Preserve in 2013 due to its value as one of the last remaining ravine and bluff ecosystems in the Chicago metropolitan region.

When you hear "lakeshore," it's easy to conjure images of swimming, boating, and fishing, but Openlands Lakeshore Preserve is not that kind of place. Its list of prohibited activities (*NO swimming, wading, paddling, boating, fires, camping, drones, alcohol, smoking, firearms*) might be off-putting to some, but banning

Where: 3136 Patten Road, Highland Park, IL 60035

Learn More: Openlands, 312/863-6250, www.openlands.org/livability/lakecounty/openlandslakeshorepreserve, www.facebook.com/openlandslakeshorepreserve

Hours: 6:30 a.m. to sunset daily, year-round

Quick Review: A nearly 80-acre Illinois Nature Preserve with steep ravines, gravel and clay bluffs, and one mile of lakefront access. Dogs are allowed (but they must be leashed, and they're not allowed on the beach). (#18 on the map on page 8)

What You Can Do There: Bicycling, Birdwatching, Hiking, Photography, Picnicking, Running/Exercise, Snowshoeing

these activities protects the preserve from overuse and positions it as a true natural place. Despite these restrictions, there are plenty of things you can do at the preserve, including:

Go hiking. There are three trails that allow you to walk atop the bluffs (70 feet above the lakeshore), through a ravine (via the Bartlett Ravine Trail), or along one mile of beach, and the paved trails (including one that travels to the beach) are accessible for visitors who have a disability. Visit www.openlands.org/wp-content/uploads/2021/03/1-OLP-Trail-Map-2020.02.18.pdf for a trail map, but check with the preserve before visiting for information on trail expansions or closures. Note: Trails are closed when ice or snow are present.

Enjoy the wildflowers and autumn colors. In the spring, look for large-flowered bellwort, white and red trillium, bloodroot, early-meadow rue, white trout lily, wild geranium, mayapple, Jack-in-the-pulpit, and spring beauty. During summer walks, you'll see wild bergamot, jewelweed, woodland sunflower, black-eyed Susan, golden Alexanders, zigzag goldenrod, and other flowers. In the fall, you can watch the leaves of the white, bur, red, and black oak; paper birch; and other trees come alive with deep reds and oranges and vibrant yellows.

Go birdwatching. Birds such as robins, sparrows, blue jays, woodpeckers, owls, and hawks live in the preserve year-round, but spring and fall migration is the time to really enjoy birdwatching. During these times, more than 300 bird species pass through the preserve. Some of the migrating birds that have been recorded at the preserve include redheaded mergansers, Caspian terns, double-breasted cormorants, American kestrels, indigo buntings, and ruby-throated hummingbirds.

Enjoy Lake Michigan. As Chicagoland residents, we are lucky to live along one of the Great Lakes, but sometimes don't take the time to appreciate it. During your visit, savor the opportunity to relax and observe our beautiful lake, the waterfowl who visit it in all seasons, the sandy shore, the cliffs, and everything else that makes this ravine and bluff ecosystem so special.

View some art. There are not too many preserves that combine nature and art, but this is one of them. As you hike, look for *Reading the Landscape* (which was designed by Kate Friedman), *Erode* (Vivian Visser), *Arc of Nature* (Chicago Public Art Group), *The Soil is Alive* (Sharon Bladholm), and *Lake, Leaf, and Earthbark Prism Series* (Olivia Petrides). You can read descriptions and view photos of these works of art at https://openlandsdotorg.files.wordpress.com/2016/04/olp-visitors-guide.pdf.

NEARBY NATURE DESTINATIONS

Captain Daniel Wright Woods Forest Preserve, Chicago Botanic Garden, Edward L. Ryerson Conservation Area, Fort Sheridan Forest Preserve, Green Bay Trail, Mellody Farm Nature Preserve, Middlefork Savanna Forest Preserve, Robert McClory Bike Path, Skokie Lagoons, Somme Woods

RIVER TRAIL NATURE CENTER

BIRDWATCHING, HIKING, GREAT VIEWS OF THE DES PLAINES RIVER, AND MUCH MORE

Turtle time at the nature center
© Andrew Morkes

Are we really in a Chicago suburb?, I asked myself as my young son and I hiked trails that brought us close to the Des Plaines River and then took us through wetlands and woodlands that were ubiquitous with mayapples that resembled a mini-forest on the ground beneath the real trees. We were at the River Trail Nature Center in Northbrook, Illinois, about 11 miles northwest of our home, but that seemed like a world away. This area of the river was stunning and appeared as if it belonged in some wild stretch of America—not in a Chicago burb. We'd come

Where: 3120 Milwaukee Avenue, Northbrook, IL 60062

Learn More: Forest Preserves of Cook County, 847/824-8360, https://fpdcc.com/places/locations/river-trail-nature-center, www.facebook.com/River-Trail-Nature-Center-101211133291824

Hours: Grounds and trails: open seven days a week, from 8 a.m. to 4 p.m.

Visitor Center: March to October: 9 a.m. to 5 p.m., November-February: 9 a.m. to 4 p.m., closed Fridays all year

The entire center is closed on Thanksgiving/Christmas Day/New Year's Day.

Quick Review: Beautiful views of the Des Plaines River; great birdwatching; three easy-to-hike trails through forest and wetlands; and a Noah's Ark–menagerie of other animals for viewing—from flying squirrels, frogs, turtles, snakes galore, and lizards indoors, to a coyote, bald eagle, owls, and an impressive bee colony outdoors. Sorry, no lions, tigers, or bears. The nature center has a large children's indoor play and exploration area. No dogs allowed. (#19 on the map on page 8)

What You Can Do There: Birdwatching, Educational and Self-Enrichment Opportunities and Classes, Hiking, Nature Center, Photography, Snowshoeing

View of the Des Plaines River from near the Visitor Center.
© Andrew Morkes

on a Friday, when the visitor center was closed, so we had the grounds mostly to ourselves. My son eventually got over his disappointment at the closed nature center as we checked out the bald eagle in his enclosure (he'd been shot in one of his wings and would live the rest of his life at the center), a curious coyote, and, stoic, but fascinating, owls.

We first hiked the Grove Portage Trail (0.5 miles), which is an easy and pleasant ramble through the woods. Then, we headed to my favorites, the Little Fort Trail and Green Bay Trail (a combined 0.8 miles). I like these trails because the terrain is a little more interesting, the paths are closer to the river and wetlands, and it seems like there are more opportunities to view birds and other wildlife. Visit http://fpdcc.com/downloads/maps/nature-centers/english/FPCC-River-Trail-Nature-Center-Map-4-17.pdf for a map of the trails.

Back at the nature center, my son and I took a break from hiking to sit and watch the river. We looked up and saw what seemed like a "winged creature superhighway." Tree swallows periodically alit from the wetlands and swooped down to the water for a quick bug meal. Canada geese descended and landed en-mass a few hundred feet from us. Other birds chirped and chased one another mid-air, occasionally settling down on jutting rocks and logs at this Hollywood-quality stretch of the Des Plaines River. The dragonflies were not to be outdone. They conducted their own feeding, playing, and mating games above the river and in the field between the river and the nature center. High

BIRDWATCHING AT RIVER TRAIL NATURE CENTER

Birds are everywhere. A nature center ranger gave me this report: "At the feeders, we regularly get ruby-throated hummingbird, blue jay, red-winged blackbird, mourning dove, house sparrow, woodpeckers (red-bellied, downy, and hairy), Baltimore oriole, cardinal, and Cooper's hawk. Near the river are Canada goose, mallard, tree swallow. Soaring overhead are red-tailed hawk and turkey vulture. There are also house finch, goldfinch, black-capped chickadee, and white-breasted nuthatch. Besides the regulars, there are more than 96 species recorded here and in the surrounding forest preserve. Happy birding!"

© Andrew Morkes

above us, a lone red-tailed hawk circled in the warm sun, waiting patiently for lunch.

And the birds and dragonflies watched us humans below: a father and his son enjoying each other's company—sipping water, having a snack, throwing twigs into the water, kidding around, looking for fish and other wildlife, and talking about everything and nothing. I savored the privilege of being a parent and the opportunity to share my love of nature with my son.

I could go on and tell you about the importance of the area's wetlands to wildlife and humans, of the Native Americans who lived in these woods until as recently as 200 years ago, of the attempts to remove invasive species such as garlic mustard, and much more. But sometimes a memorable nature trip involves nothing more than time with your son hiking through wetlands and woods and watching the beauty of a meandering river amidst birdsong as the wind gently rustles the leaves of the trees around you.

TIPS FOR A SUCCESSFUL VISIT

✔ Bring bug repellent. The mosquitoes can be fierce in shadier spots in the forest.

✔ The hikes I mentioned are perfect for children of any age, but if you're looking for lengthier trails, you can connect to the Des Plaines Trail System (DPTS, http://fpdcc.com/downloads/maps/trails/english/FPCC-Des-Plaines-Trail-Map-10-15.pdf) near the nature center. The DPTS follows the Des Plaines River for 22 miles south in Cook County and another 31 miles north through Lake County.

The nature center has a large children's indoor play and exploration area, where kids can climb into an "eagle nest," crawl in a "fox den," view Native American artifacts, play checkers on a tree stump, read nature books, climb through massive logs (just outside one of the center's doors), and do much more.   © Andrew Morkes

✔ The center offers a wealth of educational programs for people of all ages. Visit https://fpdcc.com/places/locations/river-trail-nature-center for a list of upcoming events.

NEARBY NATURE DESTINATIONS

Caldwell Woods, Chicago Botanic Garden, Edward L. Ryerson Conservation Area, Harms Woods, LaBagh Woods, Potawatomi Woods, Sidney Yates Flatwoods, Skokie Lagoons, Somme Woods

CHICAGOLAND NORTHWEST, WEST, AND BEYOND

Belmont Prairie © Andrew Morkes

BELMONT PRAIRIE

A GLIMPSE OF ILLINOIS' PRAIRIE PAST + 25 OTHER PRAIRIES IN CHICAGOLAND TO VISIT AND ENJOY

Willa Cather, one of my favorite authors, once described the Midwest (especially Nebraska) as a "Sea of Grass." But farms, miles of pavement, and cities and suburbs have replaced much of this vast ecosystem. This is especially true in Illinois, which is misleadingly known as the "Prairie State." Approximately 60 percent of Illinois, or about 22 million acres, once was prairie. Today, only about 2,300 acres of high-quality prairie remain.

    Prairies are a special part of our natural world, and they're sometimes overlooked amidst the forests and Great Lakes of the Midwest. But a walk in a prairie is a wonderful thing in any season. We're living in extremely stressful times, but studies show that a walk in nature is a proven stress buster. The wildflowers, grasses, and wild creatures of Belmont Prairie are a prescription any nature doctor would write to fix the modern-day blues. This small neighborhood prairie is surrounded by homes and located near the interstate—yet you'll feel as if you're in another time the moment you leave the small parking lot at the edge of the prairie and walk the narrow paths surrounded by flowers and tall grasses. A time when a prairie like this covered much of Illinois.

Purple coneflower at Belmont Prairie
© Andrew Morkes

SOME THOUGHTS ON PRAIRIES

✔ I love that there's always something new to see at a prairie depending on the time of year—even the time of day—you visit.

✔ It's a joy to follow the journey of a prairie from the first green shoots fighting their way through the soil in the earliest days of spring, through the heat and wild growth of summer, to the late fall when some flowers take their final bow, while others are just debuting their lovely colors. Select a prairie near you and visit it every month to enjoy this entertainment spectacular. No admission fee required.

Where: Belmont Prairie is located in Downers Grove, Illinois, west of the Downers Grove Golf Course at Haddow Avenue and Cross Street.

Learn More: Downers Grove Park District, www.dgparks.org/belmont-prairie

Hours: Dawn to dusk, year-round

Quick Review: A neighborhood prairie that is a place of peace, beauty, and birdsong. It supports more than 300 species of plant and animal wildlife, including many bird species, fox, raccoons, toads, meadow voles, opossums, ground squirrels, garter snakes and, occasionally, coyotes and white-tailed deer. No dogs, bikes, or cross-country skiing are allowed. (#20 on the map on page 10)

What You Can Do There: Birdwatching, Hiking, Photography

✔ We're so often surrounded by concrete and buildings in our modern world—especially if you live in the city as I do. A visit to a prairie takes you away from this sometimes-claustrophobic world of stone pavement and walls and returns you to a land of lush grasses, big skies, and the good earth.

✔ A prairie is a great place to take your kids to teach them about nature or simply to relax and have some fun. Bring a wildflower book that you can refer to with your kids. I suggest *Prairie Plants of Illinois: A Field Guide to the Wildflowers and Prairie Grasses of Illinois and the Midwest*, by Steve W. Chadde.

✔ I love the interplay of the flowers and prairie grasses with the sky—especially on bright sunny days when the so blue sky is only occasionally shielded by wispy white clouds. Crouch low and gaze at the flowers and sky or, better yet, lie down (not on the flowers!) and soak in a view that humans have enjoyed since time immemorial.

✔ Prairies are key to the health of the natural world, and they must be preserved, protected, and appreciated so that they can be passed on to future generations. It's a shame that only 2,300 acres of high-quality prairie remain in Illinois, but dedicated volunteers throughout our state are working to increase this acreage. We do not need another Wal-Mart or McDonalds, but we do need many more prairies.

I hope you'll visit Belmont Prairie. Budget anywhere from 30 minutes to an hour for your visit, but I wouldn't be surprised if you stay longer. Here are a few other things to keep in mind when you visit Belmont Prairie.

✔ Bring water, bug repellent, and sunscreen.

✔ Wear long pants and long sleeves if you visit during the summer and fall when the prairie is densest.

✔ Wear waterproof boots if you visit after a heavy rain. Parts of the prairie have poor drainage.

✔ Be sure to stay on the narrow trails. All prairies feature delicate ecosystems that can easily be destroyed when people venture off the paths.

✔ Help the Belmont Prairie volunteers maintain the prairie by not picking flowers or collecting seeds, or otherwise gathering anything from the prairie.

✔ This is a small prairie, so don't rush through the trails. Take the time to savor each area. A visit to a prairie is a form of meditation, and my best wishes for you include a blanket of fragrant flowers, tall grasses that make you feel small in the world (but big in your heart), beautiful blue skies, and the chance to be alone amongst your thoughts amidst this beauty.

✔ Visit www.dgparks.org/upload/Belmont_Prairie.pdf for a map, but it will be very hard to get lost.

NEARBY NATURE DESTINATIONS

Bemis Woods, Blackwell Forest Preserve, Herrick Lake Forest Preserve, Morton Arboretum, Salt Creek Woods Nature Preserve, Springbrook Prairie Forest Preserve

MORE PRAIRIES TO VISIT

Here are 25 other beautiful prairies to check out in Chicagoland (many are covered in this book):

- ✔ Bartel Grassland (Tinley Park, IL)
- ✔ Burnham Prairie (Burnham, IL)
- ✔ Cap Sauers Holding Nature Preserve (Palos Park, IL)
- ✔ Elmhurst Great Western Prairie (Elmhurst, IL)
- ✔ Fermilab Prairie (Batavia, IL)
- ✔ Gensburg-Markham Prairie Nature Preserve (Markham, IL)
- ✔ Glacial Park (Ringwood, IL)
- ✔ Goose Lake Prairie State Natural Area (Morris, IL)
- ✔ Illinois Prairie Path (multiple towns)
- ✔ Kankakee Sands (Newton County, IN)
- ✔ James Woodworth Prairie Preserve (Glenview, IL)
- ✔ Kloempken Prairie (near Des Plaines, IL)
- ✔ Lockport Prairie Nature Preserve (Lockport, IL):
- ✔ Midewin National Tallgrass Prairie (Wilmington, IL)
- ✔ Morton Grove Prairie Nature Preserve (Morton Grove, IL)
- ✔ Nachusa Grasslands (Franklin Grove, IL)
- ✔ Orland Grassland (Orland Park, IL)
- ✔ Powderhorn Marsh and Prairie (Chicago, IL)
- ✔ Prairie Wolf (Highland Park, IL)
- ✔ Rollins Savanna (Libertyville, IL)
- ✔ Morton Arboretum (Schulenberg Prairie) (Lisle, IL)
- ✔ Somme Prairie Nature Preserve (Northbrook, IL)
- ✔ Swift Prairie Nature Preserve (DuPage County, IL)
- ✔ Wentworth Prairie (Calumet City, IL)
- ✔ Wolf Road Prairie Nature Preserve (Cook County, IL)

Children enjoy a visit to Bartel Grassland. © Forest Preserves of Cook County

CORAL WOODS CONSERVATION AREA

SPRING FLOWERS, PLEASANT HIKING TRAILS, AND STUNNING FALL COLORS

Trillium © Andrew Morkes

If you're looking for four-season, outdoor fun in Chicagoland, you should visit Coral Woods Conservation Area in McHenry County, Illinois. There are three hiking trails that can be enjoyed in any season. The 1.2-mile Nature Loop Trail is renowned for its woodland wildflowers in the spring. The Sugar Maple Loop Trail is a 0.4-mile walk just off the parking lot. It's a perfect path for people with young children or those who prefer a quick hike. This trail is celebrated for its fall colors. Finally, the 1.2-mile Hiking/Ski Trail takes you through oak and maple groves and provides opportunities for cross-country skiing (when conditions warrant). As you walk the trails, look for chorus and leopard frogs, tiger salamanders, and painted turtles in ephemeral (or vernal) ponds, and see if you can catch sight of deer, raccoons, or even a coyote.

In the spring, walk the woods to see the colorful blooms of Jack-in-the-pulpit, wood anemone, spring beauty, sharp-lobed hepatica, toothwort, bloodroot, wild geranium, blue phlox, and red trillium.

Where: 7400 Somerset Drive, Marengo, IL 60152

Learn More: McHenry County Conservation District, www.mccdistrict.org/visit__explore/places_to_go/find_a_site/coral_woods.php

Hours: Sunrise to sunset, year-round

Quick Review: Nearly 800 acres of red and white oak, hickory, and sugar maple woodlands. Beautiful spring flowers and fall colors. Enjoyable hiking trails. A Festival of the Sugar Maples is held in late February and early March, and outdoor classes are offered year-round. (#21 on the map on page 10)

What You Can Do There: Birdwatching, Cross-Country Skiing, Educational and Self-Enrichment Opportunities and Classes, Hiking, Photography, Picnicking, Running/Exercise, Snowshoeing

Coyote on the hunt © Shutterstock

In the summer, head to Coral Woods for more hiking and wildflower viewing. Enjoy lunch in a picnic area near the parking lot. There is also a reservable picnic shelter (for up to 80 guests) that has a fireplace. **In the fall,** walk the beautiful trails of Coral Woods to see the leaves of red and white oaks, sugar maples, and hickory trees turn a wide array of eye-popping colors. **In the winter,** enjoy the solitude of the trails. The bare trees and snow-covered land have a unique beauty and stillness that is soothing and relaxing as most of nature sleeps beneath the earth or recreates in warmer climes. Don your snowshoes or cross-county skis and explore the preserve on a 1.5-mile, ungroomed trail for cross country skiing.

Birdwatching is popular in all seasons, but best during the spring and fall migrations and in the summer. You might see white-breasted nuthatches, scarlet tanagers, American goldfinches, northern flickers, red-eyed vireos, indigo buntings, blue jays, owls, downy and hairy woodpeckers, robins, great-crested flycatchers, and cedar waxwings, among many other species.

You can also participate in a variety of classes and other educational opportunities at Coral Woods. Recent classes included Discovery Days: Rabbits and Spring Wildflower Walk.

Pair your visit with stopovers at Pleasant Valley Conservation Area (see page 133) and Moraine Hills State Park (see page 117) for a full day of nature adventures.

NEARBY NATURE DESTINATIONS

Brookdale Conservation Area, Kishwaukee Headwaters Conservation Area, Marengo Ridge Conservation Area, Pleasant Valley Conservation Area

CRABTREE NATURE CENTER

TOP-NOTCH HIKING PATHS, AN OUTDOOR PLAY AREA FOR KIDS, AND A BEAUTIFUL NATURE CENTER

© Forest Preserves of Cook County

Crabtree Nature Center is one of six nature centers that are operated by Forest Preserves of Cook County. We're lucky to have such beautiful nature centers in the county. They provide access to hiking trails, nature exhibits and classes, and much more. They also help city folks and suburbanites learn about the importance of protecting the environment and the connection between healthy grasslands, forests, wetlands, lakes, and rivers and our own health and the well-being of society.

Where: 3 Stover Road, Barrington Hills, IL 60010

Learn More: Forest Preserves of Cook County, 847/381-6592, https://fpdcc.com/places/locations/crabtree-nature-center, www.facebook.com/Crabtree-Nature-Center-303888889747096

Hours: March to October: 9 a.m. to 5 p.m., closed Fridays; November to February: 9 a.m. to 4 p.m., closed Fridays. Closed Thanksgiving, Christmas, New Year's Day

Quick Review: More than 1,000 acres of rolling, glacier-formed landscape that features woodlands, wetlands, a lake, ponds, and prairies; 3.4 miles of hiking trails; excellent bird-watching; and beautiful spring flowers and fall colors. No dogs (except service dogs) allowed. (#22 on the map on page 10)

What You Can Do There: Birdwatching, Hiking, Nature Center, Photography, Running/Exercise, Self-Enrichment and Educational Programs, Snowshoeing (rentals available)

88   Nature in Chicagoland

Nature explorations   © Andrew Morkes

But beyond all these "big ideas," nature centers are fun—especially for children. Crabtree Nature Center is a fun place to take your kids. Just a short hike from the nature center, there is a Nature Play Area, where your kids can participate in a variety of hands-on nature activities to develop their imaginations and creativity and learn about the natural world. They can climb a row of tree stumps or a pile of wood chips, observe frogs in a tiny pond, crawl across a massive "spider web," lift up log slices to see what's under them, and explore the nearby woods via a boardwalk trail. On a recent visit, my son enjoyed these activities, as well as breaking out his nature exploration kit he'd brought from home to peer at ants and other bugs with his magnifying glass and collect leaves and rocks for further study. Crabtree Nature Center offers scheduled events in which children can learn how to safely shoot a bow and arrow (the arrows feature soft, blunt tips), learn how to climb a tree (while wearing a harness and safety gear), and participate in other hands-on activities.

Your kids will also love the nature center, where they can view many types of fish, map turtles, a woodland thrush, an eastern screech owl, snakes, and other animals; learn about ecosystems; and participate in a variety of enjoyable activities. There are also outside enclosures that house a barred owl, red-tailed hawk, and great horned owl. Crabtree Nature Center has a lot more to offer visitors. For example, you can:

Hike the nature center's beautiful trails that travel along Crabtree Lake, Sulky Pond, and Bulrush Pond, as well as through forest, gentle hills, prairies, and marshes. Paths include the Bur Edge Trail (1.4 miles), Phantom Prairie Trail (1.4 miles), and Giant's Hollow Trail (0.2 miles). The trails connect in a loop, so you can make a short trek or a long one depending on your interests. Note: There is not a lot of shade on the Phantom Prairie Trail, so be sure to wear sunscreen and a hat. Visit https://fpdcc.com/downloads/maps/nature-centers/english/FPCC-Crabtree-Nature-Center-Map-4-17.pdf for a trail map.

Go birdwatching. Some birds you might see include red-winged blackbirds, woodcocks, lesser scaups, great horned owls, black-capped chickadees, white-throated sparrows, sandhill cranes, dark-eyed juncos, nuthatches, red-bellied woodpeckers, chickadees, mallard ducks, song sparrows, green-winged teals, northern shovelers, double-crested cormorants, bald eagles, pelicans, great blue herons, and geese. Visit https://ebird.org/hotspot/L152623 for an extensive list of birds sighted at the nature center.

See a variety of other animals—such as deer, coyotes, beavers, muskrats, foxes, green frogs, spring peepers, turtles, butterflies, and dragonflies.

View colorful wildflowers such as Jack-in-the-pulpit and Dutchman's breeches (in the spring), swamp rose mallow (in mid-summer to early fall), and goldenrods and bottle gentian (in late fall).

Participate in an outdoor education activity. Recent classes and events include Wake Up with Nature: Amphibians; Spring Bird Walk; Wake Up with Nature: Songbirds; Celebrating Earth Day; and Winter Warm-up (i.e., s'mores beside a crackling fire).

That's just the start of what you can do at Crabtree Nature Center. Visit the center for a hike, some nature play, or to see the wildflowers or fall colors—or check out a nature center in your area. You won't be disappointed.

NEARBY NATURE DESTINATIONS

Arthur L. Janura Preserve, Cuba Marsh Forest Preserve, Deer Grove Forest Preserve, Ned Brown Preserve, Paul Douglas Preserve, Poplar Creek Forest Preserve, Spring Lake Forest Preserve, Spring Valley Nature Center

Nature play © Amy McKenna

DICK YOUNG FOREST PRESERVE

GREAT HIKING TRAILS, BIG SKIES, AND ONE OF THE BEST BIRDING SPOTS IN KANE COUNTY

The sky is king (and queen) at Dick Young.
© Andrew Morkes

Dick Young Forest Preserve is a stunning place with vast views that reach the horizon. It's the kind of destination that makes you feel like a tiny speck navigating the landscape, but big in your heart because you are surrounded by what seems like miles and miles of open space. For someone who lives on the Northwest Side of Chicago—who can count 20 or so homes from his backyard—this is a refreshing and invigorating feeling. I visited the preserve on an unseasonably hot (mid-80s) day in late April. The winds were howling, which cooled me a bit as I hiked, but the sun was fierce on an almost cloudless sky. Dragonflies and birds whizzed around the prairie, and I was in nature nirvana. A place where I was alone in nature for probably 99.9 percent of my visit.

Where: Batavia, Illinois. The main entrance (north) is located at 39W115 Main Street, Batavia, IL 60510 (approximately two miles west of Randall Road). The east entrance is located at 2S326 Nelson Lake Road, Batavia, IL 60510.

Learn More: Forest Preserve District of Kane County, https://kaneforest.com/location/dick-young

Hours: Sunrise to sunset, year-round

Quick Review: Nearly 1,300 acres of woodlands, marsh, wetlands, and prairies, along with kettle ponds, streams, and scenic Nelson Lake. Dogs are allowed (but must be leashed). (#23 on the map on page 10)

What You Can Do There: Bicycling, Birdwatching, Hiking, Horseback Riding, Photography, Picnicking, Running/Exercise, Snowshoeing

Dick Young Forest Preserve is one of the best-known and most ecologically important preserves in Kane County. The preserve was named after Dick Young, a naturalist; the chief environmental officer of Kane County for many years; the author of *Kane County Wild Plants and Natural Areas*; and a prime mover, along with other environmentalists, in identifying and protecting rare natural environments in the county. He died in 2011 at age 86.

There are many things to do at the preserve including picnicking, horseback riding, and trail running, but hiking and wildlife watching are my favorites. There are nine miles of trails, some that circle Nelson Lake Marsh, which enjoys special ecological protection because of its designation as an Illinois Nature Preserve. Other trails pass through oak and hickory forests; wetlands; a large, open prairie with native grasses; and croplands (in one area, the horizon was dusty dark due to a farmer busily preparing his fields for spring planting). The trail surfaces are either mowed grass or paved. As I hiked on the paved trails, I vowed to bring my son to the preserve for a fun day of biking. Visit https://kaneforest.com/upload/24-DickYoungTRAILMAP2016.pdf for information on specific trails and a trail map. Note: No horseback riding is allowed in the Illinois Nature Preserve.

Dick Young Forest Preserve is a wildlife mecca. More than 250 bird species have been sighted there. As you hike, there's a good chance you might see American bittern, dickcissels, ring-necked pheasants, white-breasted nuthatches, dark-eyed juncos, bobolinks, goldfinches, ducks, and geese. On the right day, you might see Wilson's phalaropes, sandhill cranes, northern harrier hawks, and black terns. A special treat is the early April arrival of American white pelicans—

A bridge crosses the Lake Run Tributary at Dick Young Forest Preserve. © Andrew Morkes

sometimes numbering up to 250 in a single day. But the pelicans only stay for two to three weeks, so head to the preserve as soon as possible once you hear about their arrival. Visit https://ebird.org/hotspot/L152688 for a list of birds that have been sighted at the preserve.

American white pelican   © Qunge Zhang, Shutterstoock

On a quiet day at the preserve, you might see white-tailed deer or even a coyote. Dozens of muskrat and beaver lodges are a common sight on Nelson Lake in the fall. Of course, you'll see plenty of frogs (they were very active—and loud in the marsh area when I visited), toads, fish, rabbits, and other wildlife.

A portion of the preserve (Nelson Lake Marsh Preserve) was dedicated as an Illinois Nature Preserve by the Illinois Nature Preserves Commission in 1981. These preserves protect the highest quality natural lands in the state. The commission says that the preserve is "very important to wildlife including rare and endangered types. Significant populations of invertebrates include localized species of butterflies such as swamp metalmark, meadow fritillary, purplish copper, and Baltimore checkerspot. Interesting birds such as American bittern, Wilson's phalarope, black tern, sandhill crane, and northern harrier have been observed in the spring and summer months." Visit www2.illinois.gov/dnr/INPC/Pages/Area2KaneNelsonLakeMarsh.aspx to learn more.

Dick Young Forest Preserve is a special and protected place because Dick Young and other environmentalists did the hard work to save this area from development and educate people about its worth. Its value was apparent to me within minutes of first arriving to the preserve. A value that is not tied

Meadowlark Trail © Andrew Morkes

to the short-term profits that could have been made by building a strip mall, an apartment complex, or an industrial park, but the more important long-term worth of creating a place that both protects wildlife and rare ecosystems and brings joy and peace to the masses. As I hiked the trails at the preserve, I thanked Dick Young for his work and wondered what I could do in my town to protect the environment and leave something of value for future generations.

NEARBY NATURE DESTINATIONS

Almon Underwood Prairie Nature Preserve, Aurora West Forest Preserve, Batavia Riverwalk, Johnson's Mound Forest Preserve, LeRoy Oakes Forest Preserve, Peck Farm Park

FULLERSBURG WOODS NATURE EDUCATION CENTER AND FOREST PRESERVE

BIG BUGS, TONS OF FUN ACTIVITIES FOR KIDS, AND TOP-NOTCH HIKING TRAILS

Massive bugs are everywhere at Fullersburg Woods Nature Education Center (FWNEC), which is located in Fullersburg Woods Forest Preserve. A five-foot-long praying mantis perches atop the entrance to the center, a large grasshopper peers down from the roof when you walk behind the center to view the calming currents of Salt Creek, and a massive ant greets kids and parents when they venture inside. But don't worry, this is not some nuclear experiment gone amuck. You will not need a massive fly swatter or a towering can of bug spray to battle these gigantic beasts. They are just whimsical mega-reproductions of local insects that have been placed throughout the center and preserve.

The big bugs provide a nice introduction to FWNEC and the surrounding Fullersburg Woods, but there are many other reasons to visit. Here are five reasons why you should visit this great destination just west of Chicago:

The nature education center is top notch. When you walk inside, you'll be greeted by friendly staff, tons of exhibits (including one that shows birds that have been recently spotted in Fullersburg Woods), books, informational maps

---

Where: 3609 Spring Road, Oak Brook, IL 60523

Learn More: Forest Preserve District of DuPage County, 630/850-8110, www.dupageforest.org/fullersburg-woods-nature-education-center

Hours: The preserve is open daily from one hour after sunrise until one hour after sunset. The Nature Education Center is open Monday through Saturday, 9 a.m. to 5 p.m. and Sundays from 1 to 5 p.m. It's closed on select holidays.

Quick Review: A top-notch nature center with live animals, the skeleton of a 13,000-year-old woolly mammoth, hands-on exhibits in the kids' area, and much more. Good hiking (with trails that range from 0.2 miles to 2.3 miles in length), creek views, and much more. Dogs are allowed in certain areas. (#24 on the map on page 10)

What You Can Do There: Birdwatching, Cross-Country Skiing, Educational and Self-Enrichment Opportunities and Classes, Hiking, Kayaking/Canoeing, Local History, Nature Center, Photography, Picnicking, Running/Exercise, Snowshoeing

and flyers, and other resources. The kids can view live animals (snakes, toads, etc.), learn about the prints made by different types of creatures in the woods via a hands-on exhibit (this was a favorite of my eight-year-old son), check out the skeleton of a 13,000-year-old woolly mammoth, and use microscopes and spotting scopes to study various animals and organisms. Kids can play with all types of hands-on exhibits in the kids' area and climb into a "bird's nest" (another favorite of my son). He tried to convince me to climb the narrow stairs up to the bird nest, but a quick look inside made me conjure images of myself as the lead story on the local news: "BREAKING NEWS! Chicago man gets stuck in bird nest!"

King of the stump © Andrew Morkes

Many places to relax and watch nature. There is a secluded and peaceful area with benches and chairs behind the center, where you can watch wildlife on Salt Creek, read a book, or just close your eyes and savor in the sounds of nature.

You can participate in a variety of scheduled programs for individuals, families, and groups that explore nature and outdoor activities. These include spring flower hikes, kayaking lessons, and fitness walks, as well as lessons on how to track resident and migrant wildlife, how to fish, and how to tap maple trees for syrup. There are also occasional seminars about the area's natural and human history.

There's great hiking. Novice and experienced hikers will enjoy several trails ranging in length from 0.2 miles (Monarch Trail and Oriole Trail) to 2.3 miles (Night Heron Trail) amidst the oak woodlands and marshes and wetlands bordering Salt Creek.

Bug invasion © Andrew Morkes

GRAUE MILL AND MUSEUM

Graue Mill © Andrew Morkes

When you're done visiting the nature center and woods, hike southeast about half a mile on the Night Heron Trail (or jump in your car or head over on your bike) to check out **Graue Mill and Museum** (3800 York Road, Oak Brook, IL 60523-2738, 630/655-2090, www.grauemill.org). You'll step back in time during a visit to this underappreciated local gem, which is listed in the National Register of Historic Places. It is the only operating waterwheel gristmill in the Chicago area. The museum features rooms that depict life in the mid-to-late 1800s; an exhibit about the Underground Railroad (Frederick Graue sheltered African slaves who had escaped from southern plantations as they made their way north to freedom); milling, spinning, weaving, and living history presentations by docents; and special events such as the museum's annual Fine Arts Festival, Craft Beer Tasting Event, Civil War Encampment, and Christmas at the Mill Holiday Boutique. The mill and museum are kid-friendly, and picnic tables are available with nice views of the mill and Salt Creek. Graue Mill and Museum are open from mid-April through mid-November. Contact the museum for the most current information on operating hours and events.

There are many nature-watching opportunities. You'll see wildflowers, towering trees, and mini wetlands at the edge of Salt Creek, as well as herons, egrets, migratory birds, songbirds, beavers, and red foxes. My son and I spotted tiny black pollywogs wiggling in the shallows, as well as a couple of ducks fishing in the creek.

NEARBY NATURE DESTINATIONS

Bemis Woods, Brookfield Zoo, Herrick Lake Forest Preserve, Hidden Lake Forest Preserve, Miller Meadow, Morton Arboretum, Salt Creek Woods Nature Preserve

GALENA, ILLINOIS

VISIT THIS HISTORIC DRIFTLESS REGION TOWN AND 30 NEARBY DESTINATIONS FOR REST, RELAXATION, AND NATURE ADVENTURES

I've only given one town in this book the full chapter treatment, and that's Galena, Illinois. I do so because I love visiting there; it's a special place, and it is the perfect home base for many nature and historical adventures in eastern Iowa, southwest Wisconsin, and northwest Illinois.

Nestled on bluffs above the Galena River, Galena is a beautiful town that has more than 1,450 buildings on the National Historic Register, including President Grant's home. This charming town features eclectic restaurants, antique shops, bookstores, art galleries, live music, and much more. There is also the Galena Canning Company, which sells sauces, salsas, dips, and jellies, and at which you can ruin your appetite for lunch or dinner by trying the copious amounts of samples that are available.

Galena is located in the Driftless Region (or the Driftless Area), which features limestone bluffs, rolling hills, wooded valleys, waterfalls, creeks, wetlands, rivers, caves, Native American Effigy Mounds, and rare ecosystems and plant and animal species. Unlike much of the Midwest, this area was not flattened and otherwise reshaped by glaciers during the Wisconsin Glaciation. The Driftless Region comprises about 24,000 square miles. Why is the area called the Driftless Region? When a glacier recedes, it leaves behind deposits such as gravel, silt, clay, sand, and boulders, which are called drift. The term "Driftless Region," comes from the fact that the area contains no drift, hence "Driftless."

Where: Approximately 165 miles from downtown Chicago in the far northwest corner of Illinois

Learn More: www.visitgalena.org, http://jdcf.org

Hours: Varies by attraction

Quick Review: This eastern gateway to the Driftless Region features many nature and historical destinations in and out of town. More than 1,450 buildings in Galena are listed on the National Historic Register. There are art galleries, restaurants, antique shops, bookstores, and other attractions. (#25 on the map on page 10)

What You Can Do in the Area: Bicycling, Birdwatching, Camping, Canoeing/Kayaking/Boating, Cross-Country Skiing, Downhill Skiing, Educational and Self-Enrichment Opportunities and Classes, Fishing, Golf, Hiking, Horseback Riding, Hot Air Balloon Rides, Local History, Museums, Nature Centers, Photography, Picnicking, Restaurants, Running/Exercise, Shops, Snowshoeing

Downtown Galena © Andrew Morkes

My family often uses Galena as a home base for explorations of nature spots in the area. Many of the nature properties in Galena and surrounding areas were acquired and are now managed (or co-managed) by the Jo Daviess Conservation Foundation (JDCF). When you're in Galena, check out the following JDCF sites. Some are equivalent in size to a city park, while others are larger, wilder areas. You can learn more about these properties by visiting https://jdcf.org.

IN GALENA

Buehler Preserve (102 Jefferson Street, Galena, IL 61036): This 25-acre property along the Galena River features hilly woodland and a prairie restoration. You can connect to the eight-mile (one way) Galena River Trail (www.cityofgalena.org/en/city_services/parks/galena_river_trail) at the preserve.

Casper Bluff Land & Water Reserve (870 S. Pilot Knob Road, Galena, IL 61036): The 85-acre reserve offers stunning views of the Mississippi River and its backwater sloughs, where you might see bald eagles, herons, and hawks, among other birds. Casper Bluff also features the Aiken Mound Group (named for the nearby community of Aiken), which is part of the larger Effigy Mound culture that existed in the region. Effigy mounds are raised masses of earth in the shape of animals, humans, or other symbols. They were built by the Late Woodland Native American culture from about 600 through 1150 A.D., and were used to bury the dead, for clan ceremonies, and, perhaps, for celestial observations. Twenty Native American burial mounds have been visually identified, but historical records show that there may have been more than 50 mounds and a thunderbird effigy.

Galena Gateway Park (9300 W. Powder House Hill Road, Galena, IL 61036): This 180-acre park preserves the first view visitors have of Galena when driving west on Highway 20. It features pleasant hiking trails through oak

WHERE TO STAY AND DINE IN GALENA

I won't provide a comprehensive list of lodging and dining suggestions in Galena because you can find that information on social media, in tourist guides, and through word of mouth. But I would like to mention a few of my favorites. On the outskirts of Galena, check out the **Irish Cottage Inn & Suites** (www.theirishcottageboutiquehotel.com), a charming hotel that provides everything necessary for a good time: an inviting restaurant and pub (Frank O'Dowd's Irish Pub & Grill) with more than 15 draught beers and nearly 50 whiskeys, scotches and bourbons; friendly staff; a pool; and live musical performances. There's even a Faerie Ring and a hiking trail behind the hotel. I love hiking the hilly trail in the snow or even amidst a raging snowstorm—especially with the thought that a Potosi Pilsner, Rogue Dead Guy Ale, or a shot of Jameson Black Barrel Select Reserve waits for me back at the cozy bar. My son and I also enjoy snowshoeing on the trail. The Irish Cottage was recently sold and is under new management, but I hope that the new owners keep the cozy, small-town vibe that the hotel has had for the last decade I've visited. We've also stayed at the **Best Western Galena Inn & Suites** (www.bestwesterndesignerinn.com) next door to the Irish Cottage. It's a pleasant chain motel with an indoor/outdoor pool. Other lodging options include The DeSoto House Hotel (the oldest hotel in Illinois—first welcoming guests in 1855) in downtown Galena, Eagle Ridge Resort & Spa (which offers golfing, as well as other recreational options), Chestnut Mountain Resort (which offers skiing, a zipline, and many recreational activities), various bed and breakfasts in town, and a plethora of chain motels on the outskirts of the town.

A few of my favorite places to dine in Galena are Frank O'Dowd's Irish Pub & Grill, Galena Cellars, Fried Green Tomatoes, Galena Brewing Company, Durty Gurts Burger Joynt, and Vinny Vanucchi's. This is by no means a comprehensive list—just a starting point for your gastronomic adventures. Bon Appétit!

savanna and, of course, wonderful views of the historic town, which was founded in 1826.

Horseshoe Mound (1679 N. Blackjack Road, Galena, IL 61036): The 40-acre Horseshoe Mound property provides stunning views of Galena and the rolling wooded and flower-covered hills that surround it, as well as short hiking trails. Viewing scopes are available that will allow you to see three states—Illinois, Wisconsin, and Iowa. Your kids can participate in the Dorte Breckenridge Children's Adventure, in which they can learn about the time-traveling adventure of twins Neto and Natalia via five riddles that were written and etched into a series of stones to be used as clues during their adventure. While exploring nature, children learn about the value of conservation, with the goal that they will apply these lessons to their everyday lives.

Horseshoe Mound © Andrew Morkes

OUTSIDE GALENA

Schurmeier Teaching Forest (147 E. Reusch Road, Elizabeth, IL 61028): This rugged, hillside property contains the only teaching forest in Illinois (according to the JDCF). You can learn about the natural world at this property via a self-guided tour booklet that is available at a kiosk near the parking lot. Information in the booklet corresponds to signage along the trail. This is a great place to see wildflowers and fall colors.

Valley of Eden Bird Sanctuary (5559 E. Rush Creek Road, Stockton, IL 61085): This 409-acre bird sanctuary has been designated an "Important Bird Area" by Birdlife International and the Audubon Society. More than 100 different bird species have been sighted at Valley of Eden, with April through August offering the best birdwatching opportunities. During your visit, you might see Henslow's sparrows, sedge wrens, northern harriers, bobolinks, red-headed woodpeckers, owls, and woodpeckers. There are 6 miles of hiking trails to enjoy. Note: No dogs are allowed from March 1 to September 30.

Wapello Land & Water Reserve (8642 IL-84, Hanover, IL 61041): Archaeological excavations have determined that Native Americans lived in this beautiful area along the Apple River as far back as 11,000 years ago. A historical center has been proposed to tell their story. Let's hope it gets built. This is a beautiful place—full of wildflowers, birdsong, and scenic views—that you should definitely visit. There are short hiking trails that wind their way around the protected site of a former Native American village.

Chicagoland Northwest, West, and Beyond Destinations 101

Witkowsky State Wildlife Area (7 miles north of Hanover, Illinois, on Blackjack Road): This 1,100-acre property has more than 10 miles of trails that wind through prairies and forests.

OTHER NEARBY DESTINATIONS

The charming little town of **Elizabeth, Illinois** (www.villageofelizabethil.com/ve) is located about 15 miles southeast of Galena. While you're there, check out:

✔ The **Apple River Fort State Historic Site** (311 E. Myrtle Street, Elizabeth, IL 61028), a re-built fort that was the site of a battle in the Black Hawk War of 1832, and at which Abraham Lincoln and his militia supposedly were present. Great for kids—especially during the warm months when reenactments and other events are held.

✔ **Elizabeth's Grand Antique Company** (300 West Street, Elizabeth, IL 61028, 815/858-9477, www.grandantiqueco.com) boasts 28,000 square feet of antiques in an old school. I've never seen so many rooms and rooms of antiques. It is so large that I lost my family multiple times during our visit. I didn't leave a trail of breadcrumbs to follow to the exit but was tempted.

✔ **Chicago Great Western Railway Depot Museum** (111 E. Myrtle Street, Elizabeth, IL 61028, 815/858-2343, www.elizabethhistoricalsociety.com/railway_depot_museumm.html), which features a variety of N-scale, HO-scale, and G-scale model railroad layouts, railroad artifacts, and a library of more than 1,000 railroad-focused books.

Wapello Land & Water Reserve © Andrew Morkes

Other destinations and events to check out in Elizabeth include the **Elizabeth Historical Museum** (www.elizabethhistoricalsociety.com), 1876 **Banwarth House & Museum** (www.banwarthmuseum.com), and the **Midwest Annual Garlic Fest** (held in August, www.midwestgarlicfest.com).

Pair visits to these destinations with stops at the aforementioned Schurmeier Teaching Forest, Valley of Eden Bird Sanctuary, Wapello Land & Water Reserve, and/or the Witkowsky State Wildlife Area.

Additionally, check out Apple River Canyon State Park (which is about 17 miles northeast of Elizabeth), Tapley Woods Conservation Area (6 miles northwest of Elizabeth), Hanover Bluff Nature Preserve (9 miles southwest of Elizabeth), Rall Woods State Natural Area (about 10 miles south of Elizabeth), and Mississippi Palisades State Park (18 miles south of Elizabeth).

Apple River Canyon State Park (8763 E. Canyon Road, Apple River, IL 61001, 815/745-3302, www2.illinois.gov/dnr/Parks/Pages/AppleRiverCanyon .aspx) is a pretty park with nearly 2,000 acres of limestone bluffs, deep ravines, streams, and springs. Hiking trails wind through these areas, as well as along the scenic Apple River. There are opportunities for camping, fishing (smallmouth bass, sunfish, crappie, suckers, and carp), hunting, and picnicking.

Tapley Woods Conservation Area (3742 US Highway 20, Galena, IL 61036, www2.illinois.gov/dnr/hunting/FactSheets/Pages/TapleyWoods.aspx) is a 260-acre timbered property that consists of very steep, unglaciated ridges. There are opportunities for hiking, nature viewing, and hunting.

At **Hanover Bluff Nature Preserve** (10600-10700 S. Whitton Road, Hanover, IL 61041), you can hike (although the terrain is very steep), fish, and hunt.

Rall Woods State Natural Area (11039 S. Airhart Road, Hanover Township, IL 61041) offers hiking (although the hills are very steep), excellent views of the Mississippi River flood plain, and hunting.

Mississippi Palisades State Park (16327A IL Route 84, Savanna, IL 61074, www2.illinois.gov/dnr/Parks/Pages/MississippiPalisades.aspx) offers 2,500 acres of rolling hills and towering cliffs above the confluence of the great Mississippi and Apple Rivers. There are amazing views and excellent bird watching (my son and I saw two bald eagles during our last visit). You can enjoy 15 miles of hiking trails that range from .4 miles (Prairie View) to 1.5 miles (Aspen) in length. Camping is also available. (See page 115 for more information.)

DUBUQUE, IOWA, AND NEARBY AREAS

Another daytrip option from Galena is to head across the Mississippi River to the charming river town of Dubuque, Iowa (www.traveldubuque.com). It is Iowa's oldest city (founded in 1833), and one of the oldest settlements west of the Mississippi River. Dubuque has been featured on many "best small city" lists. One of our favorite destinations in Dubuque is the **National Mississippi River**

TAKE A ROAD TRIP ON YOUR ROAD TRIP

If you're interested in Native American history and love a good hike and beautiful scenery, consider a road trip to **Effigy Mounds National Monument** (151 Highway 76, Harpers Ferry, IA 52146), which is about 1.5 hours northwest of Galena by car. There are 206 prehistoric mounds at Effigy Mounds, including 31 animal effigies. The mounds are typically 2 to 4 feet high, 40 feet wide, and 800 feet long, although the bird mounds have wingspans that range from 124 to 212 feet. There are excellent—but often demanding—hiking trails through what many consider to be one of the most beautiful areas of the Upper Mississippi River Valley. On our visit, we hiked the Fire Point Trail, which begins at the back door of the visitor center. On this 2-mile circle trail, you'll journey through dense woods, enjoy stunning views of the Mississippi River, and see many conical mounds, a few compound mounds, the Little Bear Mound Group, and the Great Bear Mound Group. There are plenty of other trails and things to do at Effigy Mounds. Visit www.nps.gov/efmo for more information.

View of the Mississippi River from the cliffs of Effigy Mounds National Monument
© Andrew Morkes

Museum and Aquarium (350 East 3rd Street, Port of Dubuque, IA 52001, 800/226-3369, www.rivermuseum.com). It's a fun place for the kids that features live animals, historical exhibits, a 4D theater, and beautiful grounds. During many subfreezing or rainy weekends in Galena, the museum has been a warm and entertaining place to take our son for a few hours. Highly recommended. Other options in Dubuque and the surrounding area include **Mines of Spain Recreation Area and E.B. Lyons Interpretive and Nature Center** (8991 Bellevue Heights Road, Dubuque, IA 52003, 563/556-0620, www.minesofspain.org), **Crystal Lake Cave** (6684 Crystal Lake Cave Road, Dubuque, IA 52003, 563/556-6451, www.crystallakecave.com), **Dubuque Museum of Art** (701 Locust Street, Dubuque, IA 52001, 563/557-1851, https://dbqart.org), **Maquoketa Caves State Park** (9688 Caves Road, Maquoketa, IA 52060, 563/652-5833, www.iowadnr.gov/Places-to-Go/State-Parks), and **Backbone State Park** (1347 129th Street, Dundee, IA 52038, 563/924-2527, www.iowadnr.gov/Places-to-Go/State-Parks).

GLACIAL PARK

ONE OF THE WILDEST PLACES IN MCHENRY COUNTY

Wow! Just wow! These are the three, not-too-descriptive words I uttered when I first visited Glacial Park because it is a place of awe-inspiring beauty and it offers a wide variety of fun outdoor activities. These traits make it a popular destination for people of all ages. The McHenry County Conservation District describes 3,439-acre Glacial Park as its "most treasured open space holding, characterized by its rolling prairie, delta kames, oak savanna, and the tranquil presence of the meandering Nippersink Creek." The word "Nippersink" is probably of Potawatomi origin and stands for "at the little water/lake." This is apropos because there are many streams that feed into Nippersink Creek, as well as marshes and wetland at Glacial Park. Plan to spend at least half a day—but, ideally, a full one—at this northern Illinois gem that's only 62 miles from downtown Chicago. Here are some fun things to do at Glacial Park.

Check out the Lost Valley Visitor Center and nearby historic areas. There are nature-oriented exhibits at the visitor center, and you can tour the historic Powers-Walker House to learn what it was like to be a settler during the 19th century. At the visitor center, pick up a Self-Guided Family Exploration Pack, a backpack that you can borrow that contains seasonal nature-oriented activities you can do while walking the trails.

Go hiking. Glacial Park has five miles of hiking trails to enjoy. Some travel along scenic Nippersink Creek and pass by glacial kames, which are large hills

---

Where: 6705 Route 31, Ringwood, IL 60072

Learn More: McHenry County Conservation District (MCCD), 815/678-4532, www.mccdistrict.org/visit__explore/places_to_go/find_a_site/glacial_park.php

Hours: Grounds: Sunrise to sunset, year-round

Lost Valley Visitor Center: April to October, 9 a.m. to 5:30 p.m.; November to March, 10 a.m. to 4 p.m.

Quick Review: Nearly 3,500 acres of rolling prairie, delta kames, oak savanna, and Nippersink Creek. Glacial Park is perfect for hiking, horseback riding, paddling, and other outdoor activities. (#26 on the map on page 10)

What You Can Do There: Bicycling, Birdwatching, Canoeing/Kayaking/Boating, Cross-Country Skiing, Educational and Self-Enrichment Opportunities and Classes, Fishing, Hiking, Horseback Riding, Library, Local History, Nature Center, Photography, Picnicking, Running/Exercise, Sledding, Snowmobiling, Snowshoeing (rentals available)

Nippersink Creek © Andrew Morkes

of sand and gravel that were deposited by glaciers about 10,000 to 12,000 years ago. There are four kames at Glacial Park including the "Camelback Kames," which have two humps that are shaped like a camel's back. These kames reminded me more of massive brontosauri crouched over the lush landscape having lunch, but to each his or her own. Other trails pass through restored prairies, grasslands, marshes, savannahs (with oak and hickory trees), and sedge meadows. There are a variety of hiking trails. Try the two-mile interpretive nature trail that follows the Deerpath Trail loop (you can access it near the visitor center). Guidebooks at the trail head provide information on four different topics: Plant Communities, Wildlife, History of the Land, and Geology. If you're looking for an even longer hike, you can connect to the MCCD's Prairie Trail, which travels through the eastern side of Glacial Park. You can hike or bike it north to the Wisconsin state line or south to Kane County.

Go biking along a 5-mile portion of the 26-mile Prairie Trail.

Enjoy a kayaking or canoeing adventure on beautiful Nippersink Creek, which travels more than 10 miles through Glacial Park. I've taken two 7-mile kayaking trips on the creek, and they provided wonderful moments with my son and my friend Dave and his son. Much of the Nippersink Creek ecosystem has been laboriously and lovingly restored by conservationists and volunteers. You can learn more about kayaking/canoeing on the creek (which is more like a small river, at times) by checking out my essay, "Nippersink Creek Provides a Great Kayaking or Canoeing Adventure Just an Hour From Chicago" on page 283.

© Andrew Morkes

Go birdwatching. During a recent kayaking trip, I sighted herons, red-winged blackbirds, and white egrets, as well as a line of about 10 ducks on a log that looked at our group as if we were on stage for their amusement. Additional birds that frequent Glacial Park include red-bellied and red-headed woodpeckers, chickadees, wood ducks, black and white bobolinks, yellow-cheeked dickcissels, grasshopper sparrows, meadowlarks, harrier hawks, and many other species.

View wildflowers, grasses, and other plants. As you hike the trails or paddle Nippersink Creek, you might see purple coneflowers, sunflowers, pretty pink Joe Pye weed, tall bright yellow prairie coreopsis, purple prairie blazing star, blue spiderwort, red cardinal flower, big bluestem, beautiful Virginia wild rye, switchgrass, bottle brush grass, and bright white boneset, as well as hazelnut, wild plum, and hawthorn bushes.

Cast a fishing line into Nippersink Creek. The waterway is home to bass, walleye, bluegill, channel catfish, carp, bullhead, green sunfish, and many other types of fish. You can fish at Keystone Road Landing and Pioneer Road Landing.

Saddle up and head out on the trails. There are 4.78 miles of horse trails at Glacial Park.

Enjoy winter sports such as snowmobiling, cross-country skiing, and snowshoeing. Snowshoes are available for rental.

NEARBY NATURE DESTINATIONS

Chain O'Lakes State Park, Grant Woods Forest Preserve, Moraine Hills State Park, Turner Lake Fen Nature Preserve, Volo Bog State Natural Area

HAL TYRRELL TRAILSIDE MUSEUM OF NATURAL HISTORY

NATURE CLASSES AND EXPERIENCES, GREAT HIKING TRAILS, AND STUNNING SPRING WILDFLOWERS AND FALL COLORS

The Hal Tyrrell Trailside Museum of Natural History was the first public nature education facility established by Forest Preserves of Cook County. It is located in a historic 1876 mansion, which served for a time as the district's headquarters. In 1931, its Board of Commissioners voted to make it a "trail side" museum displaying "every plant and animal in Cook County, live or mounted, for the education of the public."

The museum offers indoor and outdoor live animal exhibits, where you can see fish, frogs, turtles, black rat snakes and other snakes, a red-tailed hawk, and other animals. There is also a nature play area outdoors near the museum. Trailside Museum offers a variety of classes and outdoor exploration activities. Recent offerings included Morning Bird Walk, Children's Story Trail and Craft, and Going on a Gnome Hunt.

There are nearly five miles of unpaved walking trails that trek through Thatcher Woods' beautiful oak woodlands and floodplain forest, past Thatcher Pond, and

---

Where: 738 Thatcher Avenue, River Forest, IL 60305

Learn More: Forest Preserves of Cook County, 708/366-6530, https://fpdcc.com/places/locations/trailside-museum-natural-history, www.facebook.com/TrailsideMuseumofNaturalHistory

Hours: Grounds: 8:00 a.m. to 4:00 p.m.

Walking Trails: Sunrise to sunset, year-round

Museum: March to October, 9 a.m. to 5 p.m.; November to February: 9 a.m. to 4 p.m.; closed Fridays all year

The grounds and museum are closed Thanksgiving, Christmas, and New Year's Day.

Quick Review: This nature museum features live native animals, beautiful wildflower gardens, a nature play area, and hiking trails. No dogs allowed. (#27 on the map on page 10)

What You Can Do There: Bicycling (only in nature center parking lots), Birdwatching, Educational and Self-Enrichment Opportunities and Classes, Fishing, Hiking, Local History, Museum, Nature Center, Photography, Running/Exercise, Snowshoeing

Trailside Museum of Natural History © Forest Preserves of Cook County

along the Des Plaines River (where you might see white-tailed deer, foxes, coyotes, and evidence of beavers at work). The area is known for its beautiful wildflowers [such as yellow trout lily, Virginia bluebells, spring beauty, butterfly weed (a host plant for monarch butterflies), blue spiderwort, and wild bergamot] and vivid fall colors. A trail map is available at https://fpdcc.com/places/locations/trailside-museum-natural-history. The museum's proximity to the woods, Thatcher Pond, and the Des Plaines River also makes it a birding hotspot. Visit https://fpdcc.com/things-to-do/birding for a birding checklist.

Finally, you can fish at Thatcher Pond. This 1.5-acre pond is an old oxbow of the Des Plaines River and is prone to flooding. (An oxbow pond or lake is formed when a U-shaped bend in a river is cut off and no longer connects to the river.) Black bullhead, bluegill, and orange-spotted sunfish comprised approximately 65 percent of the fish in Thatcher Pond, according to a recent survey by Forest Preserves of Cook County. Other fish that were recorded included golden shiner, gizzard shad, common carp, bluegill, orange-spotted sunfish hybrid, and largemouth bass.

NEARBY NATURE DESTINATIONS

Algonquin Woods, Bemis Woods, Catherine Chevalier Woods, Chicago Portage National Historic Site, Jerome Huppert Woods, Ottawa Trail Woods, Robinson Woods, Salt Creek Woods Nature Preserve, Schiller Woods

JOHNSON'S MOUND FOREST PRESERVE

SEE A GLACIAL KAME AND ENJOY A RELAXING HIKE

Sledding hill © Andrew Morkes

The forested hills of Johnson's Mound Forest Preserve reminded me of some sort of nature castle looming above the mostly flat farm fields that surrounded it. As I drove towards the preserve on a late-April day, farmers were at work tilling the deep black soil of their fields, which sharply contrasted with the bright blue sky. Farmers in their fields is a common sight in rural Kane County, but as a city person, it's wonderful to see so much open space not covered by concrete and to see the hard work that it takes to make the food we often taken for granted when we head to our local grocery store.

Johnson's Mound Forest Preserve is a heavily forested nature area with a glacial kame, which is a large hill of sand and gravel that was deposited by glaciers about 10,000 to 12,000 years ago. The kame rises 900 feet above the surrounding tributaries of Blackberry Creek and the glacial outwash plain. A portion of

Where: 41W600 Hughes Road, Elburn, IL 60119

Learn More: Forest Preserve District of Kane County, https://kaneforest.com/location/johnsons-mound

Hours: Sunrise to sunset, year-round

Quick Review: A pretty, forested preserve with steep topography, a great sledding hill, and a large mowed field, where you can fly a kite, enjoy a picnic, or participate in a sporting activity. A stone cabin that was built by the Civilian Conservation Corps in the 1930s can be rented for small gatherings. (#28 on the map on page 10)

What You Can Do There: Bicycling, Birdwatching, Educational and Self-Enrichment Opportunities and Classes, Hiking, Photography, Picnicking, Running/Exercise, Sledding, Snowshoeing

Mayapple plants blanket the floor each spring at Johnson's Mound Forest Preserve.
© Andrew Morkes

Johnson's Mound Forest Preserve was designated as an Illinois Nature Preserve by the Illinois Nature Preserves Commission in 1992. These preserves protect the highest quality natural lands in the state. Visit www2.illinois.gov/dnr/INPC/Pages/Area2KaneJohnsonsMound.aspx to learn more.

This is a good destination for those who want a peaceful hike. Johnson's Mound Forest Preserve has 955 acres of woodland (sugar maples, white ash, slippery elm, basswood, and white and bur oaks), grassland, wetland, and cropland. There are 2.64 miles of trails, including East Loop Trail (0.25 miles, mowed), North-South Connector Trail (0.32 miles, gravel), North Loop Trail (1.29 miles, mowed), North Prairie Trail (0.44 miles, mowed), and West Woodland Trail (0.34 miles, foot trail). For a trail map, visit https://kaneforest.com/upload/49-J_MoundTRAILMAP2018.pdf.

More than 165 species of birds have been observed at Johnson's Mound, according to Ebird.org. They include turkey vultures, red-tailed hawks, black-capped chickadees, golden-crowned kinglets, great horned owls, northern shrikes, yellow-throated vireos, scarlet tanagers, Nashville warblers, black-and-white warblers, great crested flycatchers, and ring-necked pheasants.

The wildflower viewing is also excellent. Look for shooting stars, violet wood sorrel, Dutchman's breeches, declined and large white trillium, Short's aster, and blue cohosh. The hills were blanketed with Virginia bluebells, birdsfoot violets, and smooth yellow violets when I visited. The heavily forested kame makes for great fall leaf peeping. Unlike many preserves, Johnson's Mound comes alive in the winter, with excellent opportunities for sledding and snowshoeing. Look for the mysterious face that's carved in a tree at the top of the sledding hill near the stone cabin. Research has shown that it's been present at the preserve for more than 50 years, but no one knows who carved it.

FINAL THOUGHTS

On the day I visited Johnson's Mound, I drove 215 miles (roundtrip) around Chicago's western suburbs to within an hour of the Mississippi River to explore five nature destinations. During my travels, I was enchanted by the beautiful farms, sights of horses and bison (at Nachusa Grasslands, see page 125), the charming towns and scenery along the Fox River, the miles of parkland and trails, and the wide-open spaces in many parts of the area. I came home recharged and eager to spend a weekend in the area with my family. People in Illinois are sometimes so focused on vacationing in Indiana, Michigan, or Wisconsin (or heading to exotic beach locales or overseas) that we forget destinations in our own backyards. I encourage you to vacation locally and explore the Fox River Valley and other local areas. You can learn more about destinations in the Fox River Valley and other places to explore throughout Illinois by visiting www.enjoyillinois.com. Additionally, On the Fox! (https://onthefox.com) offers information on dining, shopping, and festivals and other events in the Fox Valley towns of Batavia, Geneva, and St. Charles.

The mysterious face at Johnson's Mound.
© Andrew Morkes

NEARBY NATURE DESTINATIONS

Almon Underwood Prairie Nature Preserve, Aurora West Forest Preserve, Dick Young Forest Preserve, Elburn Forest Preserve, LeRoy Oakes Forest Preserve, Peck Farm Park, Sauer Prairie Kame Forest Preserve

LEROY OAKES FOREST PRESERVE

ENJOY GREAT HIKING TRAILS, A NATURE CENTER, AND HISTORICAL SITES

I visited LeRoy Oakes on a warm, windy day in late-April and wasn't disappointed. The preserve seemed much larger than its nearly 460 acres, with a variety of ecosystems and activity areas. There's a lot to do at this beloved preserve in St. Charles, Illinois. Activities include:

Going hiking. There are almost nine miles of trails that travel through woodlands, a high-quality dry prairie (the Murray prairie), a

Pioneer Sholes School
© Andrew Morkes

Where: 37W700 Dean Street, St. Charles, IL 60175

Learn More: Forest Preserve District of Kane County, https://kaneforest.com/location/leroy-oakes

Hours: Grounds: Sunrise to sunset, year-round

Nature Center: Monday to Thursday, 10 a.m. to 4 p.m.; Saturday and Sunday, Noon to 4 p.m.

Quick Review: This nearly 460-acre preserve offers a variety of hiking trails through high-quality prairie, floodplain forests, oak woodlands, and grassy fields. Ferson Creek travels through a portion of the preserve. There's also a nature center (with very friendly staff and informative exhibits). The starting point for the Great Western Trail is located at the preserve. Dogs are allowed (on leashes). (#29 on the map on page 10)

What You Can Do There: Bicycling, Birdwatching, Camping (for youth groups only), Cross-Country Skiing, Educational and Self-Enrichment Opportunities and Classes, Fishing, Hiking, Horseback Riding, Indoor Event Rentals (for birthday parties, showers, classes, and meetings), Local History, Nature Center, Photography, Picnicking, Running/Exercise, Snowshoeing

prairie restoration (Horlock Hill, which has 130 species of prairie plants), and grasslands. Additionally, the preserve features the starting point for the 17-mile Great Western Trail (www.enjoyillinois.com/explore/listing/great-western-trail), which provides opportunities for hiking, biking, and snowshoeing and snowmobiling (when there is four inches of snow on the ground). Visit https://kaneforest.com/upload/53-LeroyOakesTRAILMAP2018.pdf for a trail map.

Ferson Creek © Andrew Morkes

Checking out Ferson Creek. This beautiful creek winds through the northern area of the preserve. I enjoyed hiking along its pretty green banks, which were covered with Virginia bluebells.

Visiting the Creek Bend Nature Center to view interactive exhibits that include a woodland exhibit that features Illinois' State Tree (the White Oak), a bison exhibit, and a wetland exhibit that provides information on natural life in the Fox River. The center's charming gallery space is available for rental for special events.

Learning about local history by visiting historic sites at the preserve. Visitors to the Durant House Museum (which was built in 1843) can learn what life was like in the mid-19th century. The Pioneer Sholes School (circa 1872) is a restored and furnished one-room country school. These sites—which are managed by Preservation Partners of the Fox Valley—are located near a towering, historic barn and are easy to access from nearby parking lots.

Visitor Center exhibits © Andrew Morkes

Enjoying a picnic. Sit by Ferson Creek or enjoy lunch at one of the preserve's picnic groves or picnic shelters. I enjoyed a quick lunch in the pretty picnic grove that's located near Ferson Creek in the northeastern section of the preserve.

Taking an outdoor education class. Recent courses included Singing Insects, which provided more information about grasshoppers, cicadas, crickets, and katydids; Mighty Mosses, which educated par-

> **DID YOU KNOW?**
>
> LeRoy Oakes has one of the finest dry prairies in the Chicago region. As a result, a portion of the property was named an Illinois Nature Preserve by the Illinois Nature Preserves Commission (INPC) in 1992. These preserves protect the highest quality natural lands in the state. "Despite encroachment from a pine tree plantation and use as a dumping ground for spoil piles in the 1950s, the prairie continues to support a diverse and very uncommon plant community," according to the INPC. "Among the more unusual plants found here are short green milkweed, scurfy pea, and Richardson's sedge." More common plants that you can see at the prairie include prairie and bird-foot violet, cylindrical blazing star, leadplant, false toadflax, downy gentian, grooved yellow flax, and prairie cinquefoil. Visit www2.illinois.gov/dnr/INPC/Pages/Area2KaneLeRoyOakes.aspx to learn more.

ticipants about the ways in which mosses help soils and microorganisms; and Sense of Place, which detailed the long history of LeRoy Oakes Forest Preserve as a homestead, farm, country estate, and religious retreat before becoming a natural area.

NEARBY NATURE DESTINATIONS AND OTHER ATTRACTIONS

Blackhawk County Forest Preserve, Brewster Creek Forest Preserve, Dick Young Forest Preserve, Fox River Bluff Forest Preserve, Fox River Trolley Museum, James Pate Philip State Park, Johnson's Mound Forest Preserve, Jon J. Duerr Forest Preserve, Tekakwitha Woods Forest Preserve

View of the farm from the Durant House Museum © Andrew Morkes

MISSISSIPPI PALISADES STATE PARK

GREAT VIEWS, MUDDY SHOES, AND EAGLES IN TWOS

The stairs to the viewing platform.
© Andrew Morkes

"Is it worth it?," asked the well-dressed couple—who looked as if they'd be more comfortable at a country-club than on a hike amidst the woods and rolling hills of northwestern Illinois. "It" was the view of the confluence of the Mississippi and Apple Rivers from the cliffs in Mississippi Palisades State Park (MPSP). I answered a hearty "yes," although as I looked down at their muddy dress shoes, I thought, "as long as you don't mind tossing those shoes when you get back to your hotel."

My wife, our six-year-old son, and I took a short day trip from Galena, Illinois, to Mississippi Palisades State Park in mid-February, a time of the year that typically requires parkas, hand warmers, and snowshoes. But, during our visit, it was sunny and in the 40s. MPSP is known for its great views, rugged

> **Where:** 16327A IL Route 84, Savanna, IL 61074
>
> **Learn More:** Illinois Department of Natural Resources, 815/273-2731, www2.illinois.gov/dnr/Parks/Pages/MississippiPalisades.aspx
>
> **Hours:** Sunrise to sunset, year-round
>
> **Quick Review:** 2,500 acres of rolling hills and towering cliffs above the confluence of the Mississippi and Apple Rivers. Amazing views, excellent birdwatching, 15 miles of hiking paths. Recommended as either a short-day trip from Galena, Illinois, or a one- or two-night camping destination. Pets must be leashed. (#30 on the map on page 10)
>
> **What You Can Do There:** Bicycling, Birdwatching, Camping, Canoeing/Kayaking/Boating, Cross-Country Skiing, Equestrian, Fishing/Ice Fishing, Geocaching, Hiking, Hunting, Photography, Picnicking, Rock Climbing, Running/Exercise, Sledding, Snowshoeing

View of the Mississippi River © Andrew Morkes

terrain, wildflower-covered hills in the spring, and eagle-watching in the winter. It's about a half-hour southwest of the historic town of Galena, which boasts the home of President Ulysses Grant, a thriving shopping district, tons of outdoor activities, and many historic buildings. The views at MPSP were awe-inspiring (my son and I even spotted two eagles fishing in the Mississippi), but hikers beware—there was only a short stretch of boardwalk where we hiked, with the rest of the quickly-descending trails consisting of wet and slippery leaves, mud, and rocks (my wife and her bad back were not happy with me). Here are a few fun things to do at the park. For example, you can take a hike on 15 miles of trails. There are many good trails but, in the North Trail System, try the High Point Trail (3.5 miles) and Aspen (1.9 miles) Trails. In the South Trail System, hike the Sentinel Trail (1.2 miles, including spurs) for a challenging outdoor experience. Note: Hiking trails are closed during the park's three-day hunting season—which is typically held before Thanksgiving Day weekend. You can also camp at one of 241 sites, with electrical hookups available at 110 sites. Fishing (bluegill, crappie, bass, catfish, and carp) is popular. And many people enjoy the wildlife, including white-tailed deer, red and gray fox, weasels, wood cucks, and badgers—as well as the aforementioned eagles, wild turkeys, and waterfowl, and shorebirds.

NEARBY NATURE DESTINATIONS AND OTHER ATTRACTIONS

Apple River Canyon State Park; Apple River Fort State Historic Site; Galena, Illinois; Hanover Bluff Nature Preserve; National Mississippi River Museum and Aquarium (Dubuque, Iowa); Rall Woods State Natural Area; Upper Mississippi River Wildlife and Fish Refuge; Wapello Land & Water Reserve

MORAINE HILLS STATE PARK

ROLLING HILLS, TOP-NOTCH HIKING TRAILS, WINTER SPORTS, AND MUCH MORE

Biking is popular at Moraine Hills State Park.
© Andrew Morkes

If you're looking for a little adventure just an hour from Chicago, you should visit Moraine Hills State Park. That's what I did recently on an early spring day that started out in the high 40s and reached 62 degrees under a bright sun and blue skies. The trees were still bare, but the forest floor was starting to green. The marshes were noisy with the sounds of spring peepers (frogs) and birds (including geese, ducks, and cranes). After a difficult February weatherwise in Chicagoland, even the earliest signs of spring were heartening. Here are some fun things you can do at Moraine Hills State Park.

Visit the nature center to view displays about the park's natural features, pick up brochures and maps, and talk with rangers regarding suggested activities.

Go hiking. There are 10 miles of trails to enjoy via hiking, biking, or skiing. They are color-coded and one-way, although I saw plenty of people breaking that rule during my hikes. The main trails are the 2-mile Fox River Trail (Yellow), the 3.2-mile Leatherleaf Bog Trail (Blue), and the 3.7-mile Lake Defiance Trail (Red). These trails are surfaced with crushed limestone. A fourth

---

Where: 1510 S. River Road, McHenry, IL 60051

Learn More: McHenry County Conservation District, 815/385-1624, www2.illinois.gov/dnr/Parks/Pages/MoraineHills.aspx

Hours: Vary with the season

Quick Review: 2,200 acres of hills, ridges, wetlands, marshes, and lakes. Ten miles of beautiful and diverse trails for hikers, cyclists, and skiers. A perfect short road trip from Chicago. Dogs are allowed (on leashes). (#31 on the map on page 10)

What You Can Do There: Bicycling, Birdwatching, Canoeing/Kayaking/Boating (including boat rentals), Cross-Country Skiing, Educational and Self-Enrichment Opportunities and Classes, Fishing, Hiking, Horseback Riding, Hunting, Nature Center, Photography, Picnicking, Playgrounds, Running/Exercise, Sledding, Snowshoeing

Leatherleaf Bog © Andrew Morkes

trail—the 1.7-mile River Road Trail—is paved. I hiked the Leatherleaf Bog Trail, which takes you through rolling hills and prairie and eventually to the Leatherleaf Bog, which the Illinois Department of Natural Resources says is an "excellent example of kettle-moraine topography." Leatherleaf is an evergreen bog shrub with narrow leathery leaves (hence the name) that has rhizomes (a modified stem that stores food and assists in propagation) that can extend up to 12 inches below the bog. Because it is shade intolerant, it can grow up to three feet tall above other plants to reach the sunlight. In Illinois, leatherleaf is a threatened species. A kettle is a depression in the land that was formed by the melting of an isolated block of glacial ice. A moraine is an accumulation of stones, boulders, and other debris that were deposited by a glacier. The gravel-rich deposits (called kames) in Moraine Hills State Park remained after glacial ice melted at the conclusion of the Wisconsin Glaciation Episode.

You do not have to hike the full length of these trails. There are 10 day-use areas (Kettle Woods, Pine Hills, Hickory Woods, Oak Opening, etc.), where you can park, picnic, and hike a bit. There are also enjoyable foot trails on the east side of the main park road. I parked at the Pine Hills day-use area, walked across the road, descended a rustic stairwell, and enjoyed a short hike through a forest of massive oak trees to check out Pike Marsh, which has a 230-foot boardwalk. At the marsh, you'll see Ohio goldenrod, Kalm's lobelia, dwarf birch, hoary willow, and other plants and trees. After I visited, I learned that there are carnivorous plants in the marsh. In fact, one of the largest known colonies of pitcher plants (which attract, trap, and digest insects) in Illinois are found in the marsh.

Check out Lake Defiance. This pretty body of water was formed when a large mass of ice broke off a glacier during the last ice age, then melted and formed a lake. It is largely undeveloped, making it one of the few glacial lakes in Illinois that remains in near-pristine condition.

View birds and other wildlife. More than 200 species of birds have been sighted at the park. Birds seemed to be everywhere I went during my visit. I saw a pair of geese having a noisy battle—first on the water, and then in midair—over a fish at Leatherneck Bog, and I enjoyed seeing two sandhill cranes methodically working their way across Pike Marsh searching for food. Other migratory birds that you might see include mallards, teal, and wood ducks. Great blue herons and green herons reside in the marsh in the summer. As you hike, you might spot white-tailed deer, eastern cottontails, minks, opossums, red foxes, coyotes, raccoons, frogs, and toads.

Go fishing. You can drop a line at Lake Defiance and on the Fox River. The peat shoreline of Lake Defiance is too dangerous to walk near, so fishing is only available from designated piers along the boardwalk and via rowboat rental. You can also access the Fox River via the McHenry Dam in the southwest corner of the park. A concession stand sells refreshments and bait and rents boats and bicycles. A fishing pier is available for those who have a disability.

Sandhill cranes © wildnerdpix, Shutterstock

Have a picnic. There seemed to be a picnic table—or at least a bench to take a rest—every time I rounded a turn as I drove or walked. In fact, there are picnic tables, drinking water, and rustic toilet facilities at the park's 10 day-use areas, and there are reservable picnic shelters at the Pike Marsh, Pine Hills, Whitetail Prairie, and the Northern Woods day-use areas.

Savor the fall colors. Moraine Hills is heavily forested, and you should visit in the fall to watch the woods ignite with brilliant hues of red, yellow, and orange. Additionally, the leatherleaf plants at Leatherleaf Bog turn a deep red, then brown, in the fall, which also makes for stunning views.

Enjoy winter sports such as cross-country skiing, ice fishing (on the Fox River and Lake Defiance), sledding (in the Whitetail Prairie area), and snowshoeing.

NEARBY NATURE DESTINATIONS

Glacial Park, The Hollows Conservation Area, Nippersink Forest Preserve, Stickney Run Conservation Area, Volo Bog State Natural Area

MORTON ARBORETUM

A NATURE WONDERLAND FOR KIDS AND NEARLY 4,700 TYPES OF PLANTS AND TREES TO ENJOY

A fall hike at the arboretum
©2021 The Morton Arboretum. All rights reserved.

If you love nature, Morton Arboretum is the place to be. It's a special place filled with nearly 222,000 specimens representing 4,650 different kinds of trees and plants from the temperate regions (those that lie between the Tropic of Cancer and the Arctic Circle) in North America, Europe, and Asia. The arboretum has been popular since its founding in 1922 but received increased public interest due to the Troll Hunt exhibit (six whimsical and massive creations that were hidden across the arboretum's 1,700 acres), which ran from 2018 to early 2021. The exhibition brought my son and

---

Where: 4100 Illinois Route 53, Lisle, IL 60532

Learn More: 630/968-0074, www.mortonarb.org

Hours: 7:00 a.m. to sunset (last entry at 6:00 p.m.). There are seasonal hours for the Visitor's Center, Children's Garden, Maze Garden, Arboretum Store, and other facilities; check with the arboretum for current hours.

Quick Review: Spend a few hours or an entire day at this 1,700-acre arboretum with beautiful forests, grasslands, lakes, wetlands, streams, and other natural areas. The Morton Arboretum is a "bucket list" kind of place and one of my favorite destinations in the area. An admissions fee is required. Dogs and other pets are not permitted (except on specially designated days or as service animals). (#32 on the map on page 10)

What You Can Do There: Bicycling, Birdwatching, Café/Restaurant, Cross-Country Skiing, Educational and Self-Enrichment Opportunities and Classes, Gift Shop, Hiking, Library, Local History, Photography, Picnicking, Running/Exercise, Snowshoeing, Tram Tours, Visitor Center

Children's Garden ©2021 The Morton Arboretum. All rights reserved.

me—as well as hundreds of thousands of others—out to the arboretum. My son and I loved the trolls, but we also found so much more to enjoy in this vast nature area.

The arboretum has both East and West Sides, and there are trails, picnic areas, and pull-off parking areas throughout the grounds. Detailed maps of the grounds are available on-site and at the arboretum's website. There is also a Morton Arboretum app that will be extremely useful to you during your visit. You can download it for free at the arboretum's website, at the Apple® App Store®, or at Google Play®.

Here are just a few things that you can do at Morton Arboretum:

Head to the four-acre Children's Garden, which is a wonderful place for kids to learn about nature and have a lot of fun. There are many things to see and do, such as Adventure Woods, where your children can walk through forested pathways and climb on adventure-oriented playground equipment; a Secret Stream, where kids can learn about the properties of moving water and actually play in the stream; Evergreen Walk and Lookout, where visitors can climb a series of stairways that take them 14 feet above the garden; and Wonder Pond, which has stepping stones, a faux beaver dam, and pretty water plants. My son LOVED splashing in Wonder Pond amidst cattails, frogs, and fish. There are steppingstones that the kids can traverse across the pond but, on warm days, it's almost inevitable (and encouraged by the arboretum) that kids will splash around in the water. Tip: Bring sandals or aqua shoes that your child can change into before going into the Wonder Pond or the Secret Stream. An extra set of clothes will also come in handy once the fun is done.

Maze Garden ©2021 The Morton Arboretum. All rights reserved.

Enjoy the arboretum's 16 miles of trails that are maintained year-round for hiking, running, cross-country skiing, and snowshoeing. Bring your bike and enjoy nine miles of paved trails. When there are four inches or more of snow on the ground, you can cross-country ski or snowshoe. Rentals are available at the Visitor Center. Popular areas for these winter activities include The Conifer Collection (recommended for kids and families), Thornhill Education Center Lawn, Main Trail Loop 4 on the East Side, Spruce Plot near Parking Lot 12, and Daffodil Glade at Parking Lot 22. Finally, the arboretum is an excellent spot for hiking. There are 16 miles of mulched, pedestrian-only trails that allow you to explore deep woods, wetlands, and prairies. If you're looking to get away from the crowd, try the 1.11-mile Heritage Trail, which starts at Parking Lot 13 and takes you to Big Rock, a 14-ton granite boulder. At Big Rock, you can connect to the 0.56-mile Woodland Trail, which you can use to return to Parking Lot 13. (Note: The Heritage Trail is a loop path, so it will also return you to the parking lot if you complete the trail.) I highly recommend taking a long hike at the arboretum. My son and I had a wonderful time exploring the trails—especially in the heavily forested areas, the 0.74-mile Prairie Trail that winds its way

Snowshoeing on the Conifer Trail
©2021 The Morton Arboretum. All rights reserved.

through beautiful Schulenberg Prairie, and the 0.55-mile Meadow Lake Trail that circles the lake and features beautiful views.

View the fall colors. The arboretum's trees are a color wonderland in the fall. Visit www.mortonarb.org/news-tags/fall-color for the arboretum's weekly Fall Color Report.

Enjoy the flowers. Although the arboretum is best known for its trees, there are beautiful displays of wildflowers to enjoy starting in the spring all the way through fall. Visit www.mortonarb.org/trees-plants to learn more about the various types of plants and trees you can see at the garden, as well as special gardens such as the Fragrance Garden, Ground Cover Garden, Herb Garden, and Maze Garden.

Take a class or participate in other learning opportunities. There are hundreds of events, classes, and other activities available at the arboretum. Visit www.mortonarb.org/visit-explore/plan-visit/events-and-programs to learn more.

Picknicking at Crabapple Lake　　　©2021 The Morton Arboretum. All rights reserved.

Finally, **consider becoming a member of the Morton Arboretum.** Membership benefits include free parking and admission; discounts at the Arboretum Shop, as well as discounts on arboretum events; free subscriptions to *ArbConnect* e-newsletter and *Seasons*; user privileges at the Sterling Morton Library, and reciprocal privileges at more than 300 arboreta and gardens across North America. If you make several trips to the arboretum, your membership will pay for itself. Visit www.mortonarb.org/join-support/membership for more information.

Here are some tips for your visit to the arboretum:

✔ Arrive early to beat the crowds. The arboretum opens daily at 7:00 a.m. and closes at sunset. Arrive early if you're not a crowd person and want to increase your chances of seeing wildlife or enjoying popular exhibitions with-

> **FAST FACTS**
>
> Here are some interesting facts provided to me by the Morton Arboretum.
>
> ✔ Founded: The Morton Arboretum was established in 1922 by Morton Salt Company founder Joy Morton.
>
> ✔ Collections: The Morton Arboretum's living collections represent one of the most comprehensive assemblages of woody plants in North America. Trees and plants have been collected from 40 countries in the northern temperate zone.
>
> ✔ Conservation: 90 different kinds of trees and plants on the grounds are considered threatened or endangered on state, federal, or world lists.
>
> ✔ Oldest Tree: While we cannot know the oldest tree with certainty, one of the oldest trees on-site is a bur oak (Quercus macrocarpa) in the East Woods that has a pith date (rough establishment date) of 1771. It's likely other trees are even older, but we cannot ascribe definite dates at this time.
>
> ✔ The Sterling Morton Library: Contains collections of 27,000 volumes on botany, horticulture, natural history, and ecology; rare books, periodicals, and catalogs; and 12,000 botanical artworks.
>
> ✔ Plant Clinic: Experts answer inquiries about plant selection and care from 615 U.S. zip codes and nine countries.
>
> ✔ Guests: 971,257 visitors; 57,544 memberships in 2020. The nonprofit organization served 1.2 million visitors before pandemic-related closures and capacity limitations.
>
> © Morton Arboretum, 2021, All rights reserved.

out being surrounded by crowds. But keep in mind that the arboretum is so vast that you can find solitude (especially in the forested areas) if you look for it.

✔ Wear sunscreen and a sunhat—you'll be exposed to the sun often as you explore the arboretum.

✔ Use insect repellent that contains DEET—some of the forested areas swarm with mosquitoes during certain times of the year. Be aware of ticks, too.

✔ Bring plenty of water if you visit on a hot day.

✔ Wear hiking boots or other water-repellent footwear. Low-lying areas can be muddy.

✔ Bring binoculars or a camera with a telephoto lens if you want to view and/or capture images of wildlife.

NEARBY NATURE DESTINATIONS

Belmont Prairie, Blackwell Forest Preserve, Cantigny Park, Danada Forest Preserve, Greene Valley Forest Preserve, Herrick Lake Forest Preserve, St. James Farm Forest Preserve

NACHUSA GRASSLANDS

SEE BISON, SAVOR SOLITUDE, AND HIKE THROUGH BIODIVERSITY HOTSPOTS

Stone Barn Savanna Trail
© Andrew Morkes

Nachusa Grasslands is a wild and wonderful place and an environmental restoration success story. And to top that, it has bison on-site. What more can you ask for?

The Nature Conservancy had a goal of restoring a large and diverse grassland in Illinois, so it purchased what is now Nachusa Grasslands in 1986. Then the staff and volunteers got to work. They conducted controlled burns to improve habitats for native plants and animals and reduce the risk of uncontrolled wildfires, collected more than 2,500 pounds of seed from remnant habitats on the preserve (and then planted them), and observed and recorded wildlife to better understand life at the preserve. In all, volunteers donated more than 200,000 hours of labor to improve the biodiversity of the site and make it more enjoyable for visitors.

You need to head to Nachusa Grasslands now! OK, maybe not right this

---

Where: 2075 Lowden Road, Franklin Grove, IL 61031 (visitor center); about 98 miles west of downtown Chicago

Learn More: The Nature Conservancy, www.nachusagrasslands.org/visitor-center.html, www.nature.org/en-us/get-involved/how-to-help/places-we-protect/nachusa-grasslands

Hours: Sunrise to sunset, year-round

Quick Review: A 3,600-acre nature wonderland with hiking trails in a variety of ecosystems; some of the Midwest's only bison; 700 native plant species and more than 215 species of birds. An Autumn on the Prairie festival is held each year when conditions permit. No dogs or other pets allowed. (#33 on the map on page 10)

What You Can Do There: Bicycling (trail nearby), Birdwatching, Hiking, Photography, Picnicking, Running/Exercise, Snowshoeing, Visitor Center

Stone Barn Savanna Trail © Andrew Morkes

moment, but tomorrow, or this weekend. You need to visit especially if you're a birder, love viewing wildflowers, want to see bison, or are simply the kind of person who wants to wander the natural world (Nachusa encourages you to explore off trail) and make discoveries on your own.

I visited Nachusa on an 86-degree day in late April. It was my last stop on a day in which I had visited five nature destinations. I arrived late in the afternoon—4:10 p.m. and stayed till nearly 7 p.m.—which had its pros and cons. My late arrival left me virtually alone in the grasslands—alone to wander the trails and almost alone (along with one other visitor) to marvel at the herds of bison in the Bison Viewing Area. I was amazed at the large number of bison in one spot. My view reminded me of the times I'd seen large herds of bison in Yellowstone National Park.

The con of arriving so late is that I had to race the slowly descending sun to fit in as many hikes as possible before sunset. I didn't get to try all the trails, but the upside is that I have a very strong reason to return to explore Nachusa when I have more time. Here's some information on what you can do (and not do) at Nachusa.

Go hiking. This is one of the most popular activities at Nachusa. There are five trails:

✔ Stone Barn Savanna Trail: 250 acres of oak savanna (under restoration), restored prairie openings, wetlands, and sandstone cliffs (no climbing). This trail was my first stop at Nachusa, and I loved it! I enjoyed the rolling hills, sometimes demanding hiking, and the beautiful sandstone cliffs, which just sort of jump out at you as you round a bend on the trail. It was wonderful to be alone and see these beautiful rock outcroppings. (Kind of the exact opposite of a weekend, summer day at Starved Rock State Park.)

✔ Clear Creek Knolls Trail: 300 acres of restored prairie, remnant hill prairies, and a creek. The conservancy offers the following advice regarding the creek: "Remove your socks and shoes and enjoy the refreshing water. Wear a swimsuit, for the creek ford is fun to play in on a hot day."

✔ Meiners Wetlands Trail: 60 acres of wetlands, a portion of Franklin Creek, a remnant prairie, and a pond with a bur oak hillside.

✔ Carpenter Prairie Trail: 60 acres of prairies, a fallow meadow, and an old farm pond.

✔ Big Jump Trail: 350 acres of oak woodlands, hilly prairie, a creek (which you might need to wade through), cliffs, and crop fields. The Nature Conservancy asks that visitors do not climb the rock faces or walk on any crops. This was my second trail of the day. The early portions of this trail travel through green, rolling hills that reminded me of the hills of Ireland (where I got engaged), a forest area near the creek, and a farm field that was full of the bones of many deer and small mammals. I guess this area is like a coyote supermarket. I didn't get to finish this trail due to time constraints, but look forward to returning one day.

Nachusa's trails are different from what you might encounter at your local preserve. There is little signage on the trails, and you are encouraged to wander off-trail to

Wildflowers at Nachusa Grasslands
© Hank Erdmann, Shutterstock

explore your surroundings, as well as use the mowed, two-tracks (roads built for Nachusa maintenance staff) to explore. Things to keep in mind:

✔ bring sunscreen and a hat because many areas of Nachusa do not have much shade;

✔ bring ample water because the only potable water at the grasslands is found at a hand pump at the visitor center;

✔ the visitor center is not a typical indoor facility that you see at many parks—it is an outdoor facility with a few informative educational displays, washroom facilities, a hand pump for water (as I mentioned earlier), and a short nature trail;

128 Nature in Chicagoland

Bison viewing area © Andrew Morkes

✔ wear bug repellent: I came home unwittingly with a tick, which was the only bad memory of my visit to Nachusa; and

✔ wear sturdy shoes because the ground can be rocky and uneven, and long pants because some plants can be thorny and to reduce contact with ticks and other bugs.

Visit www.nachusagrasslands.org/hiking-destinations.html for more information on hiking and trail maps.

View bison. Nachusa is one of fewer than 10 places you can see bison in the Midwest (see page 191 for a list of bison-watching destinations). But seeing them won't be like viewing them at a zoo. Nachusa's bison herd roams across 1,500 acres of hilly landscape, and they may not be visible from the road. You'll have to be patient and have a little luck to see the bison. Binoculars will be useful. Note: No hiking is allowed inside the fenced bison unit. Visit www.nachusagrasslands.org/bison-viewing.html for more information on viewing bison.

Check out blooms and birds. Nachusa is home to 700 native plant species and more than 215 species of birds. The Nature Conservancy provides a helpful guide to what's in bloom and in which area of the grassland it is located at www.nachusagrasslands.org/whats-in-bloom.html. For example, in July you can see compass plant, wild bergamot, queen of the prairie, purple prairie clover, and prairie blazingstar, while in September, rattlesnake master, big bluestem grass, field milkwort, fringed gentian, rough blazingstar, and showy goldenrod grace the preserve's grasslands, wetlands, and forests.

Nachusa Grasslands is a birding hotspot and during your visit you might see wood, redhead, mallard, and other types of ducks; trumpeter and tundra swans; wild turkeys; American white pelicans; double-crested cormorants; great blue, green, and other types of herons (including state-endangered black-crowned night-herons); hawks, eagles, and other types of raptors; various types of cranes (including state- and federally-endangered whooping cranes); warblers such as Wilson's warblers, chestnut-sided warblers, and state-threatened cerulean warblers; eastern meadowlarks; bobolinks; indigo buntings; dickcissels; and many other species of birds. Visit www.nachusagrasslands.org/birds.html for a list of birds that you can see at Nachusa.

Volunteer. You can help make Nachusa Grasslands an even better place by volunteering on Thursdays and Saturdays (except during controlled burn season in March and April). You'll work alongside and learn from an experienced land steward. Some of the tasks you might be assigned include collecting seeds; pulling, digging, or clipping weeds and applying herbicide; and cutting trees, branches, and shrubs. You can also volunteer to adopt an area for a day, a week, or longer. You'll receive training on how to combat invasive plants, and then you can do your part to make the preserve a more ecologically healthy place.

Go Biking. The Ogle County Nachusa Bison/John Deere Loop Bike Trail (32.4 miles) takes riders across the Rock River (twice), past Nachusa Grasslands, and by the historical village of Grand Detour, where John Deere invented the modern plow in 1837. Visit https://cityoforegon.org/visitor-information/biking for more information.

Big Jump Trail © Andrew Morkes

Big Jump Trail © Andrew Morkes

FINAL THOUGHTS

I spent my last hour or so at Nachusa hiking the Big Jump Trail, which headed directly west toward the slowly setting sun. The hills were dark green and the late hour in the day created "magic light" that photographers (including amateur shutterbugs like me) crave, in which the water, trees, and grassland take on an almost otherworldly hue. I was alone (but not lonely) in a stunningly beautiful place, and I was happy that the Nature Conservancy had worked so hard to create such a special place. But at some point, I realized that I needed to head back to the car. All day, I'd been moving forward to exploring new things, and this was the first time that I had to go backwards. I felt both sad that the day had to end, but satisfied that I'd seen so much. I stood atop one of the dark green hills and took it all in— the sunlight, the woods, the wind, the creek, a pair of geese flying overhead, and a few red-wing blackbirds calling to each other from the trees—and savored the moment. And then I turned back the way I came, back toward my car, and a nearly two-hour trip home to the urban wilds of the Northwest Side of Chicago.

NEARBY NATURE DESTINATIONS

Castle Rock State Park, Franklin Creek State Natural Area, George B. Fell Nature Preserve, Lowden-Miller State Forest

NED BROWN PRESERVE

HIKING, FISHING, BICYCLING, AND ELK...YES, ELK

As you drive along Interstates 290 or 90 through Chicago's northwestern suburbs, you pass what seem like an endless row of big box stores, manufacturing facilities, and corporate headquarters. But, suddenly, these give way to reveal a vast expanse of woods, lakes, prairies, and wetlands. It's like a sudden breath of fresh air as you walk from a smoke-filled room. This breath of fresh air is the Ned Brown Preserve—but better known as Busse Woods. I like to think of popular Busse Woods as an urban outdoor vacation spot because there are so many fun things to do there. Here are just a few things you can do at this amazing preserve.

Fishing fun © Andrew Morkes

Take a hike or enjoy a bike ride. The preserve has 12.9 miles of hiking trails. The main trails are the 7.2-mile Red Loop Trail (which circles a large area of the preserve), the 2.3-mile Black Trail (in the far northwest corner of the preserve; it connects to the Red Loop Trail), and the 1.1-mile Purple Trail (in the far southwest area of the preserve; it also connects to the Red Loop Trail). There are also unmarked footpaths that branch off from these main trails.

Where: Multiple entrances/locations in and near Elk Grove Village, Illinois

Learn More: Forest Preserves of Cook County, https://fpdcc.com/places/locations/busse-woods

Hours: Sunrise to sunset, year-round

Quick Review: This nearly 3,560-acre preserve offers ancient upland forests, nearly 13 miles of paved trails, an elk pasture, and one of the largest fishing and boating waters in Cook County. Dogs are allowed (on leashes) in some areas. (#34 on the map on page 10)

What You Can Do There: Bicycling, Birdwatching, Canoeing/Kayaking/Boating, Cross-Country Skiing, Drone Flying Area, Fishing/Ice Fishing, Hiking, Horseback Riding, Ice Skating, Model Airplane Flying Field, Photography, Picnicking, Running/Exercise, Snowmobiling, Snowshoeing, Watercraft Rental

See some nature and wildlife. Forest Preserves of Cook County says that Busse Forest Nature Preserve (which is located north of Higgins Road within the preserve) is "one of the richest and most diverse natural areas in the Cook County forest preserves. The preserve's unusual combination of flatwoods, upland forests, and marshes have earned it National Natural Landmark status" (from the National Park Service). As you hike, you might see egrets, eagles, herons, and terns at or near Busse Lake and Salt Creek, and savannah and Henslow's sparrows and bobolinks in open prairies and meadows. In the marshes, look for muskrat and mink. Busse's upland forest of towering red oaks and hickories, maple, basswood, ash, elm and very large ironwoods is noteworthy because many of its trees were alive even before the first European settlers visited the area. Imagine the history they could share if they could talk.

There are 32 picnic groves at Busse Woods.
© Forest Preserves of Cook County.

View elk at the Busse Forest Elk Pasture. In 1925, Cook County commissioner William Busse transported nine elk cows and one bull from Yellowstone National Park via train to what is now Grove 4 of Busse Woods. In 1972, they were moved to their current 17-acre location at the intersection of Arlington Heights and Higgins Roads. The genetic diversity of today's herd is expanded every three to four years by the introduction of new males.

Rent a boat at the Lake Boating Center. Need a canoe or kayak? Sailboat or rowboat? Or do you prefer to sit back and let an electric motor do the work? If so, the Boating Center has a vessel for you. The rental season typically lasts from early April through late October, but call ahead (224/415-6554) to confirm the months/hours of operation and availability.

Go fishing at Busse Reservoir, which is one of the largest fishing and boating waters in Cook County. You can fish by boat or onshore for walleye, northern pike, largemouth and yellow bass, channel catfish, bluegill, sunfish, bullheads, yellow perch, and crappie.

NEARBY NATURE DESTINATIONS

Buffalo Creek Forest Preserve, Crabtree Nature Center, Paul Douglas Preserve, Songbird Slough Forest Preserve, Spring Valley Nature Center

PLEASANT VALLEY CONSERVATION AREA

EXPLORE THE LARGEST ROADLESS AREA IN MCHENRY COUNTY

Tired of roads, traffic lights, dense city blocks, or urban sprawl? If so, you should visit Pleasant Valley Conservation Area. There's a main road that will help you get to destinations in the nature area, but after that, you're on your own—whether you're walking, running, horseback riding, cross-country-skiing, or otherwise moving by your own power. Pleasant Valley is road free for 3 miles from north to south and 1.5 miles from east to west. That's a lot of nature to explore. I recently visited Pleasant Valley Conservation Area on a sunny, but very windy, spring day. It was my first time at Pleasant Valley, and I enjoyed exploring a new place, wandering amidst the towering oaks and pine trees and along Laughing Creek, listening to spring peepers welcome in the season, seeing my first butterfly of the year, and simply enjoying being outdoors. Here are a few things to do at this gem of a nature area:

Go hiking. There are more than five miles of natural surface trails—some flat, and others slightly steep and challenging. Some of the trails take you along Laughing Creek (which was named by a child who said that its gurgling reminded her of someone happily laughing). As you walk along the creek banks, look for the Iowa darter, a tiny fish (two to three inches in length), and the state-endangered Blanding's turtle.

Check out some wildlife. During your visit, you might see hawks, eagles, turkey vultures, numerous types of songbirds, pileated woodpeckers, as well as herons, terns, cranes, ducks, owls, rails, and blue-winged teals in the wetland rookery and in other areas. More than 205 bird species have been sighted at Pleasant Valley. Visit https://ebird.org/hotspot/L390107 for a list. Other animals

Where: 13315 Pleasant Valley Road, Woodstock, IL 60098

Learn More: McHenry County Conservation District, www.mccdistrict.org/visit__explore/places_to_go/find_a_site/pleasant_valley.php, www.facebook.com/MCCDPleasantValley

Hours: Sunrise to sunset, year-round

Quick Review: Nearly 2,100 acres of rolling hills, savannah, and oak woodlands, with a healthy offering of pine trees; Laughing Creek, Kishwaukee River, and wetlands; and more than five miles of hiking trails. (#35 on the map on page 10)

What You Can Do There: Amphitheater, Bicycling (in parking areas), Birdwatching, Cross-Country Skiing, Fishing, Hiking, Horseback Riding, Photography, Picnicking, Running/Exercise, Snowshoeing

© Andrew Morkes

include turtles, salamanders, white-tailed deer, and fox.

Discover nearly 275 native plant species, including 13 that are considered rare. "Plants such as the northern bog violet, short green milkweed, prairie star sedge, prairie buttercup, swamp thistle and prairie Indian plantain help give this area a high ecological rating, while the more common sunflowers, mil hallow marsh, sedge meadow, and wet-prairie complex created a wetland rookery that attracts numerous visiting herons, cranes, terns, rails and blue-winged teals," according to the McHenry County Conservation District.

Enjoy winter sports such as cross-country skiing and snowshoeing. There is a half-mile solar-lit trail (located on the east side of the Pleasant Valley entrance) that allows visitors to enjoy the park after dark. The trail is open until 9 p.m. daily, November through March, during Central Standard time.

Go fishing. Try to catch a largemouth bass or bluegill at a two-acre pond that's located near the main parking lot.

Have a picnic. Enjoy fresh apple pie, your favorite sandwich, some potato salad, and your other favorite foods (of course you'll have to make and bring these treats) at Pleasant Valley's natural amphitheater. Large parties can rent one of two picnic shelters, which come with a grill.

Saddle up and head out on the trails. If you're an equestrian (or a hiker), you can use the 1.3-mile horse trail that transects the conservation area near the western edge and runs north/south between Pleasant Valley Road and Hensel Road. Note: No horse trailer parking lot is available on-site.

NEARBY NATURE DESTINATIONS

Boone Creek Conservation Area, Coral Woods Conservation Area, Kishwaukee Headwaters Conservation Area

TEKAKWITHA WOODS FOREST PRESERVE

ENJOY PEACEFUL TRAILS, BEAUTIFUL BIRDS, AND VIEWS OF THE FOX RIVER

© Andrew Morkes

The Sisters of Mercy—an international community of Roman Catholic women religious—owned the property that is now Tekakwitha Woods Forest Preserve for eight decades. It was used as a spiritual retreat center and to help those in need. The FPDKC bought the land from the religious order in 1992. The Sisters requested that the site be named in honor of Kateri Tekakwitha, a 17th century Native American from the Mohawk tribe whose was life was filled with physical suffering and rejection by many of her friends and family because she converted to Christianity. Tekakwitha was beatified by Pope John Paul II in 1980 and canonized by Pope Benedict XVI in 2012. Tekakwitha is the patron saint of the environment and ecology, people in exile, and Native Americans. Visit www.katerishrine.com/st-kateri to learn more about her.

I visited the preserve on an unseasonably warm (80 degree) late-April day. A steady wind kept me cool as I walked the trails, traveled over a charming foot-

Where: 35W076 Villa Maria Road, St. Charles, IL 60174

Learn More: Forest Preserve District of Kane County (FPDKC), https://kaneforest.com/location/tekakwitha-woods

Hours: Sunrise to sunset, year-round

Quick Review: A 65-acre preserve, with trails that wind through forests and ravines. The 32-mile Fox River Trail travels through the edge of the preserve. An off-leash dog area is located next to Tekakwitha Woods at River Bend Community Park. (#36 on the map on page 10)

What You Can Do There: Bicycling, Birdwatching, Canoeing/Kayaking/Boating (on the nearby Fox River), Cross-Country Skiing, Educational and Self-Enrichment Opportunities and Classes, Fishing, Hiking, Local History, Photography, Picnicking, Running/Exercise, Snowshoeing

© Andrew Morkes

bridge, and made my way down to the Fox River to views of five islands and the loud honking of geese (I could hear them in the forest before I even caught sight of the river). I also admired the spring flowers—mayapples, bloodroot, red trillium, and trout lily—as I walked. Although the preserve is small, it is a beautiful place in which you can do a variety of activities, including:

Go for a hike. There are several trails (all 0.50-miles or less) that take you through an oak-maple forest on the uplands, a floodplain forest, wetlands, and grasslands. Some of the trees at the preserve are more than 150 years old. For a list of trails and a map, visit https://kaneforest.com/upload/74-Tekakwitha WoodsTRAILMAP2015.pdf. Note: Some of the trails are on hilly terrain that can be slippery in wet or icy conditions. Additionally, you can connect to the Fox River Trail (which runs along the former Elgin-Aurora trolley line) from the parking lot on the west side of Weber Drive. There are also unofficial trails that travel along the river. If you travel north on the Fox River Trail, you'll cross the Fox River, enter the Jon J. Duerr Forest Preserve, and then continue north along the river. The Fox River Trail is 32 miles long and offers opportunities for hiking, biking, birding, snowshoeing, and cross-country skiing.

Enjoy birdwatching. More than 25 bird species have been observed at Tekakwitha, according to eBird.com. They include hooded mergansers, yellow-bellied sapsuckers, Cooper's hawks, turkey vultures, red-bellied woodpeckers, downy woodpeckers, northern flickers, black-capped chickadees, white-breasted nuthatches, and golden-crowned kinglets. Visit https://ebird.org/checklist/S84674635 for the complete list.

Take a class. The FPDKC offers a variety of classes at the preserve. One recent class was Ethnobotany Exploration, in which a naturalist educated visitors about how the plants and trees in the preserve were used by Native Americans and settlers for food, shelter, and medicine. Another, Summer Tree Identification, introduced students to the basic plant morphology needed for tree identification.

View of the Fox River © Andrew Morkes

NEARBY NATURE DESTINATIONS AND OTHER ATTRACTIONS

Blackhawk County Forest Preserve, Brewster Creek Forest Preserve, Fox River Bluff Forest Preserve, Fox River Trolley Museum, James Pate Philip State Park, Jon J. Duerr Forest Preserve, LeRoy Oakes Forest Preserve

VOLO BOG STATE NATURAL AREA

AN ICE AGE REMNANT AND THE ONLY QUAKING BOG IN ILLINOIS

Volo Bog © Andrew Morkes

About 12,000 years ago, the last of the towering glaciers that covered parts of what is now Chicagoland began melting. As one of the massive glaciers melted, a water-filled depression was left in its wake. The depression eventually developed into a deep 50-acre lake that had steep banks and poor drainage.

About 6,000 years ago, the lake began filling with dense vegetation. According to the Illinois Department of Natural Resources, "a floating mat, consisting primarily of sphagnum moss formed around the outside edges among the cattails and sedges. As these plants died and decomposed, the peat mat thickened, forming a support material for rooted plants."

The plant-filled lake eventually became part of what we now know as Volo Bog State Natural Area, which is located about 40 miles northwest of Chicago. The site includes Volo Bog, the only quaking bog in Illinois. A quaking bog consists of lay-

Where: 28478 W. Brandenburg Road, Ingleside, IL 60041

Learn More: Illinois Department of Natural Resources, 815/344-1294, www2.illinois.gov/dnr/Parks/Pages/VoloBog.aspx

Hours: Opens at 8:00 a.m.; closing times vary by the season. Closed Christmas and New Year's Days.

Quick Review: This beautiful nature site includes Volo Bog, the only open-water quaking bog in Illinois. Enjoyable hiking trails and a top-notch nature center. Tons of wildlife. (#37 on the map on page 10)

What You Can Do There: Birdwatching, Cross-Country Skiing, Educational and Self-Enrichment Opportunities and Classes, Hiking, Nature Center, Photography, Picnicking, Running/Exercise, Snowshoeing

ers and layers of plant matter that have collected atop of the remnants of a former lake. As a boy, I once walked on a quaking bog at the Owasippe Scout Reservation in Michigan. It was amazing. I bounced up and down on the ground (of course, it was not real ground, just thick layers of plant life floating atop water), and it felt like I was hopping on a mini trampoline. We also drank water from a nearby spring that I still remember as the most refreshing water I've ever tasted.

© Andrew Morkes

You can't jump on the bog at Volo Bog or drink the water, but it's still worth a visit. Volo Bog is so unique that it was designated as an Illinois Nature Preserve in 1970. These preserves protect the highest quality natural lands in the state.

Volo Bog State Natural Area is a special place for nature viewing, hiking, and contemplation. Here are a variety of things you can do at this unique site, which has a landscape that is much closer to what you see in Wisconsin or Minnesota than what is typical of Illinois:

✔ **You can walk the Volo Bog Interpretive Trail,** a half-mile trail that takes you across deck sections (which float atop the water), boardwalks, and a wood-chip path. As you walk, you'll get a chance to observe each stage of bog succession until you get to the "eye of the bog." This was my favorite walk. Within minutes of leaving the visitor center, you'll be surrounded by tall cattails, hear the sounds of crickets and frogs, and feel like you're far from civilization. Visit www2.illinois.gov/dnr/Parks/Documents/VoloBogSiteMap.pdf for a trail map.

✔ **In the bog and surrounding areas, look for wildlife:** beavers, great blue and green-backed herons, white-tail deer, mink, muskrat, raccoon, dragonflies, sandhill cranes, little brown bats, muskrats, turtles, northern owls, and finches.

✔ **You can view plant species** such as marsh shieldfern, bottlebrush sedge fern, sensitive fern, starflower, water arum, highbush blueberry, winterberry holly, red-osier dogwood, and marsh cinquefoil.

✔ **Check out the tamarack trees that are in or near the bog.** These beautiful pine trees are one of the few types of trees that flourish in bogs. The tamaracks are only present in the northeast corner of Illinois and are considered a threatened species in our state.

✔ **Hike all or a portion of the 2.75-mile Tamarack View Trail** through woods, wetlands, and prairie. The trail begins just south of the visitor center.

✔ **Hike the Deerpath Trail and Prairie View Trails,** which consist of two miles of paths through woods, old farm fields, and areas where prairie is being restored.

✔ **Check out the nature center,** which is housed in a dairy barn built in the early 1900s. The center features nature exhibits, a hands-on discovery area, and library.

✔ **Enjoy lunch in the picnic grove near the nature center.**

✔ **Visit the Pistakee Bog Nature Preserve** just across the road from Volo Bog. Visit www2.illinois.gov/dnr/INPC/Pages/Area2LakePistakeeBog.aspx to learn more.

✔ **Snowshoe and ski at the preserve in the winter.**

Visiting places like Volo Bog and other Illinois Nature Preserves makes me ponder all the beautiful, pristine natural areas in Illinois that were not protected and that have given way to "progress." It pains me to think that places just like Volo Bog are now covered by strip malls, housing developments, and factories. We can certainly use another Volo Bog or two, but we don't need any more suburban sprawl. But what's done is done, unfortunately, and this passing thought just makes me appreciate the beautiful natural areas that remain in our state. It also makes me more motivated to protect our special places. I hope that you feel the same way, too.

NEARBY NATURE DESTINATIONS

Chain O'Lakes State Park, Glacial Park, Grant Woods Forest Preserve, Moraine Hills State Park, Turner Lake Fen Nature Preserve

VOLO AUTO MUSEUM

After checking out the bog, take a break from nature by visiting the **Volo Auto Museum** (27582 Volo Village Road, Volo, IL 60073, 815/385-3644, www.volocars.com), which is about 10 minutes away by car. It's a family-owned and -run museum and collectibles auto market that features 33 distinct exhibits in 12 buildings on 35 acres, plus many outdoor exhibits. It also features a restaurant and a large antique mall. It's a warm blast of kitschy Americana. There are hundreds of vintage and famous cars, but the museum also features everything under the sun—from 1950s jukeboxes and arcade games, to military aircraft and 100-year-old trains, to antique bikes, scooters, tractors, and snowmobiles. There's literally something for everybody at the museum. Unless you're a chronic grump, you'll find something at the museum that will make you smile, laugh, or simply say wow (like I did when I saw the 28-foot-long guitar car and the 14-foot-tall roller skate car).

CHICAGOLAND SOUTH AND BEYOND

Scenic bridge at Black Partridge Woods Nature Preserve © Andrew Morkes

BLACK PARTRIDGE WOODS NATURE PRESERVE
COOL RAVINES, GREAT HIKING, AND SIX OTHER REASONS TO VISIT

Thousands and thousands of years ago, a spring-fed stream began to carve a ravine into a bluff that overlooked a river. As time passed, the ravine grew deeper. Native Americans (including the Potawatomi chief Black Partridge) lived in and/or travelled through the forests, ravines, towering bluffs, and flood plains of the area. Life was good—especially during the warm months. Eventually, European settlers came and forcibly removed the Native Americans

> **Where:** Enter from Bluff Road, east of I-355, Cook County, IL 60439 (near Lemont, Illinois)
>
> **Learn More:** Forest Preserves of Cook County, https://fpdcc.com/places/locations/black-partridge-woods
>
> **Hours:** Sunrise to sunset, year-round
>
> **Quick Review:** Ravines and streams. Prehistoric-looking fish and endangered dragonflies. Challenging hiking. Early spring flowers. Stunning fall colors. Migratory bird watching. No dogs allowed. (#38 on the map on page 12)
>
> **What You Can Do There:** Birdwatching, Hiking, Photography, Picnicking, Snowshoeing

from their ancestral lands or created programs that forced the increasingly impoverished tribes to sell more of their land in exchange for annuities that were not fair compensation for the actual value of the land. The European settlers built beautiful little towns such as Lemont and not-so beautiful heavy industry along the river.

Today, the Native Americans are long gone, Lemont remains a charming town full of history, some of the heavy industry remains along the river, but, most importantly for nature lovers, the spring-fed ravine and bluff community—which was established and protected as Black Partridge Woods—survives amidst civilization. In fact, wise people made it one of the first Illinois Nature Preserves in 1965. These preserves protect the highest quality natural lands in the state.

Black Partridge Woods is located on sleepy Bluff Road, which runs along the Des Plaines River. At 80 acres, it's a tiny preserve, but well worth a visit. Here are many reasons why:

✔ **Great hiking on the bluffs** that tower 50 feet or so above the meandering gravel- and stone-filled creek, as well as along the creek bed and in the surrounding forests, which are dominated by red and white oak, sugar maple, and basswood.

✔ **Stunning spring wildflowers, vivid fall colors, and snow-covered hills and creeks in winter.**

✔ **The opportunity to see some of the earliest late-winter/early-spring plants and flowers** such as skunk cabbage (which generates its own heat to melt the snow and can grow to two feet in height and one foot in width) and bright yellow marsh marigold, which lined the edges of the water during my visit.

✔ **Good wildlife viewing.** Black Partridge boasts a wide range of animals, including northern water snakes, deer, red-headed woodpeckers, woodcocks, gray squirrels, wood peewees (birds that love catching and eating flies and other insects), and American toads. An especially fascinating "critter" is the mottled sculpin, a prehistoric-looking, bottom-dwelling fish that flourishes in the woods' cold and highly-oxygenated streams. Additionally, spring and fall are great times to view migratory birds who've stopped for a rest at Black Partridge.

✔ **Stunning views of the Des Plaines River** from certain bluff areas of Black Partridge Woods, from Lemont Woods County Forest Preserve, and from other nearby preserves.

© Andrew Morkes

✔ **Picnicking.** Bring a picnic lunch, sit in the shade of the picnic shelter, and watch the creek make its way through the woods. (Note: The shelter can be reserved for large groups.)

NEARBY NATURE DESTINATIONS

Cap Sauers Holding Nature Preserve, Keepataw Preserve, Red Gate Woods, Tampier Slough Woods, Waterfall Glen Forest Preserve

---

EAT, DRINK, SHOP, AND SAVOR HISTORY

After visiting Black Partridge Woods, be sure to check out the historic town of **Lemont** (https://iandmcanal.org/experiences/canal-towns/lemont) just across the Des Plaines River. The town, which was first settled in 1833, offers historic churches and other buildings made from dolomite limestone (which is known locally as Athens Marble). The limestone was also used to build the Chicago Water Tower, Holy Name Cathedral, and other Chicago landmarks). Lemont also offers a charming downtown, antique shops, boutiques, and tons of history. It's one of my favorite towns in the southwest suburbs.

BUFFALO ROCK STATE PARK

AWESOME VIEWS OF THE ILLINOIS RIVER, EARTHEN ART, AND TRANQUILITY

Trail to the top of an effigy tumuli
© Andrew Morkes

I recently visited three Illinois state parks in one day. The first two were packed with people enjoying the trails, deep sandstone canyons, and waterfalls. These parks were beautiful but, in the end, I was a little "peopled out." I longed to be alone in nature, with great views and my own company. I received my wish when I visited Buffalo Rock State Park, which is located on massive bluffs that tower above the Illinois River. As I journeyed west on its Effigy Tumuli Trail on a sunny spring day in the low 60s, I was amazed at the peace I suddenly felt atop these bluffs. The only sounds I heard were the strong winds blowing through the tall prairie grass and trees, and the busy calls of cranes, geese, and other birds in their nesting areas along the river. And I encountered only four people during my entire hike.

This park land was donated by the Ottawa Silica Company, and environ-

Where: 1300 North 27th Road, Ottawa, IL 61350; located about 86 miles southwest of downtown Chicago

Learn More: Illinois Department of Natural Resources, 815/433-2224, www2.illinois.gov/dnr/Parks/Pages/BuffaloRock.aspx

Hours: Sunrise to sunset, year-round

Quick Review: A nearly 300-acre park that features bison, hiking trails on bluffs above the Illinois River, and an outdoor earthen art exhibit with massive animal effigies. Dogs allowed (on leashes). (#39 on the map on page 12)

What You Can Do There: Bicycling, Birdwatching, Bison Viewing, Cross-Country Skiing, Hiking, Photography, Picnicking, Public Art (Effigy Tumuli), Snowshoeing

> **EFFIGY MOUNDS AND TUMULI**
>
> Effigy mounds are raised masses of earth in the shape of animals, humans, or other symbols. They were built by the Late Woodland Native American culture from about 600 through 1150 A.D., and were used to bury the dead, for clan ceremonies, and, perhaps, for celestial observations or to mark tribal or group boundaries. Tumuli is another word for a group of mounds.

mental reclamation efforts were made to restore the land after extensive coal mining. In the early 1980s, the land artist Michael Heizer (https://gagosian.com/artists/michael-heizer) was commissioned to create art that spotlighted both the natural world and the Native Americans who had lived in the area for thousands of years before being displaced by European settlers and protracted warfare with other tribes. Effigy Tumuli consists of five mounds that pay homage to both Native American burial mounds that are still found throughout the Midwest and indigenous animals of the area. The animals depicted include a water strider (a type of insect), whose artist depiction is 685 feet long; a frog, 340 feet long; a catfish, 770 feet long; a turtle, 650 feet long; and a snake, 2,070 feet long measured from head to tail (it curves). The frog, turtle, and catfish tumuli are built atop the flat bluff, while the snake and water strider incorporate existing land masses. For example, the snake curves around the bluff, with its head dipping down 90 feet to the river. The Effigy Tumuli Trail begins at the parking lot and

Water Strider Tumuli © Andrew Morkes

> **DID YOU KNOW?**
>
> "The area of Buffalo Rock was the home of the Illinois Indians when Louis Jolliet, the French explorer, and the Jesuit missionary priest Father Jacques Marquette made their trip up the Illinois River in 1673," according to the Illinois Department of Natural Resources. "Later, the Illinois tribe was virtually annihilated in protracted warfare with the aggressive Iroquois."

heads west until you reach the snake mound. You'll then return east the way you came until you reach a river observation area, where there is a fork in the trail. If you head left, you will return the way that you came on the effigy trail. If you head right, you will journey east and then north on the River View Trail back to the parking lot. There is also an option on the River View Trail to continue east to see more of the river. Dirt and grass sub paths branch off the main trails throughout the park. Be very careful because many of these trails lead to steep slopes or cliff edges.

It's not always easy to see the shapes of the animals from ground level as you walk. I found this especially true walking west on the Effigy Tumuli Trail. But it was easier to see the tumuli on the River View Trail, which also has great views of the Illinois River. Sub trails also allow you to climb the tumuli to gain a better understanding of their size and design. You can learn more about the tumuli and see aerial photos of them at http://doublenegative.tarasen.net/effigy-tumuli. One complaint: When I visited, the interpretive signs for each animal were missing. Their presence would greatly improve the visitor experience. Let's hope that they've been replaced by the time that you visit Buffalo Rock.

Other things you can do at Buffalo Rock State Park include picnicking, recreational activities, and bison viewing. There's a large picnic area with grills that's shaded by mature oak, walnut, and hickory trees. There are also two shelters, and the bigger shelter has a large stone fireplace and may be reserved. The picnic area offers views of the Illinois River. Kids will enjoy the park's playground and a baseball diamond. Finally, there are three American bison in an enclosure near the parking lot. You can also see bison about an hour east of Buffalo Rock State Park at Midewin National Tallgrass Prairie and in seven other places in the Midwest. See page 191 for a list of bison-viewing destinations.

NEARBY NATURE DESTINATIONS

Illinois & Michigan Canal State Trail Buffalo Rock Access Area, Matthiessen State Park, Starved Rock State Park

BURNHAM PRAIRIE NATURE PRESERVE

A BIRDWATCHING HOTSPOT

A prairie and a nature preserve in the middle of an urban neighborhood? I wasn't expecting much as I drove through block after block of homes. I passed kids playing in front yards, people unpacking groceries from their cars, and others cutting their grass. But after I turned right from Manistee Avenue and traveled a block or so, I glimpsed six or seven herons poised over the shimmering waters of a marsh waiting to strike at unsuspecting fish. Egrets and ducks swam in the distance, and I heard the chirp and croaks of frogs and the strong wind rustling the leaves of the trees. I was in nature heaven!

I quickly parked the car and walked to the water's edge. I was fascinated by the herons, which were only 30 feet or so away. In no time, one of the herons dove its bill into the water and came out with a small fish. Others did the same in the distance. I found this even more fascinating because as I watched the herons fish, I could glimpse people's backyards, decks, and an alley that ran behind the houses. I hope the residents of Manistee Avenue never get tired of the parade of birds and other wildlife that visit their "backyard" during the year.

There is much natural beauty at Burnham Prairie Nature Preserve, but also some urban mess. As I walked the shore, I occasionally glimpsed discarded plastic bottles and an old tire. When I hiked the savannah, I encountered remnant slag from steel mills, but that comes with the territory when visiting many nature areas in Chicago's Southland. In the 1800s and early 1900s, Chicago's bigwigs made the Southland (including delicate and unique ecosystems along or near Lake Michigan) the repository for steel mills, oil refineries, other manufacturing plants, and other types of heavy industry because they didn't want them in their own backyards on the North Side and in other areas.

Where: East 139th Street & South Manistee Avenue, Burnham, IL 60633

Learn More: Forest Preserves of Cook County, https://fpdcc.com/places/locations/burnham-prairie

Hours: Sunrise to sunset, year-round

Quick Review: A small Illinois Nature Preserve that is an excellent place to see marsh and other types of birds—including common gallinule, Virginia rail, and American bittern—and take short hikes. (#40 on the map on page 12)

What You Can Do There: Birdwatching, Hiking, Photography, Picnicking, Snowshoeing

Great blue herons © Andrew Morkes

Yet, many of the ecosystems managed to survive these industrial years and are now being restored. Burnham Prairie Nature Preserve is one of these gems. According to Forest Preserves of Cook County (which manages and protects the preserve), restoration efforts at the prairie "focus on protecting the mix of marsh, wet sand prairie, and savanna. The Forest Preserves worked with the U.S. Army Corps of Engineers to build an earthen berm to prevent polluted stormwater from entering the wetlands. And ongoing invasive species control, including prescribed burns, protect the native plants that help these marsh birds thrive."

Burnham Prairie Nature Preserve is a birding hotspot, including many migratory visitors in the spring and fall. It contains some of the highest quality wet prairie habitat in Illinois. I'm not a birding expert, but visitors report having seen the following birds at the preserve: bald eagle, barred owl, Bell's vireo, black-billed cuckoo, blue-winged warbler, blue grosbeak, bobolink, broad-winged hawk, cackling goose, Carolina wren, cerulean warbler, common redpoll, dickcissel, Forster's tern grasshopper sparrow, Henslow's sparrow, hooded warbler, Iceland gull, Kentucky warbler, least bittern, lesser black-backed gull, Louisiana waterthrush, Nelson's sparrow, northern harrier, northern parula, orchard oriole, pied-billed grebe, pileated woodpecker, red-headed woodpecker, red-shouldered hawk, red crossbill, savannah sparrow, sedge wren, short-eared owl, snowy egret, sora summer tanager, Thayer's gull, Virginia rail, white-eyed vireo, willow flycatcher, wood duck, wood thrush, yellow-billed cuckoo, and yellow-breasted chat.

Burnham Prairie Nature Preserve is a great place to see dozens of bird species, view the positive effects of environmental restoration efforts, and simply enjoy nature. It's a small area that you will probably spend an hour or two at—unless you're a dedicated birder. Regardless of its size, Burnham Prairie is worth a visit—especially during the spring and fall bird migration seasons.

NEARBY NATURE DESTINATIONS

Beaubien Woods; Big Marsh Park; Hegewisch Marsh; Indian Ridge Marsh Park; Powderhorn Lake, Marsh, and Prairie; Sand Ridge Nature Center; Wolf Lake Memorial Park

CAP SAUERS HOLDING NATURE PRESERVE

THE WILDEST PLACE IN COOK COUNTY, A RARE ESKER, AND A HIDDEN PRAIRIE

You won't find a nature center or interpretive trail signs at Cap Sauers Holding Nature Preserve in Palos Park, a southwest suburb of Chicago. But you will find beautiful oak forests, prairies, savannahs, cattail marshes, sedge meadows, and wetlands. Walking the gravel trails and footpaths in this sprawling 1,520-acre preserve is probably the closest one can get to wilderness in Cook County.

Cap Sauers is my favorite hiking destination in Chicagoland. I've hiked there for more than 25 years—sometimes twice a week when I was in my 20s and fancy free.

At Cap Sauers, there are great hiking, biking, and horseback trails; excellent opportunities to view wildlife; and much more. Cap Sauers also holds a special place in my heart. It was my place of refuge and regeneration after my father died in 1997. After he passed away, I hiked its woods constantly, regardless of the season. I loved to wade the creek shallows that shimmered with the busy activity of minnows, water beetles, and frogs. Loved the ravines that dove swiftly as if fleeing the sun. Loved to wade into Visitation Prairie's sea of grass during high summer. And loved getting "lost" in the woods for hours, searching for fossils. When I found a fossil, I felt happy momentarily, forgetting the images of my 90-pound, cancer-stricken father in bed, his skin the color of ash, his voice

Where: South Willow Springs Road (aka 104th Avenue), south of Calumet Sag Road/Route 83, Cook County, IL 60464; Park at Teason's Woods parking lot, cross Willow Springs Wood, and head west along the Sag Valley Yellow Unpaved Trail.

Learn More: Forest Preserves of Cook County, https://fpdcc.com/places/locations/cap-sauers-holding-nature-preserve

Hours: Sunrise to sunset, year-round

Quick Review: The largest roadless area in Cook County, with 1,520 acres of rolling hills, wetlands, marshes, streams, savannah, prairie, and forest. Five miles of paved and unpaved trails. Beautiful spring flowers and fall colors. The trails at Cap Sauer's Holding are part of the 20.4-mile Sag Valley Trail System. Visit https://fpdcc.com/places/trails/sag-valley-trail-system/#overview for more information. Dogs allowed. (#41 on the map on page 12)

What You Can Do There: Bicycling, Birdwatching, Cross-Country Skiing, Equestrian, Hiking, Picnicking, Photography, Running/Exercise, Snowshoeing

© Andrew Morkes

a thin whisper. That first year after he died, I found an impressive fossil almost every time I hiked. It was like a special gift from God and my dad. This went on for a year or two, and my sadness ebbed slightly. I still hike frequently, but rarely find large fossils, which just makes those first frequent finds even more special.

But there are many other reasons to love Cap Sauers Holding, including:

Stunning wildflowers. When I visited Cap Sauers recently, flowers blanketed most of the preserve—from the little creek "valleys," to Visitation Prairie, to the top of the esker trail that winds its way through the preserve. You'll find vivid wildflower displays throughout the late spring, summer, and fall.

Excellent hiking. There are five miles of paved trails and footpaths that wind through forest, prairies, wetlands, savannah, and other ecosystems.

Great opportunities for exercise. Its rolling hills provide an excellent workout. It may sound strange, but I love the feeling of pushing my body to near exhaustion—my leg muscles burning, my heart pounding—as I hike its hills and valleys. Cap Sauers isn't completely hilly, so don't let the occasionally rugged stretch deter you from visiting.

Peace and solitude. The dense woods, beautiful prairie, and meandering streams will heal your mind and soul. If you leave the main gravel trails, you'll

---

IT'S THE LAW!

Remember that it's against the law to remove fossils, arrowheads, and other historical or natural resources from forest preserves.

most likely never encounter another person for the rest of your hike—but you'll see plenty of deer, frogs, birds, squirrels, chipmunks, fish, and even a coyote, if you're lucky. A feeling of peace will wash over you as the only sounds that you hear are those of your footsteps, the song of crickets, and the wind rustling the leaves of the trees and tall prairie grass.

Birdwatching. Cap Sauers is an excellent destination for birdwatching. Birders can see summer tanagers, white-eyed vireos, Louisiana water thrushes, hooded warblers, chipping sparrows, uncommon pileated woodpeckers, eastern phoebes, blue-winged warblers, ovenbirds, herons, ruby-throated hummingbirds, and many other types of birds.

© Andrew Morkes

History. In the 1800s, European immigrants settled some areas of Cap Sauers. They're long gone, but they've left a few traces (stone foundations, 100-year-old bottles, a rusty wagon wheel, and broken china) that you might discover during your visit. Native Americans also lived in this area for thousands of years before Europeans settled this area, and they've also left their mark in these woods.

Winter hiking. Cap Sauers is a great destination for snowshoeing or just a hike. You'll enjoy even more solitude in the winter months.

The joy of discovery. Cap Sauers is so vast that it would take years of steady visits to see everything it offers.

I also recommend Cap Sauers because it's undergoing a rebirth of a sort. Until

Visitation Prairie © Andrew Morkes

recently, some of its footpaths had become almost unnavigable (although the main gravel trails are always navigable) due to the thick buckthorn—the scourge of Chicagoland forest preserves—as well as honeysuckle and dead underbrush. In the absence of natural fire cycles, which reinvigorated the forest and prairie in the past, some trails I used to hike became completely overgrown. But the Forest Preserves of Cook County, The Nature Conservancy, and dedicated volunteers are working hard to restore the habitat to its original state by conducting prescribed burns and removing buckthorn and other non-native plants and trees. On a recent trip, I learned that they've made great progress. What an improvement! In the areas where this work has been done, the forest floor is awash with flowers, and, from the treetops, a virtual never-ending chorus of birdsong "played" during a recent hike. It was really beautiful to see and hear. I look forward to the continued rebirth of my favorite hiking spot.

MY FAVORITE SPOTS AT CAP SAUERS HOLDING

If you visit Cap Sauers Holding, you can certainly enjoy a great day hiking the crushed gravel trails that wind through the preserve.

But for a really enjoyable time, venture off these paths, and take the foot trails that wind through the preserve—on 30-foot bluffs overlooking meandering streams, through beautiful meadows and prairies, and through dense forests.

WHO WAS CAP SAUERS?

Cap Sauers Holdings is named for Charles "Cap" Sauers. He was the first general superintendent of Forest Preserves of Cook County. Sauers served as superintendent from the early 1930s to the early 1960s and is credited with expanding and improving the preserves. Because of his wise stewardship and the vision of others, more than 70,000 acres have been acquired and are currently managed by the district.

My first suggestion: hike to Visitation Prairie in the middle of Cap Sauers. But before you enter, revel in the riot of white and yellow wildflowers that seem to go on forever along the trail as you approach the prairie. This area used to be a dense labyrinth of European buckthorn. Thanks to the work of Forest Preserves of Cook County staff and volunteers, it's now an awe-inspiring example of what can be done to make an unhealthy forest area into something more natural and beautiful.

Take some time to savor the wildflowers, then hike to Visitation Prairie, which offers peace and solitude that can rival the remotest monastery; prairie grasses that grow as tall as Giannis Antetokounmpo in the summer; and evening primrose, goldenrod, prairie sunflower, New England aster, and other striking blooms as beautiful as my wife. In fact, many call Visitation Prairie the most-isolated spot in Cook County (quite an achievement in a county with 5.2 million people).

Next, exit Visitation Prairie to the east and hike north on the esker trail. An esker is a narrow ridge made of sand and gravel that, thousands of years ago, was a river bottom on top of or at the bottom of a glacier. Forest Preserves of Cook County says that the esker at Cap Sauers is "one of the best examples of this rare feature in Illinois." As you walk the esker trail, you'll travel through dense forest, wetlands, and marshes,

Esker trail © Andrew Morkes

Crinoid fossils   © Andrew Morkes

which are filled with wildflowers of varying types during the warm seasons. You'll hear spring peepers (a type of chorus frog), cricket song, and other animals in the wetlands and forests on each side of the trail. It's a stunning walk (especially in late spring, summer, and early fall), and I wish this esker was my own. I would walk it every day if I could. [Note: If you follow the esker trail to its northern terminus and make a right, you'll take a series of foot trails that cross a creek, gradually climb from the creek bed into the forest, and eventually link up with the main gravel trail (turn left when you reach the gravel trail)—bringing you back to your car at the Teason's Woods parking lot.]

Another option: Head off the gravel trails to traverse one of the many footpaths that travel along the pretty streams that meander through the preserve. Some of these streams flow year-round, while others shrink to tiny little pools of frogs, turtles, and fish during times of drought. In some areas, 30- to 40-foot hills loom over these creeks, and it's almost as if you're in a deep canyon. Of course, the only true canyon in Cook County is Sagawau Canyon (see page 204), just northwest of Cap Sauers on Route 83. It can be visited by appointment. These creek "canyons," actually ravines, are a wonderful place to look for fossils, enjoy a picnic lunch, or simply watch nature. Some of my favorite creek-hiking experiences include:

✔ Discovering pretty mini waterfalls during winter hikes
✔ Seeing a great blue heron along one of the creek beds
✔ Taking a break for lunch along the banks of a creek and suddenly seeing a 10-point buck emerge from the woods and splash through the water just feet away
✔ Coming upon thousands of pollywogs in a pool of water; any time I moved the future frogs churned the water as if a shark was below them
✔ Hiking with my wife and seeing a coyote emerge from her den about 20

feet away. She was unaware of us for a few minutes, and it was breathtaking to see this animal in the wild.

✔ Taking my nine-year-old hiking there for the first time and impressing him—for some reason—with my hill-climbing abilities.

Chicagoans are blessed to have such a diverse range of preserves (including Cap Sauers) to enjoy in their back yard. Cap Sauers Holding is special place to me, and I hope it becomes one for you.

Keep the following in mind when you visit Cap Sauers Holding Nature Preserve:

✔ If you visit during the warm season, bring bug repellent and sunscreen.

✔ Bring an ample supply of water; no potable water is available once you enter the preserve.

© Andrew Morkes

✔ Wear waterproof hiking boots if you plan to hike off the gravel trails; low-lying areas can be wet and muddy after heavy rains.

✔ Bring your binoculars. There is good birdwatching.

✔ Tell someone where you're going before you head out for a hike; Cap Sauers is a big place and, if you head off the gravel trails, it's easy to get lost. Of course, getting lost is relative at Cap Sauers since it's surrounded on all sides by roads. If you get really lost, just pick a direction, and you'll eventually reach a road. Or use GPS to navigate.

NEARBY NATURE DESTINATIONS

Black Partridge Woods Nature Preserve, Cranberry Slough Nature Preserve, Keepataw Preserve, Lake Katherine Nature Center and Botanic Gardens, Orland Grassland, Red Gate Woods, Sag Quarries, Sagawau Environmental Learning Center, Swallow Cliff Woods, Tampier Slough Woods, Waterfall Glen Forest Preserve

CRANBERRY SLOUGH NATURE PRESERVE

TAKE AN ENJOYABLE HIKE AND SEE A RARE PEAT BOG ECOSYSTEM

In 1965, Cranberry Slough Nature Preserve was dedicated as only the fifth nature preserve in Illinois. These preserves protect the highest quality natural lands in the state. Cranberry Slough Nature Preserve is special because it contains one of only a handful of peat bog ecosystems in Illinois. "A unique ecological community developed in this hollow, formed by an ice block stranded during the retreat of the glacier some 14,000 years ago," according to Forest Preserves of Cook County. "Plants such as sphagnum moss, a more typical inhabitant of the cooler climes of Wisconsin, Michigan, and Minnesota, share company with familiar prairie and woodland species, such as white wild indigo, marsh blazing star, and tall bellflower." A slough is the colloquial name for a shallow pond or wetland.

If you start your travels from Country Lane Woods, travel south along the Palos Tan Unpaved Trail, which connects to the Yellow Trail, and continue heading south until you reach the slough. (Another option: Take Old Country Lane, a wide, gravel country lane, from the Country Lane Woods parking lot. Head south on this lane until you reach the Yellow Trail, where you'll first head south, then gradually travel northeast till you reach the slough.) As you walk, savor this rare Illinois ecosystem and listen for the sounds of spring peepers, green frogs, and gray tree frogs. Look for herons, egrets, gulls, ducks, and sandhill cranes in or near the slough, and pileated woodpeckers, red-headed woodpeckers, eastern bluebirds, and tufted titmice in the white and black oak forests in

Where: Entrance located on West 95th Street between S. Kean Avenue and Willow Springs Road in Willow Springs, Illinois 60480; park at Country Lane Woods and travel south along the Palos Tan Unpaved Trail or Old Country Lane. Access is also available via the Palos Yellow Unpaved Trail from multiple forest preserves.

Learn More: Forest Preserves of Cook County, https://fpdcc.com/places/locations/cranberry-slough

Hours: Sunrise to sunset, year-round

Quick Review: A rare Illinois peat bog ecosystem, great hiking, and wildlife viewing. (#42 on the map on page 12)

What You Can Do There: Bicycling, Birdwatching, Cross-Country Skiing, Hiking, Horseback Riding, Photography, Picnicking, Running/Exercise, Snowshoeing

the rolling hills near the slough. You might even see a tiger salamander in wet areas in vernal ponds near Cranberry Slough. Wildflowers are in abundance at the preserve. There are more than 250 native plant species in the preserve, although there are no cranberry plants.

Once you're finished enjoying Cranberry Slough, you can head back to your starting point or travel south and then west on the Yellow Trail to explore this large, roadless area. If you continue south and then west about 1.7 miles on the Yellow Trail, you'll reach the Little Red Schoolhouse Nature Center (see page 175), an excellent nature facility, with top-notch hiking areas. Of course, you'll have to re-trace your path (at least to Old Country Lane, which you can take north to the parking lot at Country Lane Woods) or hire a ride-share service to take you back to your starting point.

Horseback riding is popular in the Palos Forest Preserves. © Andrew Morkes

My advice: Schedule a day of free time to roam the area that is located between Kean Avenue to the east, 95th Street to the north, Archer Avenue to the north and west, and 107th Street to the south. There are excellent trails for hikers of all skill levels; opportunities for mountain biking, picnicking, camping, and fishing; a nature center; and plenty of beautiful scenery (forests, marshes, sloughs, lakes, and prairies) to savor. Use the following map to plan your adventure: https://fpdcc.com/downloads/maps/trails/english/FPCC-Palos-Trail-Map-022020.pdf.

NEARBY NATURE DESTINATIONS

Cap Sauers Holding Nature Preserve, Lake Katherine Nature Center and Botanic Gardens, Little Red Schoolhouse Nature Center, Maple Lake, Paw Paw Woods Nature Preserve, Red Gate Woods, Sagawau Environmental Learning Center, Spears Woods, Swallow Cliff Woods, Waterfall Glen Forest Preserve

THE FORGE: LEMONT QUARRIES

THE PLACE TO GO FOR OUTDOOR ADVENTURE FUN AND MUCH MORE

The Forge: Lemont Quarries is a fun-tastic outdoor adventure park that opened in 2020. The 300-acre area is located on the grounds of the Heritage Quarries Recreation Area (www.lemont.il.us/residents/about-lemont/heritage-quarries-recreation-area). The Forge: Lemont Quarries was created via a public-private partnership with the Village of Lemont and Lemont Township.

If you're looking for an amazing outdoor adventure, The Forge: Lemont Quarries has an activity for you. There is fun for people of all ages—whether you like to climb, rappel, fly through the air like a bird (reaching speeds of up to 30 miles per hour on a zipline), paddle, play augmented reality games, or simply walk around in nature. Here's some more information about its popular attractions:

Eight Towers Adventure. The Forge: Lemont Quarries says that the Eight Towers Adventure is the "largest aerial challenge course in the world." In this challenging 10-acre adventure course, you will climb rock walls and rope courses, use ziplines, and participate in other demanding activities. Note: Participants must meet minimum age, height, and weight requirements.

Two Towers Adventure: Kids Activity Zone. This area is for children ages 3 to 13. What's great about the Two Towers Adventure is that it's fully enclosed, so

Where: 1001 Main Street, Lemont, IL 60439

Learn More: 630/326-3301, www.forgeparks.com

Hours: Hours of operation change seasonally; visit www.forgeparks.com for the most current information

Quick Review: An outdoor adventure park that offers ziplining, boulder climbing, biking, rappelling, paddle sports, and many other activities. The park's grounds are open to the public for free, but visitors must pay to participate in waiver-based activities, such as the Eight Towers Adventure, Two Towers Adventure Kids Zone, Bouldering Park, Climbing Towers, mountain biking activities, paddlesports, and other activities. Annual memberships are available. Reservations are highly recommended. Trails and access points are Americans With Disabilities Act–accessible. Dogs are allowed, but they must be leashed. (#43 on the map on page 12)

What You Can Do There: Adventure Sports (bouldering, climbing, rappelling, tactical laser tag, ziplining), Bicycling, Birdwatching, Canoeing/Kayaking/Boating, Hiking, Photography, Restaurant/Fireside Dining Experiences, Running/Exercise (including organized races)

© The Forge: Lemont Quarries

visitors do not need to wear harnesses or helmets. They can climb more than 12 feet in the safety-netted structures and use ziplines, balance beams, and other structures.

Paddling. There are seven quarry lakes that provide great opportunities to kayak, canoe, or pilot a pedal boat. Rentals are available, or visitors can bring their own boats (paddle, oar, or electronic trolling motors only), which they can use in six quarries on the north side of the park.

Biking/Running/Walking. Mountain and BMX biking skills and pump tracks are available. You can bring your own bike or rent one. More than five miles of trails are available for cyclists, walkers, and runners.

Laser Tag. Visitors age five and older can play one or more of 30 tactical laser tag game types in The Forge: Lemont Quarries' arena. Popular games include Team Deathmatch, Team King of the Hill, Team Snipers, and Infection: Survivors (i.e., zombies!).

Digital Adventure Games. The Forge: Lemont Quarries describes these games as a "mixture of an escape room, scavenger hunt, and location-based adventure rolled into an unforgettable augmented reality experience." The games are available for groups of 2 to 20 participants.

When you're ready to stop ziplining, rappelling, or otherwise moving at superhuman speed, you can get a snack or a meal at The Foundry, which features outdoor seating for 150 guests. The Forge: Lemont Quarries also offers what it calls the Forgefire Adventure Dining Experience, which consists of a pre-reserved fireside meal overlooking the Forge Quarry. Not a bad way to end a day of adventure.

Paddle sports © The Forge: Lemont Quarries

There are a lot of other things to do and see at The Forge: Lemont Quarries, including live music, film screenings, and yoga classes. Visit www.forgeparks.com/events-calendar for more information about activities and amenities at this great destination. Visit www.forgeparks.com/parkmap for a facility map.

NEARBY NATURE DESTINATIONS

Black Partridge Woods Nature Preserve, Cap Sauers Holding Nature Preserve, Keepataw Preserve, Red Gate Woods, Sagawau Environmental Learning Center, Tampier Slough Woods, Waterfall Glen Forest Preserve

DID YOU KNOW?

The Skyscraper Tower at The Forge: Lemont Quarries climbs to more than 120 feet in the sky. At the top, you will enjoy breathtaking views of the Chicago skyline and suburbs. According to the company's website, the Skyscraper Tower "features 56 ropes course elements (making it the second-largest stand-alone ropes course in Chicagoland), three rappelling platforms at 80, 90, and 105 feet high, and a zipline platform at 74 feet high."

ISLE A LA CACHE PRESERVE AND MUSEUM

GREAT VIEWS OF THE DES PLAINES RIVER, MIDWEST FUR TRADE HISTORY, AND MANY OTHER REASONS TO VISIT

There's a museum and beautiful nature area just waiting to be discovered amidst all these oil refineries and a hydrogen plant! That's what I thought to myself as I headed southwest on New Avenue toward Isle a la Cache Preserve and Museum. The journey to the museum was not pretty (the sight of a refinery spewing pollutants is not what one wants to see if you're a nature lover), but once you arrive at the museum and preserve you'll forget that glimpse of post-fur-trade industrial Chicagoland.

The museum provides more information on the fur trade that occurred in the area between the French voyageurs (fur traders) and Potawatomi during the 1600s to the early 1800s. The Native Americans traded beaver and other animal pelts for European goods, including cloth, blankets, knives, brass kettles, silver ornaments, glass beads, liquor, guns, gunpowder, gun flints, and lead.

In French "Isle a la Cache" means "Island of the Hiding Place." Some people believe that the French voyageurs and Potawatomi (or other Native American tribes) may have cached, or stored, goods on the island. Others opine that these groups may have met to trade there. The island's actual use during the fur trade

Where: 501 East Romeo Road, Romeoville, IL 60446

Learn More: Forest Preserve District of Will County (FPDWC), 815/886-1467, www.reconnectwithnature.org/preserves-trails/visitor-centers/isle-a-la-cache-museum www.reconnectwithnature.org/preserves-trails/preserves/isle-a-la-cache

Open: Visitor Center: Tuesday to Saturday: 10 a.m. to 4 p.m.; Sunday: Noon to 4 p.m.; Monday: Closed.

The preserve is open 8 a.m. to sunset daily.

Quick Review: A well-organized and attractive museum on an island in the Des Plaines River. It provides information on the fur trade between the French voyageurs and Potawatomi. Things to do include visiting the museum and participating in its programs (bird hikes, craft club, etc.), taking a short hike in the preserve, and viewing and enjoying the forest, river, and wildlife. (#44 on the map on page 12)

What You Can Do There: Birdwatching, Canoeing/Kayaking/Boating, Cross-Country Skiing, Educational and Self-Enrichment Opportunities and Classes, Fishing, Geocaching, Hiking, Horseback Riding, Local History, Photography, Picnicking, Running/Exercise, Snowshoeing

Des Plaines River © Andrew Morkes

era remains a mystery, but that matters little because the FPDWC has created an informative museum and protected a beautiful natural area along the Des Plaines River. It is well worth a visit. Here are many reasons why you should check out the museum and preserve:

✔ **There are plenty of activities for kids.** They can touch an actual beaver pelt, experiment with making animal tracks, play in a wigwam, and check out a Potawatomi longhouse and traders' cabin.

✔ **You can attend the museum's annual "Island Rendezvous" celebration.** According to the museum, "rendezvous was a time when fur traders met to celebrate a successful season."…[Visitors will] "experience the connection between the past and present with activities, games, and crafts. Feel what it's like to pull back a bow and shoot an arrow. Try to start a fire with nothing but wood. See live birds of prey and celebrate historic farms with a petting zoo."

DID YOU KNOW?

The preserve provides a 0.32-mile trail connection (via 135th Street) to the paved, 3.26-mile Centennial Trail/Veterans Memorial Trail and a 0.57-mile connection to the 7.57-mile, crushed limestone I&M Canal Trail. These trails provide great opportunities to bike, hike, run, in-line skate (on a 3.26-mile paved segment north of 135th Street), cross-country ski, and snowshoe.

✔ **You can follow the journey of a beaver pelt from a beaver lodge in what is now Illinois to a Paris hat shop (via a museum exhibit).**

✔ **You can participate in educational programs** in the museum's longhouse, traders' cabin, or outdoor amphitheater.

✔ **You can view Blanding's turtles at the museum.** The Blanding's turtle has been on the state's endangered list since 2009 due to habit loss and other causes. They can live up to 80 years in the wild. Blanding's turtles usually live in wetland habitats in clear and shallow water with abundant aquatic vegetation but live in almost any type of water body.

✔ **You can take a hike** on a short trail that runs along the Des Plaines River. When I visited, the area had just experienced heavy rains, so the river was running fast and some of the island was flooded. Muddy fun!

✔ **You can see tons of wildlife:** bald eagles, osprey, and migratory birds; turtles; frogs; deer; and mink.

✔ **You can fish** for northern pike, rock bass, carp, largemouth bass, crappie, bluegill, and sunfish in the Des Plaines River.

✔ **There are opportunities to canoe and kayak.** The preserve has a canoe/kayak launch site.

I'm amazed at how many great, local nature and historical museums we have in Chicagoland, and you can add Isle a la Cache Museum to this list. If you're looking for an alternative to video-gaming, social media liking and posting, mall-visiting, or just hanging-out-at-home days, you should check out this museum and its natural areas.

NEARBY NATURE DESTINATIONS

Cap Sauers Holding Nature Preserve, O'Hara Woods Preserve, Prairie Bluff Preserve, Lockport Prairie Nature Preserve

---

MITCHELL MUSEUM OF THE AMERICAN INDIAN

If you're looking to learn more about Native American history, check out the **Mitchell Museum of the American Indian** (3001 Central Street, Evanston, IL 60201, 847/475-1030, https://mitchellmuseum.org). It's a great place to visit to see both the past and present of Native Americans—not only in Chicagoland, but throughout the U.S. and Canada. In addition to the exhibits and a library filled with books about local history, the museum hosts many events, including artist demonstrations, a film festival, a speakers series, a Weekend Arts & Stories program, and an annual Native American Fine Arts Market.

KEEPATAW PRESERVE

WILD WOODS, LOCAL HISTORY, BREATHTAKING VIEWS, AND THE CHANCE TO SEE RARE AND ENDANGERED SPECIES

The Keepataw Preserve is an excellent destination if you:

✔ Are tired of the flat, boring topography of most of Chicagoland

✔ Like a good hike or run

✔ Enjoy seeing rare and endangered species

✔ Want to see the "birthplace" of limestone that was used to construct some of Chicago's most famous downtown buildings such as the Water Tower.

The historic smokestack through the trees.
© Andrew Morkes

I was excited to experience all these things (okay, not the run), when I visited the preserve on a beautiful late-summer day. Keepataw Preserve offers a diverse range of habitats—beautiful forests, golden prairies, wet wetlands (just seeing if you're still paying attention), and a portion of the Des Plaines River Valley. There's a 0.28-mile mowed grass circle trail that provides a relaxing hike filled with enchanting scenes of natural beauty. (The views were truly enchanting; I don't use this term lightly.) Additionally, footpaths allow you to hike deeper into the woods if you so choose.

Where: Located on Bluff Road, roughly one mile east of Joliet Road in the southwest Chicago suburb of Lemont, Illinois

Learn More: Forest Preserve District of Will County, www.reconnectwithnature.org/preserves-trails/preserves/keepataw

Hours: 8 a.m. to sunset, year-round

Quick Review: A small, hilly forest preserve with beautiful views of the Des Plaines River Valley; it's the "birthplace" of limestone that was used to construct some of Chicago's most famous downtown buildings. (#45 on the map on page 12)

What You Can Do There: Birdwatching, Hiking, Local History, Photography, Picnicking, Running/Exercise, Snowshoeing

MORE ABOUT THE HINE'S EMERALD DRAGONFLY

The Hine's emerald dragonfly is an endangered species that is only found in Illinois, Wisconsin, Michigan, and Missouri, after once also living in Alabama, Indiana, and Ohio. It is endangered because of habitat loss or degradation (it lives in and near calcareous spring-fed marshes and sedge meadows that overlay dolomite bedrock), contamination of their living areas by pesticides and other pollution, and decreases in the quality or amount of ground water. Hine's emerald dragonflies are an important part of ecosystems because they are beautiful, eat nuisance insects such as mosquitoes and biting flies, and serve as a food source for aquatic animals. Their presence in an ecosystem suggests that its water quality is excellent.

One of the best aspects of the preserve are the beautiful views of the river valley that are available from atop the 60-foot bluffs. These cliffs were created as dolomite limestone was mined in the late 1800s. Ruins of the limestone quarrying operation, including a tall smokestack, can be viewed from the cliffs.

After viewing photographs and video of the smokestack, I thought it would be easy to find. Not so. The dense summer foliage made it hard to spot. But I was not deterred. I hiked east on a footpath that began just after the only bench in the preserve (the one that overlooks the river valley) and eventually spotted the tan smokestack through the trees. Success! As a nature writer, I'm not a big fan of smokestacks, but seeing that a remnant of this area's rich history had survived was pretty cool.

I carefully descended the 60-foot cliff. My goal was to get a closer look at the smokestack, the limestone quarries, and the spring-fed wetlands that are now home

© Andrew Morkes

to a beautiful natural area that features the federally endangered Hine's emerald dragonfly and other rare species, as well as plant species such as robin's plantain, Ohio horse mint, and false pennyroyal.

I tried to reach the smokestack and one of the now-water filled quarries, but the wetlands were really wet and the late-summer growth was quite dense. I turned around and headed back up the sheer cliff.

Many huffs-and-puffs, desperate grabs at roots and tree branches, and 7,000 calories burned later, I pulled myself back atop the cliff. There must be an easier path to the smokestack and the valley bottom, but maybe not. But I enjoyed the exertion and adventure. Plus, you'd never get this type of adventure as you stroll flat North Michigan Avenue in Chicago, where some of the limestone from this area ended up as Chicago was slowly built into a great, international city. When I see Holy Name Cathedral, the Water Tower, and other iconic buildings that were built with dolomite limestone, I'll always remember my hike at the Keepataw Preserve. The preserve is named after Chief Keepataw, a Potawatomi who settled in this area in the early 1800s.

After visiting the Keepataw Preserve, be sure to visit the historic town of Lemont just across the river. The town was originally named Keepetaw in honor of the Potawatomi chief, then changed to Athens, then Palmyra, and finally Lemont in 1850. Lemont, which was first settled in 1833, offers historic churches and other buildings made from dolomite limestone, a charming downtown, antique shops, boutiques, and tons of history. It's one of my favorite towns in the southwest suburbs.

NEARBY NATURE DESTINATIONS

Black Partridge Woods Nature Preserve, Cap Sauers Holding Nature Preserve, The Forge: Lemont Quarries, Red Gate Woods, Tampier Slough Woods, Waterfall Glen Forest Preserve

LAKE KATHERINE NATURE CENTER AND BOTANIC GARDENS

PLEASANT HIKING TRAILS, A STUNNING WATERFALL, BOATING, AND A NATURE CENTER

When I was in my 20s and 30s, I spent a lot of time chasing adventure in the national parks and monuments of the western and southwestern United States. When I sought to enjoy the outdoors in the Midwest, I'd head to Cap Sauer's Holding Nature Preserve (see page 149), which I believe is the wildest spot in Cook County; to other destinations with rolling hills, plunging ravines, and isolated creeks and wildflower-filled prairies (i.e., places you could get happily "lost"); or up to Pictured Rocks National Lakeshore (see page 250) in Michigan's Upper Peninsula to hike and camp along the towering bluffs above Lake Superior. I didn't have much interest in visiting manicured botanic gardens and nature centers. But as I neared age 50, I came to also embrace visits to more serene and relaxing nature spots. It also helps when you have an eight-year-old son who is not yet up for six-hour hikes–after which you come home achy, muddy, and occasionally bloodied by invasive buckthorn, yet recharged and exhilarated by an adventure in Chicago Wilderness.

One day recently, I decided to take my son to check out Lake Katherine Nature Center and Botanic Gardens, a much-beloved nature and recreational destination in Palos Heights (a southwest suburb of Chicago). Although I lived in

Where: 7402 W. Lake Katherine Drive, Palos Heights, IL, 60463

Learn More: 708/361-1873, www.lakekatherine.org, www.facebook.com/LakeKatherine

Hours: Nature Center: Weekdays, 9 a.m. to 5 p.m. and Saturdays, 10 a.m. to 4 p.m. Park Grounds: Open daily from dawn to dusk

Quick Review: A beautiful nature area with a relaxing, one-mile loop trail; a nature center with live animals and a play area for children; and more than 120 species of birds, 19 kinds of mammals, 12 types of fish, and 17 species of reptiles and amphibians; and much more. There is something for everyone at this beautiful destination. A good place to spend a few hours or even a day. Dog must be leashed. (#46 on the map on page 12)

What You Can Do There: Bicycling (where allowed), Birdwatching, Canoeing/Kayaking, Cross-Country Skiing, Educational and Self-Enrichment Opportunities and Classes, Events Facility, Fishing (but only sanctioned programs), Hiking, Nature Center, Photography, Running/Exercise, Snowshoeing

168 Nature in Chicagoland

Lake Katherine's waterfall   © Andrew Morkes

Chicago's Beverly neighborhood on the South Side for the first three decades of my life, I'd passed by Lake Katherine many times, but never visited. After our visit, I realized how much I'd missed all these years.

Lake Katherine Nature Center and Botanic Gardens is a bucolic, serene (if you visit at the right time), and thoroughly enjoyable destination that offers trails and other features for people of all ages. The 85-acre park includes woodlands, wetlands, prairie, gardens and a 10-acre lake. Here are a variety of things you should do at Lake Katherine:

✔ Take a hike, go for a run, or walk your dog along the one-mile lake loop trail or on other trails along the Cal Sag Channel.

✔ Go birdwatching: Look for warblers of many types, Baltimore orioles, indigo buntings, rose-breasted grosbeaks, white-crowned sparrows, scarlet tangiers, herons, trumpeter swans, and many other species.

✔ Search for a variety of other creatures such as painted lady butterflies, twelve-spotted-skimmer dragonflies, snapping turtles, northern water snakes (one of which we almost walked right over as we hiked…it was pretty big!, and we jumped in surprise), bullfrogs, blue spotted salamanders, coyotes, white-tailed deer, groundhogs, and dozens of other animals. Check out the center's Field Guide (www.lakekatherine.org/168/Field-Guide) for a complete list.

✔ Rent a canoe or kayak and wile away the day exploring the lake. You'll get the chance to see a variety of birds depending on the season, and may even see turtles, muskrats, and beavers. Boats are available from late-May through October, Monday-Saturday, 11 a.m. to 3 p.m. $10 per person, per hour. Contact the center for details.

✔ Cycle or walk the Cal-Sag Trail. Lake Katherine is a stopping-point on the 26-mile-long trail (www.calsagtrail.org), which runs from Lemont to the west to the Burnham Greenway near the Indiana border.

✔ Visit the Children's Forest (west of the lake), which features a salamander mound, a spider maze, and wetlands.

✔ Visit the nature center to view fossils, rocks, reptiles, and fish; check out a variety of other exhibits for kids; and enjoy the children's play area.

✔ Explore the Buzz N' Bloom Prairie (especially in June, July, and August) to view Indian grass, compass plant, bee balm, and other plants, as well as a variety of dragonflies, butterflies, and other insects.

✔ Participate in a variety of classes, workshops, summer camps, and other events for families or adults. Recent opportunities included Stories at the Lake; Stargazing; Brews & Bullfrogs; Family Yoga with Nature Walk; and a Monarch Butterfly Festival. A fee is required for some events; many events and activities are free.

✔ Enjoy the soothing sounds and sights of the human-made waterfall. This is no modest waterfall, but a series of four separate falls. The waterfall travels a distance of more than 300 feet from its source 30 feet above the ground.

✔ Do nothing but sit on a bench and soak in the sun, the sights and sounds of nature, and recharge your "batteries."

Springtime at Lake Katherine
© Andrew Morkes

Lake Katherine is a beautiful spot for hiking, pondering, canoeing, kayaking, creating art, animal-watching, celebrating life events (several venues for weddings, birthday parties, baby and bridal showers, etc. are available), and simply enjoying nature. I highly recommend a visit.

NEARBY NATURE DESTINATIONS

Cap Sauers Holding Nature Preserve, Cranberry Slough Nature Preserve, Little Red Schoolhouse Nature Center, Midlothian Meadows, Orland Grassland, Red Gate Woods, Rubio Woods, Sagawau Environmental Learning Center, Swallow Cliff Woods, Tampier Slough Woods, Waterfall Glen Forest Preserve

ENJOY A POST-VISIT TREAT

Treat yourself to some of the world's best ice cream at **The Plush Horse** (12301 South 86th Avenue, Palos Park, IL 60464, 708/448-0550, www.theplushhorse.com/hourslocation). The Plush Horse has been one of the go-to places for fantastic ice cream in the southwest suburbs since long before I was born (it was founded in 1937). It changed my life, and it will change your's, too!

LAKE RENWICK PRESERVE/HERON ROOKERY NATURE PRESERVE

EXCELLENT BIRDWATCHING, HIKING, BIKING, AND WINTER ACTIVITIES

"The geese are having a blowout of an argument" was my first thought as I began hiking along the main trail that travels along a beautiful lake at Lake Renwick Preserve. I heard a symphony of honking (although the geese lacked a conductor) that I estimated was coming from a half-mile away. The non-harmonious honks grew louder as I hiked closer, but their song began to sound more like a friendly conversation amongst old friends meeting up at the end of another day. They seemed happy, and that worked just fine for me on what was a beautiful day to hike and birdwatch.

Fall and winter are the time to view (and hear) thousands of geese and ducks—as well as the occasional bald eagles, American white pelicans, and other waterfowl—that either hunt, roost, or rest amidst migration. Of course, you can see these birds in all seasons, but they are most common at 200-acre Lake Renwick (and Turtle Lake, Budde Lake, and Darter Pond—the preserves' other bodies of water) during fall and winter.

But Lake Renwick is best known for its large heron rookery, where not only black-crowned night-herons and great blue herons—but also great egrets and dou-

The rookery © Andrew Morkes

Where: There are three access points to the preserves: Heron Rookery Nature Preserve, Copley Nature Park, and Turtle Lake Access—all in Plainfield, Illinois.

Learn More: Forest Preserve District of Will County, www.reconnectwithnature.org/preserves-trails/preserves/lake-renwick/lake-renwick-heron-rookery, www.facebook.com/Lake.Renwick.Rookery

Hours:

Lake Renwick Preserve: 8 a.m. to sunset, year round

Heron Rookery Nature Preserve

August 16 to the end of February: 8 a.m. to Sunset

March 1-August 15: Closed (except for public program dates/times as listed in the Event Calendar, www.reconnectwithnature.org/news-events/event-calendar)

Quick Review: A top-notch spot for birdwatching (geese and ducks—as well as the occasional bald eagles, American white pelicans, and other waterfowl—in the fall/winter, and black-crowned night-herons, great blue herons, great egrets, and double-crested cormorants from early spring to late summer), hiking (1.45 miles of trail), bicycling (via a 2.9-mile loop trail at the Turtle Lake Access), and other outdoor activities. Dogs are not allowed in the nature preserve. (#47 on the map on page 12)

What You Can Do There: Birdwatching, Educational and Self-Enrichment Opportunities and Classes, Hiking, Photography, Visitor Center

In Certain Areas: Bicycling, Cross-Country Skiing, Fishing, Geocaching, Picnicking, Running/Exercise, Snowshoeing

ble-crested cormorants, amongst other birds—live and raise their young from early spring to late summer. The birds roost on artificial nesting platforms that are located on islands in the middle of the lake, which was created when a quarry was closed. You can view videos of nesting season at Lake Renwick on YouTube.

The 839-acre Lake Renwick Preserve was acquired by the Forest Preserve District of Will County between 1989 and 2010, and a 320-acre portion of the site (where the rookery is located) was dedicated as an Illinois Nature Preserve in 1992.

MY HIKE

I visited Lake Renwick Preserve and Heron Rookery Nature Preserve (which the Illinois Audubon Society has called a "site of outstanding statewide significance" and an "important bird area") in late January on a 35-degree day that felt more like the mid-20s due to the wind. I arrived only a little more than an hour before sundown (the preserve's closing time), so I walked quickly along the snow-covered path eager to find the source of the loud honks and hike as far as possible before having to head home.

© Andrew Morkes

As I walked, I encountered people of all ages who were as bundled up against the cold as I was. I passed a family, and the little boy unexpectedly called out "Hi!!," and I said hi back. I think he was disappointed that his parents kept walking and he couldn't stop to talk. The sun cast a long golden path across the lake as it gradually sunk to the horizon, and I was grateful for the chance to be outdoors and walk for the most part in solitude. Hiking always clears my head. It either makes me think of nothing, except nature (wind, sun, earth, trees, plants, and animal sights and sounds), or it helps me sort out the problems and challenges of everyday life. (It was a "think of nothing, except nature" hike for me that day.) I wish more people would choose to disengage from technology and get outdoors in order to recharge and refresh their perspective in these challenging times.

I followed the sounds of the geese until I reached the end of the trail before it turned right to go beneath a railroad underpass. If you stay on this path, it joins the preserve's bike trail and you will see Budde and Turtle Lakes.

There they were! Thousands of geese, ducks, and other birds resting on the ice across Lake Renwick. It was a beautiful sight, and I was glad I'd saw them in such large numbers before I had to head home. In a world where our environment is under relentless attack and some species of birds (such as the Brazilian spix's macaw, giant ibis, and New Caledonian owlet-nightjar) can be counted in the hundreds (in the entire world!), it was refreshing to see thousands of birds in one spot.

Alas, I realized that I'd need to halt my hike in order to arrive at the car just before sunset. I reluctantly returned the way I came. Groups of five to 10 geese honked overhead as they flew toward their thousands of friends on the lake. Several robins hopped amongst the branches of an evergreen tree. I passed a deer, who looked just as surprised as I was to see him. I occasionally stopped to observe the birds on Lake Renwick and enjoyed watching the shimmering sunlight on the water.

My late-hike deer friend © Andrew Morkes

Soon, I reached a hilly area that was crowned with trees that blocked my view of the lake. I occasionally glanced at the orange setting sun through breaks in the trees, and it reminded me of a bonfire in the woods. The air grew colder, and the sky turned light pink. I reached my car a few minutes before sunset. My vehicle was the last one in the parking lot, and that made me feel good for some reason. In my younger days, I closed down bars. In my middle-age days, I close down nature preserves. Night was coming on quickly, so I got in my car and began the 55-mile drive back home.

THINGS TO DO

I had a great visit at Lake Renwick and plan to return when I have more time. Here are five things you should do during your visit.

Watch birds. About 200 species have been documented at Lake Renwick Heron Rookery. In addition to the aforementioned herons, egrets, cormorants, and eagles, you might spot eastern bluebirds, purple martins, and Baltimore orioles. Spotting scopes are located in several areas. Consider bringing binoculars, or a camera with a high-quality zoom lens if you're interested in photography.

Take a hike or go for a run. There are 1.45 miles of crushed limestone trail. Most of the terrain is flat, so the hiking is relatively easy. Be sure to wear boots in wet or snowy weather because the trails get slippery.

Go for a bike ride on the Lake Renwick bikeway. There is a 2.9-mile asphalt loop trail that is suitable for all non-motorized, non-equestrian use. You can use the Bikeway year round. It can be accessed at the Renwick Road entrance to the preserve.

Go fishing. You can shoreline fish at Turtle Lake (park at the Turtle Lake

© Andrew Morkes

Access point) for bass, catfish, bluegill, sunfish, and other fish. Catch and release is encouraged. You can also access the Bikeway at this access point.

Go snowshoeing or cross-country skiing. The flat terrain is perfect for both winter activities. Use the Turtle Lake Access point. If you've never snowshoed, check out my article, First-Time Snowshoer Tells All: 10 Tips for Success and My Son's Thank You on page 290, for more information.

THINGS TO KNOW BEFORE YOU GO

Important: Lake Renwick Preserve and Heron Rookery Nature Preserve are open to visitors from 8 a.m. to sunset from mid-August through February. During the breeding season from March 1 through mid-August, *Heron Rookery Nature Preserve* is only open for public programs and guided bird viewing to protect the nesting activities of migratory birds. Check www.reconnectwithnature.org/news-events/event-calendar for information on how to sign up for tours from March 1 through mid-August. Keep in mind that *Lake Renwick Preserve* (which comprises more than 500 acres) remains open year-round, so the preserves are worth a visit regardless of the season.

I parked at the Heron Rookery Nature Preserve (Renwick Road, east of Route 30/Lincoln Highway in Plainfield). At this parking lot, you will find a small visitor center (which is the meeting point for bird tours and other activities) and a long hiking path that connects with other sections of the preserve. There are two other access points to the preserve: Copley Nature Park and Turtle Lake Access, both in Plainfield.

NEARBY NATURE DESTINATIONS

Hammel Woods, Lower Rock Run Preserve, Mather Woods Forest Preserve, Prairie Bluff Reserve, Rock Run Preserve, Van Horn Woods

LITTLE RED SCHOOLHOUSE NATURE CENTER

THIS IS NOT YOUR PARENTS' LITTLE RED SCHOOLHOUSE

Nature adventures © Andrew Morkes

I often write about unique or off-the-beaten-path nature destinations, but there's nothing secret, but a lot that's special, about the Little Red Schoolhouse Nature Center (LRSNC). The LRSNC has been a school field trip destination for decades, and tens of thousands of people visit each year. But the Little Red Schoolhouse Nature Center is a far different place than I remember from when I was a little boy. In fact, an entire new facility was built in 2010. It's now one of the best nature centers in

Where: 9800 Willow Springs Road, Willow Springs, IL 60480

Learn More: Forest Preserves of Cook County, 708/839-6897, https://fpdcc.com/places/locations/little-red-schoolhouse-nature-center, www.facebook.com/LittleRedSchoolhouseNatureCenter

Hours: March to October: 9 a.m. to 5 p.m., November to February: 9 a.m. to 4 p.m.

Nature center buildings are closed on Fridays, but the trails are open. The nature center and grounds are closed Thanksgiving, Christmas, and New Year's Day.

Quick Review: One of the crown jewels of the many great nature centers in Chicagoland. The center offers a large and fun kids' indoor play area with live animals, a reading section, games, and much more; an outdoor play area for kids; a two-story museum; a historic schoolhouse; easy and enjoyable hikes; and a large garden for those with disabilities. No pets are allowed. (#48 on the map on page 12)

What You Can Do There: Birdwatching, Educational and Self-Enrichment Opportunities and Classes, Hiking, Local History, Nature Center, Photography, Snowshoeing

The Little Red Schoolhouse was built in 1886 in a nearby area and hosted classes until 1948. It was moved to its present site in 1952. The Schoolhouse now serves as a time capsule of education from another era. My son liked sitting in the old desks. He had no idea what the inkwell holders were in the desks. © Andrew Morkes

Chicagoland. I recently visited the nature center with my son. Here are several reasons why we had such a good time—and you will, too:

✔ A large and fun kids' indoor play area with live animals, a reading section, games, and much more. And an outdoor play area for kids.

✔ A two-story museum that traces the geological history of the area and features live snakes, turtles, frogs, fish, and other fauna.

✔ **Great scenery and wildlife viewing.** The LRSNC is situated on the banks of Long John Slough, a pretty body of water with viewing platforms that is surrounded by dense forests. Look for the permanent resident lodgings of the American beaver and muskrat in the slough. American white pelicans, blue herons, and sandhill cranes make stopovers during the spring and fall migrations. Also, check out the beautiful spring and summer wildflowers and stunning fall colors.

✔ **Easy and enjoyable hikes.** The Farm Pond Trail (0.25 miles) is a relaxing hike for families. The Black Oak Trail (1.75 miles) is the longest trail, but when I visited there were gaggles of kids and their moms and dads walking this trail, too. It follows the slough for a portion of the path, giving hikers the opportunity to view wildlife and the fall colors from an observation blind. Then it heads through a rolling glacial highland of prairie and oak woods. Another option is the one-mile White Oak Trail. Hikers seeking longer hikes can connect to other trails that weave through the 42.1-mile Palos Trail System (https://fpdcc.com/places/trails/palos-trail-system).

✔ **Plenty of events** such as an annual art fair, bird walks, stargazing and solstice events, and much more; visit https://fpdcc.com/events for the latest info.

NEARBY NATURE DESTINATIONS

Cap Sauers Holding Nature Preserve, Cranberry Slough Nature Preserve, Red Gate Woods, Sagawau Environmental Learning Center

MATTHIESSEN STATE PARK

AWE-INSPIRING CANYONS, COLORFUL CLIFFS, AND A BIODIVERSITY HOTSPOT

I heard the soothing sounds of falling water striking soft sandstone as soon as I descended the steep steps from the Dells Area parking lot to the trails below. By the sound, the water was falling fast and in large volume to the canyon floor below. It was a beautiful 60-degree morning in mid-April, sunny and breezy, and I was excited to see Matthiessen's waterfalls and mile-long main canyon that's nearly 100 feet deep in some spots and ranges from 50 to 140 feet wide. I hiked the trail and then the steps to the canyon floor, passing families with toddlers and a few older hikers who were taking a break on the steps.

Creek crossing © Andrew Morkes

Where: Located in central LaSalle County in Illinois, approximately four miles south of Utica and three miles east of Oglesby (95 miles southwest of Chicago)

Learn More: Illinois Department of Natural Resources (IDNR), www2.illinois.gov/dnr/Parks/Pages/Matthiessen.aspx

Hours: Sunrise to sunset, year-round

Quick Review: Starved Rock State Park's underappreciated neighbor. This stunning park features awe-inspiring waterfalls, a colorful sandstone canyon, excellent (and sometimes challenging) hiking trails, towering ice formations in the winter, and much more. Pets must be leashed. (#49 on the map on page 12)

What You Can Do There: Archery Range, Bicycling (in select areas), Birdwatching, Cross-Country Skiing, Hiking, Horseback Riding (including an equestrian campground), Hunting, Photography, Picnicking, Radio-Controlled Model Airplane Field, Running/Exercise, Snowshoeing

178   Nature in Chicagoland

Cascade Falls   © Andrew Morkes

And then I was at the bottom of the stairs in the sandy canyon that was probably 10 degrees cooler than the temperature on the sun-dappled cliffs above. Mosses, liverwort, and other plants were growing from outcrops in the sandstone walls, which were "painted" light and dark orange in spots with oxidizing minerals from the groundwater above. Ferns and wildflowers were growing on the sandy floor of the canyon, and the towering canyon loomed above me like the walls of a cathedral.

I followed the creek toward the sounds of the water, walked by massive boulders, stepped in thick mud and atop piles of leaves from the past fall, and crossed the water occasionally on cement circles installed by the park and rocks and tree limbs placed by nature and visitors. Birdsong filled the canyon, and I noticed how everything was greener in this canyon microclimate.

And there it was: Cascade Falls in all its glory—gushing from the top of the cliff to a sandstone outcropping just a few feet above a pretty pool of water. The pond's surface shimmered in the sunlight and also cast ever-changing reflections on the canyon walls nearby. Cliff swallows and rock doves flitted back and forth between the canyon walls, where it seemed they'd set up house. I found a boulder to rest on and enjoyed the sounds and sights of the waterfall and canyon for about 20 minutes. I eventually stood up and began exploring the little nook-and-cranny caves that were located in the cliff walls and took a few photos. I looked down the canyon and saw a black Labrador retriever joyfully running back and forth through the creek and amongst the large rocks. The owners—a young couple, with a six- or seven-year-old—soon caught up with their lab. We greeted one another, and the lady said, "I know she's off leash, but don't worry if she comes up to you. She's the friendliest dog. She just loves to be unleashed." I said, "No problem [pregnant pause]…I love to be unleashed, too!" We all laughed, and I wished them a great day at the park. It was true. After being stuck at home for much of the pandemic, I was happy to be unleashed from the monotony and worries of pandemic times at one of the most beautiful state parks in Illinois.

Matthiessen State Park features nearly 1,950 acres of natural wonders: a main canyon (which consists of the Upper and Lower Dells) and sub canyons, cliffs, streams, prairies, and forests (comprised of white, black, and bur oak, hickory, white pine, and red and white cedar). In addition to the stream that traverses its canyon, you can visit Matthiessen Lake in the north of the park and the Vermillion River in the park's western side. There are two units, or areas, in the park. The Dells Area features the canyon, several beautiful waterfalls, an archery range, picnic areas, 3.2-miles of hiking trails, and a restored fort that is representative of the fortifications the French built in the area during the 1600s and early 1700s. The Vermillion River Area has nearly two miles of hiking trails, picnic areas, and a model airplane field. You can travel between the areas by car or by two or four feet via a one-mile horse trail.

Lake Falls © Andrew Morkes

In addition to hiking and canyon viewing, there are many other things you can do at Matthiessen, including:

Enjoy the wildflowers. In the spring, look for shooting stars, columbine, Jack-in-the-pulpits, hepaticas, and spring beauties, while the summer brings yellow partridge peas, black-eyed Susans, and tick-trefoils, amongst other beauties.

Savor the fall colors. The beautiful forests come alive with color during the fall, and Matthiessen's hiking trails provide many opportunities to enjoy the show.

Have a picnic. The Dells Area has picnic tables, water fountains, playground equipment, ample parking, and washroom facilities. The picnic grove is relaxing and a great place to rest and re-fuel before or after a hike. The Vermilion River Area also has picnic facilities.

Enjoy winter activities such as cross-country skiing and snowshoeing. There are six miles of cross-country ski trails, and skis are available for rental during weekends from December through March. The park advises visitors to call the Do It, To It Ski Shop to check on rentals and snow conditions at 815/343-7125 or 815/343-9014 before heading to the park.

View from the canyon floor © Andrew Morkes

Go mountain biking or horseback riding. These activities are listed together because bike riders and equestrians share nine miles of multi-use mountain bike/horseback riding trails at the park. (Mountain bikes and horses are prohibited on all other trails.) The trails are open from May 1 to November 1, weather permitting or as determined by park staff. The park advises visitors to call 815/667-4726 to check trail conditions and status before heading to Matthiessen. There is also a campground for equestrians.

FINAL THOUGHTS

While Matthiessen State Park is typically less crowded than nearby Starved Rock State Park—which is packed during warm weather—it can still get very busy. This may reduce your enjoyment level if you don't like crowds. The IDNR says that "Matthiessen Dells area and Vermillion River Area typically shut down on weekends May through October when they have reached full capacity (parking lots are full) around 10 a.m. and will not reopen again until 3 p.m." Keep this in mind as you plan your visit. The best times to visit are early in the morning and late in the afternoon. Mild days in early spring and late fall may also be less busy. Final advice: Have a few park backups ready in case you arrive and the parking lots are full. Two suggestions: Margery C. Carlson Nature Preserve and Buffalo Rock State Park, which are about a 10-minute drive from Matthiessen.

NEARBY NATURE DESTINATIONS

Buffalo Rock State Park, Illinois & Michigan Canal State Trail-Buffalo Rock Access Area, Margery C. Carlson Nature Preserve, Starved Rock State Park

MCKINLEY WOODS

ENJOY BREATHTAKING VIEWS OF THE DES PLAINES RIVER AND I&M CANAL, EXCELLENT HIKING TRAILS, AND MORE

© Andrew Morkes

McKinley Woods is a beautiful preserve that features bluffs, deep ravines, and forest along the Des Plaines River and I&M Canal. There are two access points: Frederick's Grove and Kerry Sheridan Grove. I recently spent several hours on a warm spring day hiking the trails at Frederick's Grove, which has north and south parking areas. I first parked at the north parking lot and tried the Upland Ski Trail (.26-mile loop) and Riverbend Lookout Trail (.46-mile loop). Heavy rains had soaked the area in recent days, so the trails were wet and flooded in spots, but the spring flowers were stunning and I had fun sloshing through the boggy trail. When I'd tested the waterproofing on my boots enough (it held), I headed back to the parking lot and tried the Trail of the Old Oaks (1.15 miles)—which

Where: Located in Channahon, Illinois. There are two access points: Kerry Sheridan Grove (which is located on Walnut Lane, east of Blackberry Lane) and Frederick's Grove (which can be accessed on McKinley Woods Road, south of Route 6/Eames Street).

Learn More: Forest Preserve District of Will County, www.reconnect withnature.org/Preserves-Trails/Preserves/McKinley-Woods/McKinley-Woods-Fredericks

Hours: 8 a.m. to sunset

Quick Review: A beautiful, hilly preserve along the Des Plaines River and Illinois & Michigan (I&M) Canal that offers hiking, wildflowers and fall colors, birdwatching, and cross-country skiing and snowshoeing. You can also access the Illinois Department of Natural Resources' 61.5-mile, crushed limestone I&M Canal State Trail. (#50 on the map on page 12)

What You Can Do There: Bicycling, Birdwatching, Camping (at Frederick's Grove), Canoeing/Kayaking, Cross-Country Skiing, Educational and Self-Enrichment Programs, Fishing, Geocaching, Hiking, Indoor Event Rentals (for birthday parties, showers, classes, and meetings), Local History, Nature Center, Photography, Picnicking, Running/Exercise, Snowshoeing

View of the I&M Canal and the Des Plaines River
© Andrew Morkes

was my favorite trail of my visit. This rugged trail gradually takes you through ravines; past redbud, blue ash, and chinquapin oak trees; and down to a pretty creek that drains into the I&M Canal. The Trail of the Old Oaks also provides nice views of the Des Plaines River at times, and some excellent birdwatching. Nearly 100 bird species—including cedar waxwings, purple martins, and bald eagles—have been sighted at the preserve. If you're looking to get a workout amidst stunning scenery, take the Trail of the Old Oaks. If you prefer shorter hikes on a relatively level surface, take the Upland Ski and Riverbend Lookout Trails. Visit www.mobilemaplets.com/showplace/8365 for a trail map.

I eventually headed to the south parking area. There are great views of the I&M Canal and Des Plaines River from the lookout. You can hike the Heritage Trail (a 0.4-mile loop trail) or—if you're feeling ambitious, access the Illinois Department of Natural Resources' 61.5-mile, crushed limestone I&M Canal State Trail. If you walk 2.3 miles northeast on this trail, you'll reach the Four Rivers Environmental Education Center. Interested in camping? If so, there is a campground with four primitive campsites near the south parking area. Other fun activities include picnicking, fishing, canoeing/kayaking (no launch pass is required), and bicycling (on the I&M Canal State Trail).

Once you've had some fun at Frederick's Grove, get back in your car (or hike or bike the I&M Trail) and travel about four miles to Kerry Sheridan Grove, where there is excellent birdwatching (the area is known as a great place to see bald eagles, herons, and American white pelicans, and other waterfowl). There's also a 0.56-mile natural surface trail and a 1.75-mile paved trail. The Four Rivers Environmental Education Center is located at Kerry Sheridan Grove. It features public programs, facility rentals (especially for wedding ceremonies/receptions), and nature education opportunities. At the first parking area, you can look north across the DuPage River and see Briscoe Mounds, the site of the largest Native American burial grounds in Northern Illinois. The site is undeveloped, but a museum and visitor/cultural center has been proposed that will educate visitors about Native American history.

NEARBY NATURE DESTINATIONS

Briscoe Mounds, Des Plaines State Fish and Wildlife Area, Hammel Woods, Lower Rock Run Preserve, Rock Run Preserve, Rock Run Rookery Preserve

MESSENGER WOODS NATURE PRESERVE

FAMOUS SPRING FLOWERS, BEAUTIFUL FALL COLORS, CAMPING, AND YEAR-ROUND FUN

© Andrew Morkes

After months of gray, dreary winter in Chicago, the Virginia bluebells, great white trillium, and other flowers that blanket the gently rolling hills of Messenger Woods Nature Preserve almost hypnotize you when you suddenly see them in all their glory. That's what Ellen, my wife's cousin (I consider her my cousin, too), and I thought as we hiked the trails at this stunning Illinois Nature Preserve. These preserves protect the highest quality natural lands in the state.

Where: 13800 W. Bruce Road, Homer Glen, IL 60491

Learn More: Forest Preserve District of Will County (FPDWC), 815/727-8700, www.reconnectwithnature.org/preserves-trails/preserves/messenger-woods, www.facebook.com/Messenger.Woods

Hours: 8 a.m. to sunset

Quick Review: Stunning swathes of spring flowers (I've never seen anything like them in the Chicago area), ravines, a pretty meandering creek, prairie, oak savannas, and wetlands. Perfect for hiking (easy-to-moderate hiking trails), birdwatching, and camping. (#51 on the map on page 12)

What You Can Do There: Bicycling, Birdwatching, Camping, Cross-Country Skiing, Educational and Self-Enrichment Opportunities and Classes, Hiking, Photography, Picnicking, Running/Exercise, Snowshoeing

Virginia bluebells along Spring Creek. © Andrew Morkes

Messenger Woods offers what many consider to be the most beautiful and impressive display of Virginia bluebells in the Chicagoland area. (O'Hara Woods Preserve in Romeoville, Illinois, and Pilcher Park Nature Center in Joliet, Illinois, also offer great bluebell displays.) These vast stretches of beautiful flowers went on for as far as my eyes could see as we walked a trail that ran along Spring Creek. They were a stunning and awe-inspiring reminder of the beauty of nature—something I think we sometimes forget as we are glued to our various digital devices. Better yet, Ellen and I were completely alone in the preserve on a beautiful 70+-degree day in May. No crowds; just the sounds of birds, the wind rustling the young leaves, and the gentle sounds of Spring Creek.

Take my word for it if the photographs in this book don't convince you. (As I viewed the photos I took at the preserve, I soon realized that, while beautiful at times, they did not capture the full effect these spring blossoms have on your eyes.) This is a place you need to see in person to believe.

According to the FPDWC, here are some other spring flowers that are in bloom at Messenger Woods and other district properties: buttercups, violets (common, yellow, lance-leaved, and bird's foot), rue anemone, meadow rue, trilliums, wild geranium, woodland phlox, cleft phlox, spring beauties, violet wood sorrel, marsh marigold, hoary puccoon, shooting star, blue-eyed grass, and wood betony.

So, now that I'm done rhapsodizing about the fantastic display of spring flowers, here are some practical details about Messenger Woods:

> **DID YOU KNOW?**
>
> There is an annual Bluebell Festival at Maple Leaf Park in Earlville, Illinois.

✔ **Lots of land.** The 441-acre preserve features forest (including ravines and massive oaks), prairie, savanna, wetlands, and a portion of Spring Creek.

✔ **Pristine.** Environmental organizations report that Messenger Woods is one of the few forests in northeastern Illinois that has never been grazed, cut, farmed, or developed.

✔ **Birds galore.** More than 135 bird species are found at the preserve, including red-bellied woodpeckers, pileated woodpeckers, white-breasted nuthatches, ruby-crowned kinglets, double-crested cormorants, Cooper's hawks, warbling vireos, great crested flycatchers, great-horned owls, and American kestrels.

✔ **There is great hiking.** The preserve features nearly two miles of natural surface trail. You can also connect to other trails in nearby forest preserves.

✔ **There's camping.** The preserve has four primitive campsites for family or group rental. Campers have access to fire pits and latrines.

✔ **You can picnic.** The preserve offers nice stretches of flat, grassy areas for picnicking. You can also rent one of two picnic shelters if you want to have a large get-together.

Busy beavers © Andrew Morkes

THINGS TO KNOW BEFORE YOU GO

✔ Park in the second, most-northern, lot, and then hike the trail that parallels Spring Creek to view the most impressive stretch of Virginia bluebells (at least when we visited). Visit https://map.reconnectwithnature.org/publicwebmap/?type=P&id=12MWN for a trail map.

✔ Bring bug spray, sunscreen, and water.

✔ Pack binoculars. There is excellent birdwatching.

✔ Early morning and late afternoon/early evening are the best times to take photographs.

✔ Leave your dog at home; they are banned because of the environmentally sensitive and protected natural areas.

© Andrew Morkes

✔ Spring is an amazing time at Messenger Woods, but don't forget to visit during the summer (for camping, hiking, camping, birdwatching, etc.), fall (hiking, fall colors), and winter (snowshoeing, cross-country skiing).

✔ After heavy rains, some areas of the woods can flood and make trails impassable. After a downpour, check with the forest preserve for current conditions.

✔ The Forest Preserve District of Will County offers a variety of nature hikes, presentations, and other activities at Messenger Woods. Visit www.reconnectwithnature.org/preserves-trails/preserves/messenger-woods for the latest opportunities.

NEARBY NATURE DESTINATIONS

Cap Sauers Holding Nature Preserve, Hadley Valley, Hickory Creek Preserve, Orland Grass-land, Red Gate Woods, Sagawau Environmental Learning Center, Swallow Cliff Woods, Tampier Slough Woods

MIDEWIN NATIONAL TALLGRASS PRAIRIE

VAST OPEN SPACES, A BIODIVERSITY HOTSPOT, AND SEVEN OTHER PLACES TO SEE BISON IN THE MIDWEST

Bison are an enduring symbol of the old American West—and our national mammal. Massive, powerful, and free, they linger in the American imagination unlike any other land animal except perhaps the bald eagle and grizzly bear. At their peak in the mid-1800s, an estimated 30 to 60 million bison ranged from Canada to northern Mexico and from the plains to eastern forests. The diaries of early settlers recorded herds of bison so vast that they took hours to pass. But the completion of the Transcontinental Railroad in 1869, the indiscriminate killing of bison by white hunting parties (they often only took the animal's tongue and hide, leaving the carcass to rot on the prairie), and a concerted effort by the U.S. military to deprive Native American tribes of one of their principal food sources during the Indian Wars decimated these vast herds. The tens of millions of bison were reduced to massive piles of bones and hides, and by about 1890, only 1,000 or so bison remained, including two dozen in Yellowstone National Park.

All seemed lost for the bison, but ranchers such as James "Scotty" Philip, the U.S. government, and others stepped in to save the last remaining bison. Today, there are approximately 150,000 bison in the United States, with nearly all found in the West—especially in Yellowstone National Park (Wyoming, Montana, and Idaho), Custer State Park and Wind Cave National Park (South Dakota), Theodore

---

Where: 30239 S. State Route 53, Wilmington, IL 60481

Learn More: USDA Forest Service, 815/423-6370, www.fs.usda.gov/midewin

Hours: Grounds: 4:00 a.m. to 10:00 p.m., year-round

Visitor Center: April to October, Monday-Saturday, 8:00 a.m. to 4:30 p.m.; November to March, Monday-Friday, 8:00 a.m. to 4:30 p.m.

Quick Review: Approximately 13,000 acres of tallgrass prairie, streams, wetlands, and forests. There are 34 miles of trails and a wide variety of bird, reptile, mammal, and aquatic species—including 20 endangered or threatened species—but the bison are the biggest draw for many visitors. Check out the visitor's center for kids' activities, a small museum, and the current location of the bison in this vast preserve. (#52 on the map on page 12)

What You Can Do There: Bicycling, Birdwatching, Cross-Country Skiing, Educational and Self-Enrichment Programs, Equestrian, Hiking, Photography, Picnicking, Running/Exercise, Snowshoeing, Visitor Center/Museum

Nature in Chicagoland

Our group on the hunt for bison.
© Andrew Morkes

Roosevelt National Park (North Dakota), and Santa Catalina Island (California). Those who live in the West have plenty of opportunities to see bison, but did you know that there are nearly 10 places you can go to view bison in the wild in the Midwest? I recently visited one of these destinations: Midewin National Tallgrass Prairie, which is about 60 miles from downtown Chicago. Approximately 13,000 acres, including 34 miles of trails, are open to the public for hiking, bicycling, and horseback riding. Midewin, which was established in 1996, is the first national tallgrass prairie in the country. Nearly 150 bird species have been sighted at the prairie, 23 species of reptiles, 40 aquatic species, and 27 species of mammals make Midewin their home. But the bison are the main draw.

HIGH HOPES

My son and I, as well as Greg, a good friend of mine, and his children, started out from the Northwest Side of Chicago with high hopes to see bison—which last roamed wild in Illinois in 1808. (This was just a few years after Lewis & Clark returned from their epic exploration of the American West.) But when we arrived at Midewin, our first thoughts were on our growling stomachs, so we headed to its visitor center to have a picnic. The small, but interesting, facility offers exhibits that detail the site's history from its Native American era, to the time of European settlers, to its use as the Joliet Army Ammunition Plant, and now as a grassland (and larger ecosystem) in the process of restoration. The kids will enjoy the bison hide they can touch and the small exhibits on bison bones and fossils. A bookstore, a pleasant outdoor picnic area, and guided tours and presentations on certain days of the year round out the offerings at the visitor center.

When it comes to bison-human interactions, fences make good neighbors because bison can run 30 to 45 miles per hour.
© Jack Dykinga, U.S. Forest Service

MORE BUNKERS THAN BISON

After lunch, we headed to the Iron Bridge Trailhead, then began hiking in the hot sun. We walked amongst golden Alexanders, prairie Indian plantains, porcupine grass, tufted hair grass, and other wildflowers and grasses beneath vivid blue skies. The songs of birds and crickets were like a natural symphony as we traversed long stretches of prairie intermingled with savanna, wetlands, and the occasional breaks of forest. As we hiked, it was hard to believe that this area housed a massive ammunition facility during World War II. The ecological restoration efforts by the USDA Forest Service and volunteers are impressive.

We eagerly scanned the horizon for bison, asked other hikers if they had sighted our quarry, and climbed a bench or two to get a better view of the long flat prairie—but to no avail. We didn't see any bison, but we did see the remnants of two military armament storage bunkers, which the kids enjoyed investigating.

THE QUEST CONTINUES

A male bison can weigh as much as 2,000 pounds and reach 5'6" at the shoulder, but despite their massive size, the 27 bison at Midewin were missing in action amidst the 13,000-acre prairie. They are highly mobile animals and are often on the move in a search of food. We searched and searched with no luck.

The day grew hotter and our kids' patience grew shorter, so we headed back to the car, disappointed, but not defeated. Midewin is a work in progress, and so

© Andrew Morkes

is our search for the bison. With nature, sometimes you must play the long game and wait to be rewarded. What's comforting is that the USDA Forest Service and dedicated volunteers are slowly creating an environmental jewel in a Chicago suburb. Midewin is an excellent destination for hiking and nature watching and, someday soon, we'll head back to see the bison.

A FEW TIPS FOR VISITORS:

✔ Be prepared to walk, and wear good hiking shoes, a hat, and lots of sunscreen. Midewin features vast stretches of prairie (without much shade), and you may have to hike long distances to see the bison (something our kids, ages seven to 10, did not want to do on a hot summer day).

✔ Give yourself at least four hours on-site to enjoy the prairie and increase your chances of seeing some bison.

✔ Take advantage of the maps, animal and plant guides, and other resources at the Visitor Center. They'll make your visit go smoother and allow you to spot and enjoy some of the other natural life out on the prairie in case you don't see any bison. You'll be amazed at the exotic-looking spiders, lizards, and other animals that also live on the prairie.

✔ Bring a good supply of water. No water is available once you leave the visitor center.

✔ Pack binoculars. There is excellent birdwatching, and you can use the binoculars to spot the bison at a distance.

✔ Be patient. This is not a zoo, so you may have to work (i.e., hike far) to see the bison. Enjoy the journey, soak up the sun and solitude (unless you're trailed by three excitable children as Greg and I were), and don't get caught up just pursuing the goal of seeing bison. There's plenty more to do, and always another time to see the bison.

OTHER SPOTS TO SEE BISON IN THE MIDWEST

Illinois

✔ Fermilab (Batavia): www.fnal.gov/pub/visiting

✔ Nachusa Grasslands (Franklin Grove) (see page 125): www.nachusagrasslands.org

Indiana

✔ Kankakee Sands (Newton County) (see page 237): www.nature.org/en-us/get-involved/how-to-help/places-we-protect/kankakee-sands

Iowa

✔ Broken Kettle Grasslands Preserve (near Sioux City): www.nature.org/en-us/get-involved/how-to-help/places-we-protect/broken-kettle-grasslands-preserve

Minnesota

✔ Blue Mounds State Park (near Luverne): www.dnr.state.mn.us/state_parks

✔ Minneopa State Park (near Mankato): www.dnr.state.mn.us/state_parks

Wisconsin

✔ Sandhill Wildlife Area (near Wisconsin Rapids): https://dnr.wisconsin.gov/topic/Lands/WildlifeAreas/sandhill

Bison at Nachusa Grasslands
© Andrew Morkes

NEARBY NATURE DESTINATIONS

Braidwood Dunes and Savanna Nature Preserve, Des Plaines State Fish and Wildlife Area, Hitts Siding Prairie Nature Preserve, Kankakee River State Park, Laughton Preserve, Sand Ridge Savanna Nature Preserve

ORLAND GRASSLAND

VISIT FOR A RESPITE FROM MALLS, MOTORWAYS, AND MODERNITY

Banded garden spider   © Andrew Morkes

This doesn't look promising, I thought to myself, as I drove south on LaGrange Road toward Orland Grassland. LaGrange Road would be better named LaGrange Consumer Superhighway, with every possible big box store, mall complex, and chain restaurant imaginable in these densely packed suburbs. How could the Grassland be wild and serene if it was located so close to such a busy, retail thoroughfare?

Yet, once my wife's cousin Ellen (I consider her my cousin, too) and I pulled into the Grassland's parking lot near 167th and LaGrange and began hiking in the 90-degree heat, I realized I was wrong. Very wrong. In moments, we were surrounded by six-foot-tall prairie grasses, the soothing sounds of crickets, and a medley of wildflowers. Thoughts of malls, McDonalds, and motorways were replaced by the joys of nature. We were quickly taken back to a time before humans marked the land with asphalt roads, massive homes, bridges, and not-so golden arches.

Where: 167th Street & South LaGrange Road, Cook County, IL 60467 (near Orland Park)

Learn More: Forest Preserves of Cook County, https://fpdcc.com/places/locations/orland-grassland

Hours: Sunrise to sunset, year-round

Quick Summary: A large, restored grassland with prairie, oak savannas, shrublands, ponds, wetlands, and woodlands. Perfect for hiking and bird-watching. Approximately 13 miles of paved and unpaved trails. Dogs allowed (on-leashes only). (#53 on the map on page 12)

What You Can Do There: Bicycling, Birdwatching, Cross-Country Skiing, Hiking, Photography, Picnicking, Snowshoeing

© Andrew Morkes

We hiked the gently rolling hills of the Birdsong Trail in the stifling heat, with just a few wispy clouds overhead. (Visit www.orlandgrassland.org/bird-checklist for a trail map.) At one point, my cousin turned to me and declared, "Isn't this wonderful." And I wholeheartedly agreed as we walked and talked, savoring the chance to enjoy nature and each other's company.

Only .001 percent remains of the millions of acres of prairie that existed in Illinois prior to the arrival of European settlers. The 960 acres that comprise Orland Grassland (including more than 750 acres of open prairie) are not original prairie, but a lovingly undertaken restoration that began in 2002 with the purchase of farmland. The U.S. Army Corps of Engineers-Chicago Region, the Forest Preserves of Cook County, Openlands (a Chicago-based nonprofit conservation organization), and other organizations provided $7.7 million in funding for the restoration. Audubon-Chicago Region, the Conservation Design Forum, and Orland Grassland Volunteers have—and continue to play—a major role in the farm's return to its natural state.

And the work continues. According to Forest Preserves of Cook County, "Orland Grassland is one of the largest grassland habitat restoration projects in Cook County. The area...is now being restored as a grassland complex with prairie, wetlands, open ponds, oak savannas, shrublands and woodlands."

The backstory of Orland Grassland is interesting, but let's return to the present. Depending on the time of year you hike, you'll encounter the following at Orland Grassland:

✔ Rolling grass-covered hills, creeks, and ponds
✔ An amazing array of flowers in bloom

© Andrew Morkes

✔ Coyotes, spiders (including a nifty banded garden spider that I spotted), and many other wild creatures

✔ More than 140 bird species, including prairie birds such as the grasshopper sparrow, bobolink, sedge wren, dickcissel, Eastern meadowlark, Northern harrier, Henslow's sparrow, and short-eared owl; shrubland- and savanna-loving birds such as the black-billed cuckoo, brown thrasher, willow flycatcher, field sparrow, yellow-breasted chat, and eastern kingbird; wetland birds such as the American bittern, pied-billed grebe, Wilson's snipe, Wilson's phalathrope, marsh wren, Virginia rail, sora, great egret, and Caspian tern; majestic harrier and Cooper's hawks riding the thermals overhead hunting for lunch; and migrating sandhill cranes, solitary sandpipers, greater yellowlegs, Smith's longspurs, and rusty blackbirds. Visit www.orlandgrassland.org/bird-checklist for a birding checklist.

✔ Rare, endangered, and simply beautiful plants including scurfy pea, leadplant, hoary puccoon, prairie gentian, purple prairie clover, grass-leaved goldenrod, compass plant, and prairie dock

✔ Grass species such as little bluestem, prairie dropseed, big bluestem, indian grass, and Scribner's and Leiberg's panic grasses

✔ The biggest sky you'll find in Cook County—no buildings allowed

I've hiked at Orland Grassland several times, yet still feel the urge to revisit areas that I've not yet visited. I hope you will visit, too. It is well worth a trip.

NEARBY NATURE DESTINATIONS

Cap Sauers Holding Nature Preserve, Hadley Valley, Hickory Creek Preserve, Messenger Woods, Orland Grove Forest Preserve, Rubio Woods, Swallow Cliff Woods, Tampier Slough Woods

Rock Creek © Andrew Morkes

RACCOON GROVE NATURE PRESERVE

STUNNING SPRING WILDFLOWERS, A SUN-DAPPLED CREEK, SPLENDID FALL COLORS, AND EASY HIKING

I didn't see any raccoons, but I did savor acres and acres of stunning wild geraniums and mayapples during a recent hike at Raccoon Grove Nature Preserve. This 213-acre Illinois Nature Preserve is a great destination for a short hike and wildflower viewing (blue-eyed Marys and Virginia bluebells, among other blooms), as well as a great place to soak up the golden hues and other colors of

Where: 5851 W. Pauling Road, Monee, IL 60449

Learn More: Forest Preserve District of Will County, www.reconnectwithnature.org/preserves-trails/preserves/raccoon-grove

Hours: 8 a.m. to sunset, year-round

Quick Review: A great destination for a short hike and wildflower viewing, birdwatching, and fall colors. No dogs are allowed. (#54 on the map on page 12)

What You Can Do There: Birdwatching, Hiking, Photography, Picnicking, Running/Exercise, Snowshoeing

© Andrew Morkes

the white, bur and black oak; shagbark hickory; and sugar maple trees in the fall. I bet the snowshoeing is pretty fun in the winter, too, when a deep layer of snow blankets the forest floor. Illinois Nature Preserves are special places because they protect the highest quality natural lands in the state.

Soon after you exit the parking lot and begin walking the 0.27 mile loop trail, you will leave civilization behind and quickly be overwhelmed by a forest of green, wildflowers, and a birdsong (including more than 80 species such as the scarlet tanager and eastern wood-pewee) that I wish had a decibel meter to measure.

The trail eventually takes you to Rock Creek, a pretty meandering waterway that runs through the preserve. Take the time to explore the sub trails that travel along the creek and take a break by sitting on a fallen tree branch and simply experiencing the sights, sounds, and smells of the forest. Don't rush back to your car. There's no need to get back to the "rat race" anytime soon. Take some time to explore, look for fossils in the creek bed, enjoy the spring flowers or fall colors, and otherwise savor this pretty stretch of nature in a Chicago south suburb. And take a moment to thank the visionaries who loved this spot so much that they protected it from being paved over and turned into yet another subdivision or strip mall.

NEARBY NATURE DESTINATIONS

Goodenow Grove Nature Preserve, Monee Reservoir, Wayne Lehnert Forest Preserve, Plum Grove Forest Preserve

RED GATE WOODS

HAWKS AND HILLS, SLOUGHS AND SNAKES, AND GHOSTS AND BURIED NUCLEAR WASTE, OH MY!

I usually have a plan when I hike. I'll take this branch of the trail, check out this lake or flower-filled meadow, or hike for a specified amount of time. But, sometimes, it's just fun to wander wherever your legs take you. That's what I decided to do when I recently visited Red Gate Woods. I was a blank slate in the woods ("Tabula Rasa Morkes," if you will). I took the paths I wanted; lingered to watch hawks, ducks, and deer; wandered off trail into ravines and through dense woods when the mood hit; ignored my watch; got lost once or twice off trail; and had a terrific time in the 89-degree heat. It was a great hike, and here are seven things you should know about Red Gate Woods:

There is wildlife galore. In my 3.5 hours walking hill and dale, I saw hawks, countless frogs (including some noisy bullfrogs), a convention of blue jays, turtles, a water snake, a trail snake (which I nudged into the woods after seeing his squashed friend earlier on my hike…I said to him, "you'll thank me later"), deer, butterflies and spiders, and many other bird species. And there were also tons of wildflowers blooming. The woods were alive with motion, sound, and color, and it felt good.

Speaking of that dead snake, there are a lot of mountain bikers. If you like mountain biking, you'll love these winding trails that roam through hills and prairie. Please note that some areas of Red Gate Woods are off-limits to mountain bikers, which provide a little peace to those who like a good walk.

Where: Enter from South Archer Avenue, northeast of 107th Street, Cook County, IL 60480 (near Willow Springs, IL)

Learn More: Forest Preserves of Cook County, https://fpdcc.com/places/locations/red-gate-woods

Hours: Sunrise to sunset, year-round

Quick Review: Hiking trails that range from paved flat paths, to boggy, muddy single-person-wide trails, to challenging hilly terrain. Many lakes and sloughs (perfect for a picnic lunch or fishing). Wildlife in abundance. Mountain biking. Camping opportunities at Bullfrog Lake. And remnants of the top-secret Manhattan Project above and below ground (bring your Geiger Counter…just kidding). (#55 on the map on page 12)

What You Can Do There: Bicycling, Birdwatching, Camping (at nearby Bullfrog Lake), Cross-Country Skiing, Fishing, Hiking, Horseback Riding, Local/National History, Photography, Picnicking, Running/Exercise, Snowshoeing

© Andrew Morkes

You can go camping! There are 32 campsites and 11 cabins at Bullfrog Lake, which is near the Little Red Schoolhouse Nature Center (see page 175), Sagawau Environmental Learning Center (see page 204), which features the only canyon in Cook County—reservations are required), and other local attractions. The campsites and cabins are affordable, and a good place to camp if you don't want to leave Chicago and its collar counties.

You can hike for miles without ever crossing a road—and enjoy some solitude. If you hike at the right time, you might not see another person for hours. Kind of nice in a metropolitan area with nearly 10 million people.

There is a trail for everyone. There are flat, easygoing trails (on the Orange Trail Loop by Tomahawk Slough), wooded footpaths, grassland paths, and hilly, challenging trails (north of Bullfrog Lake on the Blue Trail and in the far south edge of the woods on the Orange Loop Trail). Visit https://fpdcc.com/downloads/maps/trails/english/FPCC-Palos-Trail-Map-022020.pdf for a trail map.

ST. JAMES AT SAG BRIDGE

If you like history and old churches, check out **St. James at Sag Bridge Catholic Church** (10600 S. Archer Avenue, Lemont, IL 60439, www.historicstjames.org), which sits at the far southwestern edge of Red Gate Woods, near the intersection of Archer Avenue and 107th Street. I was married at this beautiful limestone church that was built in 1853 (a log cabin church had been constructed at the site in 1833). St. James was built by Irish immigrants who came to America to work on the construction of the Illinois & Michigan Canal. A walk through the ancient graveyard tells a moving story of the Irish diaspora in America. A few gravestones provide a detailed history of certain families. This hilltop overlooking the Sag Valley has a long history of habitation. A Native American village was located there for many years and, later, a French fort was built at this site. In 1673, it is believed that Father Jacques Marquette said Mass at the French fort. St. James at Sag Bridge Catholic Church is listed on the National Register of Historic Places and is worth a visit.

You almost can't get lost if you stay on the main trails. Forest Preserves of Cook County has installed an amazing system of trail signage that tells you where you are in this vast preserve, what trail you're on, and which direction to take if you want to stay on a specific trail or switch to another one. The signs use a numbering system that helps you find your destination.

At times, you'll walk through and over history—and you will not emit a radioactive glow thereafter (if you can believe the U.S. Department of Energy). Yes, it's true. Buried deep in some of Chicagoland's most rugged and dense forest are the remains of the world's first nuclear reactor at the original site of Argonne National Laboratory (ANL), which was a major nuclear research facility for the Manhattan Project during World War II. Albert Einstein and Enrico Fermi both visited ANL. After World War II, the U.S. government decommissioned the site. Between 1955 and 1956, Forest Preserves of Cook County reports that the Atomic Energy Commission "systematically dismantled the reactors and removed the remaining radioactive fuel and the radioactive heavy water coolant to Oak Ridge National Laboratory in Tennessee for disposal. Other low-level waste at Site A, such as CP-3's biological shield, was encased in concrete, dislodged with explosives, and buried in a 40-foot-deep trench." Visit https://fpdcc.com/site-a-the-worlds-first-nuclear-reactor for detailed information about this era.

I tried to re-visit what's left of ANL (the U.S. government calls this place "Site A"), but I ran out of time (reality did eventually creep into my day). (I'd seen Site A on a Scout hike, but that was decades ago.) I did visit Plot M, where nuclear waste was dumped from the laboratory. It's sobering to think that amidst such natural beauty, radioactive material still lingers beneath the soil, although it's hopefully still safely encased in concrete. (When I neared Plot M, my phone's GPS started going haywire, but perhaps that was just a coincidence.)

More than 75 years later, it seems odd that the U.S. government would build such a top-secret installation that developed nuclear energy amidst a forest preserve filled with hikers, picnickers, and fishermen and fisherwomen, but those were different times. (Note: The plutonium used in the atomic bombs that were detonated over Hiroshima and Nagasaki, Japan, was produced on the West Coast.)

But during this hike, I was just happy to soak up a little history, the sounds of birdsong, and the bright sunlight on my face as I hiked in some of the nicest woods in Chicagoland. I hope you'll check out Red Gate Woods someday, too.

Plot M   © Andrew Morkes

SEARCHING FOR RESURRECTION MARY

If you stay in the area late into the night, see if you can catch a glimpse of Resurrection Mary, who is purported to have haunted Archer Avenue from the Willowbrook Ballroom to Resurrection Cemetery (7201 Archer Avenue, Justice, IL 60458) since the 1930s. She is the most-famous ghost in Chicago. Some say that Red Gate Woods itself is haunted, but I think Resurrection Mary is a better story. Her story falls into the vanishing hitchhiker genre. As the legend goes, Resurrection Mary was a beautiful young lady who was killed in a hit-and-run accident while walking along Archer Avenue after having an argument with her boyfriend at the Oh Henry Ballroom, which was later renamed the Willowbrook Ballroom. Mary's parents buried her at Resurrection Cemetery in a pretty dress and dancing shoes, in which her ghost appears in most stories.

The first sightings of Resurrection Mary began in the late 1930s. A man named Jerry Palus met a stunning woman at a dance hall. They made beautiful music together all night on the dance floor. At the end of the evening, she asked Palus for a ride home down Archer Avenue. When they reached the gates of Resurrection Cemetery, she exited his car and promptly disappeared. In the ensuing decades, similar stories emerged of a beautiful woman in a white dress hitching a ride down Archer Avenue and then vanishing near or at Resurrection Cemetery. Stories also abound of a young woman in a white dress jumping out in front of cars on Archer or walking on the side of the road crying. Ghost hunters have linked the story of Resurrection Mary to the tragic deaths of two young women in the 1920s and 1930s—one who died on the way home from the Willowbrook Ballroom.

When I was a little boy, my friend's dad, who drove a bread delivery truck, claimed he picked up Resurrection Mary on one of his delivery runs. I never knew if he was serious. While on bread deliveries, this guy also loved to whip loaves of bread through the open car windows of unsuspecting friends (including us) whom he spotted waiting at stoplights. So, who knows.

If you like ghost-hunting and Chicago area history, you might be interested in my article, "Visit Bachelor's Grove Cemetery Not Only for Spooks and Scares, But Also For Its Rich Local History," at my blog, https://natureinchicago.wordpress.com/list-of-articles. Bachelor's Grove is considered to be the most-haunted cemetery in Chicagoland, if not America.

NEARBY NATURE DESTINATIONS

Black Partridge Woods Nature Preserve, Cap Sauers Holding Nature Preserve, Keepataw Preserve, Tampier Slough Woods, Waterfall Glen Forest Preserve

ROCK RUN ROOKERY PRESERVE

SEE BALD EAGLES, GREAT BLUE HERONS, AND OTHER BIRDS AND ENJOY PLEASANT HIKES, BOATING, AND FISHING

Looking for an excellent spot for birdwatching, short hikes, fishing, snowshoeing, and other outdoor activities? If so, Rock Run Rookery Preserve is a perfect destination. The 224-acre preserve features 84-acre and 13-acre lakes (which were originally created and used for quarrying), as well as breeding areas (including islands) for birds and wetland and forest ecosystems.

American bald eagle
© Jim Hudgins, U.S. Fish & Wildlife Service

I visited Rock Run Rookery Preserve on a winter day in January. I was eager to get outdoors after not hiking since December. The temperature was in the low 40s, but a stiff wind made it feel like the high-20s in open areas. Still, the sun was shining, the moon rose early and looked beautiful against the cloudless blue sky, and the slabs of ice bumping against one another on the lake sounded like

Where: 23065 S. Youngs Road, Joliet, IL 60436

Learn More: Forest Preserve District of Will County, www.reconnectwithnature.org/preserves-trails/preserves/rock-run-rookery, www.facebook.com/Rock.Run.Rookery

Hours: 6 a.m. to sunset (April-October); 8 a.m. to sunset (November-March)

Quick Review: An excellent spot for birdwatching, short hikes, fishing, snowshoeing, and other outdoor activities. (#56 on the map on page 12)

What You Can Do There: Bicycling, Birdwatching, Canoeing/Kayaking/Boating, Cross-Country Skiing, Fishing, Hiking, Photography, Picnicking, Running/Exercise, Snowshoeing

© Andrew Morkes

wind chimes as I walked along the shore. Winter nirvana (at least if you live in Chicagoland).

Here are seven things you can do at Rock Run Rookery Preserve.

Go birdwatching. This is a popular pastime for visitors to the preserve. I decided to visit the rookery after seeing stunning photos of bald eagles, great blue herons, cormorants, great egrets, and other birds on the preserve's Facebook page (www.facebook.com/Rock.Run.Rookery) as well as at Will County Wildlife (www.facebook.com/groups/willcountywildlife). Unfortunately, I did not see any eagles, nor herons, during my visit, but did see a few egrets and many ducks, geese, and swans, among other birds. American white pelicans are also known to visit during spring and fall migrations. There were thousands of birds at the preserve when I visited, so even though I didn't see any eagles, I enjoyed my visit. If you plan to birdwatch, be sure to bring high-quality binoculars and some patience. While it's easy to see large numbers of ducks and geese, you will have to search carefully for the eagles and other birds of prey. On the other hand, I've seen photos at the aforementioned websites that feature five to 10 eagles in one tree, so eagle-spotting is often a matter of the timing and the frequency of one's visits.

Go hiking. There are 0.41 miles of flat, paved trail at the preserve, and probably 0.5 to 1 mile of foot trails. If you walk to the end of the paved path, there is a large wooden platform/walkway that is good for nature viewing and photography. Smaller viewing platforms can be found in other areas around the lakes. The foot trails begin at the end of the main viewing platform (and there are others throughout the preserve). Some traverse hilly areas along the edge of the lakes. Be careful on wet or icy days. During my hike, I was one false step and missed tree branch grab away from a frigid dip in the lake. Other trails head east through wetlands and around a pretty creek that flows into the nearby Des Plaines River.

Go canoeing or kayaking. The preserve features a canoe/kayak launch on the large east lake. You do not need a launch pass. Nippersink Creek (see page 283) is my favorite area kayaking destination, but I think I'll check out Rock Run this spring or summer.

Enjoy a picnic. Bring your favorite treats and enjoy lunch or dinner in the great outdoors.

Go fishing. You can catch large or smallmouth bass, sauger, walleye, bluegill, sunfish, and channel catfish at the shore or by boat. Note: Part of the large east lake is off-limits to boats in order to protect the rookery, and boats are not allowed on the small west lake.

Go snowshoeing or cross-country skiing. You could do worse than watching eagles or herons hunting gulls and geese over the main lake as you enjoy these winter activities.

Pick up some plastic and other trash. Although Rock Run Rookery is a beautiful and serene place, there are ongoing issues with litter—especially microplastics. Some of this trash is generated by litterbugs who don't have the class to throw out their garbage but, more significantly, from trash deposited into the rookery by the adjoining Des Plaines River when it overflows its banks after heavy rains. This is not to say that the rookery is filled with trash, but there were isolated areas that had significant collections of garbage (mainly fishing supplies and the occasional plastic bottle). Consider bringing a garbage bag or two to pick up some trash or join the volunteer meetups that occur frequently at the rookery. Participating is an easy way to make the world a better place and teach your kids the importance of volunteering and protecting the environment.

> **DID YOU KNOW?**
>
> Rock Run Rookery Preserve is one of the northernmost spots where invasive Asian carp have been detected in the Illinois Waterway System. Its lakes are periodically checked for carp. Most of these ecosystem-destroying fish are removed, while a few are mounted with tracking devices that scientists use to study their spread.

FINAL THOUGHTS

Rock Run Rookery Preserve is a wonderful place to enjoy warm weather, but I encourage you to bundle up and visit in the winter to experience the great birdwatching and other outdoor activities that are available. There are fewer people at the preserve and a cold-weather walk is the perfect way to break up the monotony of a Chicago winter.

NEARBY NATURE DESTINATIONS

Hammel Woods, Lake Renwick Preserve/Heron Rookery Nature Preserve, Lower Rock Run Preserve, McKinley Woods, Rock Run Preserve, Van Horn Woods

SAGAWAU ENVIRONMENTAL LEARNING CENTER

HIKE THE ONLY CANYON IN COOK COUNTY AND OTHER TRAILS, CROSS-COUNTRY SKI, AND LEARN ABOUT LOCAL AND NATURAL HISTORY

Sagawau Environmental Learning Center is a perfect destination in all seasons. **In the spring and summer,** visit it for wildflower viewing, birdwatching (more than 100 species of migrant and resident birds are found at the center), a diverse range of hiking trails (there are 2.6 miles of trails; visit https://fpdcc.com/downloads/maps/nature-centers/english/FPCC-Sagawau-Environmental-Learning-Center-Map-4-17.pdf for a trail map), and guided tours of Sagawau Canyon, the only canyon in Cook County, which offers uncommon and unusual plants (including bulblet fern, purple cliff brake, walking fern, hairy rock cress, and ninebark) and rock formations. A Hummingbird Festival is also held each summer.

In the fall, continue to enjoy hiking and birdwatching (visit https://fpdcc.com/wp-content/uploads/2019/01/FPCC-bird-the-preserves-checklist-mar16-011419.pdf for a Forest Preserves of Cook County Birding List), but also savor the beautiful fiery reds, gorgeous golds, pumpkin oranges, and banana yellows of the forest canopy in this heavily wooded area.

In the winter, go cross-country skiing (weather permitting, of course) and snowshoeing. When heavy snow descends, Sagawau Environmental

---

Where: 12545 West 111th Street, Lemont, IL 60439, 630/257-2045

Learn More: Forest Preserves of Cook County, https://fpdcc.com/places/locations/sagawau-environmental-learning-center, www.facebook.com/Sagawau

Hours: 9 a.m. to 4 p.m., year-round; Closed Thanksgiving, Christmas, New Year's Day

Quick Review: The only canyon in Cook County (tours are available spring through fall; registration required), 2.6 miles of varied hiking trails, an environmental education center and lodge that also features information on Native American history; cross-country skiing; a Hummingbird Festival in the summer; and weekly indoor and outdoor education programs. Pets are not permitted on nature center grounds, including in the parking lots. (#57 on the map on page 12)

What You Can Do There: Birdwatching, Cross-Country Skiing, Educational and Self-Enrichment Opportunities and Classes, Hiking, Local History, Nature Center, Photography, Running/Exercise, Snowshoeing

Sagawau Canyon © Forest Preserves of Cook County

Learning Center transforms into Sagawau Nordic—a premier full-service cross-country ski center that provides ski rentals and lessons at all levels on groomed trails that are appropriate for both novice and advanced skiers. Sagawau Nordic is open the third week of December through the first weekend in March. Contact the center for firm opening/closing dates and information on rental costs and ski lessons. You can warm up in the lodge after your skiing adventure.

In all seasons, Sagawau Environmental Learning Center's visitor center and classroom offers exhibits on geology, natural history and habitat management, Native American and early settler history, and much more. Indoor and outdoor educational classes and programs are frequently offered. Recent classes included Fall Color Palette (sketching), Fall Color Walk, Red Gate Woods: Beginning of the Atomic Age, Lichen Lab, Fossil Quarry Tour, and Winter Bird Feeding.

NEARBY NATURE DESTINATIONS

Black Partridge Woods Nature Preserve, Cap Sauers Holding Nature Preserve, Cranberry Slough Nature Preserve, The Forge: Lemont Quarries, Keepataw Preserve, Lake Katherine Nature Center and Botanic Gardens, Orland Grassland, Red Gate Woods, Sag Quarries, Swallow Cliff Woods, Tampier Slough Woods, Waterfall Glen Forest Preserve

SAND RIDGE NATURE CENTER

DIVERSE HIKES, AN EXCELLENT NATURE CENTER, A PIONEER HOMESTEAD, AND MORE

I've traveled thousands of miles to visit national parks, visited more than 200 natural and historic spots in Chicagoland, and lived in Chicago for 50 years, yet I'd still not visited the "tree-rific" (bad pun intended) Sand Ridge Nature Center (SRNC) that's less than two miles from my mother-in-law's house and not too far from my childhood home in Beverly on Chicago's South Side.

Until, that is, recently—when I checked off this south suburban gem on my "nature bucket list." I spent several hours enjoying the nature center and its grounds on a cool, but sunny, day and the space-time continuum maintained its equilibrium. There was no antimatter (me) meeting matter (SRNC) explosion. Instead, I was greeted by peace and solitude and had a wonderful time exploring the nature center and its trails that travel through forests of white and black oak, wild black cherry, hickory, sassafras, and black gum; wetlands; prairie; savannas; and the remnants of what was once the shoreline of Lake Chicago (which covered most of what we now know as Cook County after the end of the last great Ice Age). And then I went back to Sand Ridge again, and again, and again because it's such a wonderful place.

Dogwood Trail © Andrew Morkes

Where: 15891 Paxton Avenue, South Holland, IL 60473

Learn More: Forest Preserves of Cook County, 708/868-0606, https://fpdcc.com/places/locations/sand-ridge-nature-center, www.facebook.com/Sand-Ridge-Nature-Center-485394718215678

Hours: Nature Center: March-October: 9 a.m. to 5 p.m.; November-February: 9 a.m. to 4 p.m., closed on Fridays throughout the year

Grounds: March-October: 8 a.m. to 5 p.m.; November-February: 8 a.m. to 4 p.m.

The nature center and grounds are closed on Thanksgiving, Christmas, and New Year's Day.

Quick Review: Nearly four miles of easy trails that provide pleasant views of oak savannah, wetlands, prairies, and other ecosystems. There's also a top-notch nature center for kids (with live animals), an 1800s pioneer homestead, a variety of workshops and guided hikes, and annual festivals and events. No fishing or dogs allowed. There is ample parking. Washrooms and drinking water are available. The nature center and grounds have recently been renovated. (#58 on the map on page 12)

What You Can Do There: Bicycling (only allowed in nature center parking lots), Birdwatching, Camping (at nearby Camp Shabbona Woods), Educational and Self-Enrichment Opportunities and Classes, Hiking, Nature Center, Running/Exercise, Photography, Snowshoeing (including rentals)

If you're looking for a good hiking destination in the south suburbs, the 235-acre SRNC should be one of your first choices—especially if you're seeking easy trails that provide nice views of oak savannah, wetlands, prairies, and other ecosystems. I first hiked the one-mile Dogwood Trail, which alternated between dirt paths and wooden boardwalks, taking me through forest and wetlands. I hiked in solitude, the bright sun keeping me company and warming me as I walked. When the clouds or trees blocked the sun and the wind picked up, I was reminded that I was hiking on an unseasonably cold day in early November. I was glad I'd bundled up. Sand Ridge is surrounded by roads, but I was amazed at how peaceful it was once I began hiking. You know you're hiking in solitude when your steps on the slightly frozen ground are the loudest sounds you hear.

I also hiked the 1.5-mile Long Beach Trail, which I highly recommend. On a warm fall day, I returned to SRNC with my wife and son, and we were wowed by the late-season wildflowers (including cardinal flowers) on this trail. The Long Beach Trail and the Dogwood Trail are the longest paths at Sand Ridge. Other trails—which may be better for small children—include the Redwing Trail (0.3 miles) and the Pines Trail (0.3 miles). Visit https://fpdcc.com/places/locations/sand-ridge-nature-center for trail maps.

There's a lot more to Sand Ridge Nature Center than just excellent hiking. Here are a few other things you can do during your visit:

Sand Ridge has a top-notch nature center with friendly and knowledgeable staff.
© Andrew Morkes

View exhibits at the nature center about the natural and cultural history of the Calumet region, and see a variety of live animals (fish, turtles, etc.). You can even view the 65-million-year-old leg bone of a duck-billed dinosaur.

Check out a wide range of creatures outdoors; visit www.inaturalist.org/check_lists/453392-Sand-Ridge-Nature-Center-Check-List for a list of insects, amphibians (northern leopard frog, American bullfrog, Fowler's toad), mammals (opossum, chipmunk, muskrat, coyote, and white-tailed deer), reptiles (snapping turtle, painted turtle, various types of snakes), arachnids, and other critters spotted at Sand Ridge recently.

Enjoy the kids' activity area in the center with your children—perfect for a snowy or rainy day.

Enjoy great birdwatching—especially in the spring and fall. You might see red-headed woodpeckers, red-bellied woodpeckers, sandhill cranes, barred owls, turkey vultures, great egrets, green herons, red-tailed hawks, red-winged blackbirds, bald eagles, scarlet tanagers, yellow-rumpled warblers, and a variety of other bird species.

View the butterfly and interpretive gardens during warm weather.

Learn about the many varieties of trees at Sand Ridge by flipping up the numbered placards that appear along the trails.

Attend annual festivals and events such as the Underground Railroad Interactive Hike, Juneteenth Celebration, Archaeology Day (which celebrates Native American culture), Settlers' Day, and Christmas Past.

Chicagoland South and Beyond Destinations 209

The nature center has a pioneer homestead that depicts life in the early 1800s.
© Andrew Morkes

Spend a night or two just down the trail from Sand Ridge at Camp Shabbona Woods (https://fpdcc.com/places/locations/camp-shabbona-woods), which features small, three-season cabins and mulch tent pads.

Nature recharges our batteries. It calms us and improves our health. It gives us a glimpse of the wonders of the natural world before European settlement. Nature centers are islands of biodiversity and beauty amidst the sometimes sprawl of our city and suburbs. They offer dozens of free programs, classes, and other activities each year that educate us, allow us to experience nature, spend time with family, and have some fun. They're usually staffed with friendly workers who love their jobs and who are happy to share their knowledge with visitors. They're great places to take your kids, learn a new skill (such as painting, writing, or meditation), and see a variety of ecosystems, plants, and animals—some that are even rare or endangered. I encourage you to visit Sand Ridge Nature Center, or nature centers in your area, soon. You won't be disappointed.

NEARBY NATURE DESTINATIONS

Beaubien Woods; Big Marsh Park; Burnham Prairie Nature Preserve; Hegewisch Marsh; Indian Ridge Marsh Park; Powderhorn Lake, Marsh, and Prairie; Wolf Lake Memorial Park

SILVER SPRINGS STATE FISH & WILDLIFE AREA

AN OUTDOOR RECREATION HOTSPOT IN KANE COUNTY

There are two constants at Silver Springs State Fish and Wildlife Area. First, the park's namesake spring flows constantly from a gravelly spot in the woods, and then gradually works its way to the Fox River. Second, there's always something fun to do at this Kane County natural area. Here are a few things to do at Silver Springs.

Picnicking. You can dine alfresco at a picnic table or shelter at several areas along the Fox River. Charcoal grills, water, and washroom facilities are available.

Fishing. You can cast a line at Loon Lake, Beaver Lake, and the Fox River. Channel catfish, large and smallmouth bass, bluegill, and crappie are found in both lakes, and rainbow trout are stocked twice annually in Loon Lake. If you choose to shore or boat fish in the Fox River, you might catch large and smallmouth bass, northern pike, muskie, crappie, channel catfish, bullhead, carp, and bluegill.

Boating. Bring your canoe or kayak and ply the waters of Loon Lake, Beaver Lake, and the Fox River. Boats with gasoline motors are only allowed on the Fox River. You can also rent canoes and kayaks from local outfitters.

Hiking. Four miles of hiking trails meander along the river and through groves of majestic oaks and prairie grasslands that overlook the lakes.

Enjoying winter sports. Many people steer clear of the outdoors during the winter, but that's a mistake because Silver Springs and other nature areas are

---

Where: 13608 Fox Road, Yorkville, IL 60560

Learn More: Illinois Department of Natural Resources, 630/553-6297, www2.illinois.gov/dnr/Parks/Pages/SilverSprings.aspx

Hours: Sunrise to sunset, year-round

Quick Review: Nearly 1,400 acres of forests, hills, lakes, portions of the Fox River, and a natural spring. More than 130 types of wildflowers. Dogs allowed (but they must be leashed). (#59 on the map on page 12)

What You Can Do There: Archery Range, Bicycling, Birdwatching, Camping (youth groups only), Canoeing/Kayaking/Boating, Cross-Country Skiing, Educational and Self-Enrichment Opportunities and Classes, Fishing/Ice Fishing, Hiking, Horseback Riding, Hunting, Ice Skating, Photography, Picnicking, Running/Exercise, Sledding, Snowmobiling, Snowshoeing

© Andrew Morkes

beautiful during the cold months and provide lots of solitude. Winter activities include snowshoeing, cross-country skiing, ice fishing, sledding, and ice skating. A four-mile snowmobile trail is available.

Visiting Farnsworth House. When the trees are bare, you can spot the historic Farnsworth House to the north across the river. From 1949 to 1951, this National Historic Landmark was designed and built in the International Style by architect Ludwig Mies van der Rohe for Dr. Edith Farnsworth. This minimalist masterpiece is a "pilgrimage site for architects and designers worldwide and is considered one of the most important modern assets in the United States," according to the National Trust for Historic Preservation, which owns and administers the property. The Farnsworth House is open for tours. Visit https://farnsworthhouse.org for more information.

NEARBY NATURE DESTINATIONS

Big Rock Preserve, Lake Renwick Preserve, Sauer Prairie Kame Forest Preserve, Springbrook Prairie Forest Preserve

STARVED ROCK STATE PARK

STUNNING CANYONS AND WATERFALLS, BEAUTIFUL VIEWS OF THE ILLINOIS RIVER, AND CHALLENGING HIKING TRAILS

Starved Rock State Park is one of the crown jewels of the Illinois state park system. Its steep sandstone cliffs, cool canyons (and waterfalls), stunning views of the Illinois River, beautiful (but often challenging) hiking trails, and wealth of biodiversity—as well as the availability of a wide range of recreational activities—make it easy to love.

But...Starved Rock also can be overcrowded. On weekends from May through October, the park can be like a Nature Lollapalooza—and not in a good way. More than 2.8 million people visited Starved Rock in a recent year, an attendance figure that rivals only the top 10 to 20 national parks in the National Park Service system. I say this early on in this article because while Starved Rock is a wonderful place, it's not enjoyable to visit during peak periods—especially if you like peace and solitude on the trails. The IDNR says that parking lots typically fill and close by 11 a.m., May through October, which is a bummer if you've left Chicago early in the morning and arrive to see closed park gates. There are several strategies you can employ to address this reality:

✔ Visit during the week.

✔ Visit very early in the day and/or off-season.

✔ Choose to visit areas of the park that are less busy or more difficult to

Where: 2668 East 873 Road, Oglesby, IL 61348; about 95 miles southwest of downtown Chicago

Learn More: Illinois Department of Natural Resources (IDNR), www2.illinois.gov/dnr/Parks/Pages/StarvedRock.aspx

Hours: Trails: 6:30 a.m. to sunset

Visitor Center: 9 a.m. to 4 p.m. Monday-Friday (although opening hours may vary)

Campground: Gates open at 8:30 a.m. and close at 10 p.m.

Quick Review: This park features waterfalls, nearly 20 canyons, hiking trails, towering ice formations in the winter, and so much more. Pets must be leashed. (#60 on the map on page 12)

What You Can Do There: Bicycling (on select trails), Birdwatching, Boat Tours, Camping, Canoeing/Kayaking/Boating, Educational and Self-Enrichment Opportunities and Classes, Fishing, Gift Shop, Hiking, Hunting, Ice Climbing, Local History, Lodge, Photography, Picnicking, Restaurant, Running/Exercise, Trolley Tours, Visitor Center

The view from atop Starved Rock   © Andrew Morkes

reach. Some people beat the crowds by avoiding the Starved Rock Lodge and Visitor Center area and, instead, parking in the far east of the state park near Ottawa, Kakaskia, and Illinois Canyons and work their way west after exploring the aforementioned canyons.

✔ Visit nearby parks instead. For example, Matthiessen State Park (which is about 2.6-miles to the south) offers a 1-mile canyon and a smaller number of waterfalls and hiking trails but is often less crowded than Starved Rock. Other suggestions: Margery C. Carlson Nature Preserve (about 7.5 miles south) and Buffalo Rock State Park (about 6 miles east).

During a trip to visit several state parks in the area, I was tempted to skip Starved Rock because of the crowds. But it was only mid-April, the weather was beautiful (sunny and in the low 60s), and I really wanted to see the canyons and cliffs that I had last visited 20 years earlier.

I was pleasantly surprised when I arrived. The large parking lot was about one-third full, but the trails were not packed as they can be in the summer and fall. I was able to enjoy occasional solitude on the cliffs and in the canyons, but there were also times when the narrow trails were clogged with nature seekers (many of whom did not have the right footwear to navigate the steep and slippery trails). If you visit Starved Rock, you must be ready for this reality.

Starved Rock is an Illinois "bucket list" kind of place, so I recommend a visit—regardless of the crowds. With careful planning and timing, you can schedule a visit that proves more terrific than touristy. Here are just a few things you can do at Starved Rock:

French Canyon © Andrew Morkes

Check out the Visitor Center, which offers educational exhibits about the park's geology, plants and animals, and its French and Native American history. Brochures and maps are also available.

Enjoy a hike. There are more than 13 miles of trails. Some travel along the scenic Illinois River, while others involve demanding treks up and down staircases that lead to canyons or bluffs. Trails range in length from the 0.3-mile Starved Rock Trail (which offers excellent views of sandstone outcroppings and the Illinois River) to the Illinois Canyon trail (4.7 miles). Many trails in the park connect to one another, so you can organize your hiking itinerary by the distance you want to travel, the areas of the park that you want to see, and the trail's level of difficulty.

You can hike year-round, but you'll need to be especially careful when trails are wet or icy. Here's how the IDNR describes its trail organization: "Trail maps and brown trail signs with directional arrows are located at every intersection along the park's trail system. There are posts and metal discs along the trails that correspond to the color-coded maps marking the trails: Red for River Trail, Green for Interior Canyon or Connecting Trail, and Brown for Bluff Trail. Finally, yellow dots on trees or posts indicate you are moving further away from the lodge or visitor center, and white dots mean you are returning." Despite this signage, the trails can be confusing. Be sure to bring the park's hiking trail map (www2.illinois.gov/dnr/publications/documents/00000005.pdf) to help you navigate the trails. Additionally, the Prairie State Conservation Coalition offers a hiking app for Starved Rock and more than 20 other nature spots in Illinois at www.prairiestateconservation.org/pscc/hikeapp. Ranger-led hikes are also available. Use the apps or maps. It is not a good feeling to be very tired on the trail and realize that you have miles to walk to get back to your vehicle. Note: Biking is not allowed on the hiking trails.

View canyons and waterfalls. The 18 canyons at Starved Rock were formed by glacial meltwater and stream erosion. They travel for four miles beneath tree-covered (black and white oak, red and white cedar, and white pine) sandstone bluffs. I visited several canyons near the Visitor Center during my short visit, and they were all worth the hike. In the spring, all the canyons have waterfalls that are fed by rain and snowmelt. The IDNR says that the longer-lasting waterfalls are found in French, LaSalle, and St. Louis canyons. The waterfalls freeze in the winter—making them attractive destinations for visitors. You can even climb the waterfalls in four canyons, but the

© Andrew Morkes

IDNR says that those who do so "climb at their own risk." An ice climbing brochure is available at the park's website and at its visitor center.

View wildlife in the park's wide range of ecosystems. During the winter, Starved Rock is a popular eagle-watching destination. The IDNR says that the best spots to see eagles are Starved Rock, Lovers Leap Overlook, Eagle Cliff Overlook, and along the sea wall of the Illinois River by the Visitor Center. Other birds that you might see include vireos, catbirds, nuthatches, chickadees, indigo buntings, wood ducks, geese, herons, double-crested cormorants, ring-billed gulls, American white pelicans, turkey vultures, belted kingfishers, and woodpeckers. Visit https://ebird.org for a longer list of birds spotted at Starved Rock. Other creatures

Wildcat Canyon © Andrew Morkes

that you might see at the park include woodchucks, moles, beavers, muskrats, raccoons, flying squirrels, white-tailed deer, frogs, turtles, toads, and snakes.

Stay overnight. Many people spend the weekend—or even a week—in the Starved Rock area because there are so many local attractions. The Starved Rock campground is located outside of the park off Route 71. It has 133, Class A premium campsites with electricity, showers, and flush toilets; a separate youth group camping area; and a children's playground. There are seven campsites for people with disabilities. Camping is available year-round, although one campground loop closes during the winter. You can make a reservation at ReserveAmerica.com. Unfortunately, there are no trails that connect the campground to the park. You'll have to drive or bike to the park from your campsite.

If you prefer not to "rough it," you can stay at Starved Rock Lodge, which was built by the Civilian Conservation Corps in the 1930s. This charming lodge has 72 luxury hotel rooms and 22 comfortable cabin rooms, a restaurant and outdoor bar area, and an indoor swimming pool, whirlpool, and saunas. Visit www.starvedrocklodge.com for more information.

Have a picnic. A large picnic area with views of the Illinois River is available near the Visitor Center. Six picnic shelters are available on a first-come, first-served basis. Note: Alcohol is prohibited January 1 through May 31 in the picnic area.

Go fishing. You can catch white bass, sauger, walleye, catfish, bullhead, carp, bluegill, and crappie in the Illinois River, but you'll need an Illinois fishing license.

Go boating. You can bring your own kayak, canoe, or small boat and launch it from the Lone Point shelter at the eastern edge of the park, or you can rent/reserve a kayak by visiting www.kayakmorris.com. Additionally, boat and trolley tours can be booked at www.starvedrocklodge.com.

TIPS TO IMPROVE YOUR VISIT

✔ Bring insect repellent; mosquitoes, ticks, and other insect pests can be annoying during warm weather.

✔ Be careful as you walk the trails in the canyons (the sandstone can be very slick) and on the bluffs. People have been seriously injured and even killed due to accidents in the park.

✔ All rock climbing, rappelling, or exploring off trails is prohibited.

✔ If the parking lots are full, do not park along roadways such as Route 71 and 178. Those who do so will be towed at their own expense.

✔ Be patient as you navigate the crowds and know when to leave the park if your irritation level surpasses your enjoyment level. There are thousands of other destinations to enjoy in Illinois and beyond.

NEARBY NATURE DESTINATIONS

Buffalo Rock State Park, Margery C. Carlson Nature Preserve, Matthiessen State Park

Hiking path along the Illinois River © Andrew Morkes

SWALLOW CLIFF WOODS

EXERCISE AND GO SLEDDING ON A 100-FOOT BLUFF

Going up — © Forest Preserves of Cook County

Tucked amidst miles of peaceful forest preserves, Swallow Cliff Woods has been a busy place for nearly 100 years, if not more. In 1939, the Civilian Conservation Corps installed 125 steps to the top of its 100-foot bluff and built a toboggan slide there. The toboggan slide (which I enjoyed with my family growing up on Chicago's far South Side) closed in 2004. In recent decades, Swallow Cliff has become a popular fitness area, and sledding is still available. To address growing crowds and improve exercise traffic flow, Forest Preserves of Cook County added a second set of limestone stairs (with areas to rest every 10 steps) in 1996 to complete a unique fitness circuit. So, if you like a challenge, head to the Swallow Cliff stairs to run or walk up the stairs, log your progress on the lap counter at the top of the hill, and enjoy some beautiful views of the nearby forest preserves. Some advice: Arrive at Swallow Cliff Woods early in the day—especially on weekends during warm weather—because it has become an extremely popular destination for exercise and relaxation in the south suburbs.

Where: To access the exercise and sledding areas, enter off Calumet Sag Road (Route 83), just west of La Grange Road (96th Avenue), Cook County, IL 60464 (near Palos Park). Additionally, a South Unit can be accessed by entering off La Grange Road, south of 119th Street.

Learn More: Forest Preserves of Cook County, https://fpdcc.com/places/locations/swallow-cliff-woods

Hours: Sunrise to sunset, year-round

Quick Review: Features popular workout stairs that travel to the top of a 100-foot bluff, sledding, and sometimes challenging hiking trails that allow visitors to trek through hilly, forested terrain. There's also access to the 42.1-mile Palos Trail System. Dogs allowed (on leash only), but they're prohibited on the stairs. (#61 on the map on page 12)

What You Can Do There: Bicycling, Birdwatching, Cross-Country Skiing, Hiking, Horseback Riding, Indoor Event Rentals (for birthday parties, showers, classes, and meetings), Photography, Picnicking, Running/Exercise (including fitness stairs), Sledding, Snowshoeing

Swallow Cliff Woods is not just a scenic overlook and a fitness and sledding destination. It also features a variety of trails that travel through hills and ravines, near rocky creeks, and through pretty forests filled with wildflowers. From the top of the hill at Swallow Cliff North, you can head south on the Brown Trail toward Swallow Cliff South, which has a picnic grove and the pretty Laughing Squaw Sloughs. Go west on the Yellow Trail near the Swallow Cliff Woods North parking lot to reach the spectacular Cap Sauers Holding Nature Preserve (see page 149), which is the largest roadless area in Cook County and which features a beautiful prairie and glacial esker. Head east on the Yellow Trail at the parking lot to reach the scenic McClaughry Springs Woods.

Heading down © Forest Preserves of Cook County

NEARBY NATURE DESTINATIONS

Cap Sauers Holding Nature Preserve, Cranberry Slough Nature Preserve, Lake Katherine Nature Center and Botanic Gardens, McClaughry Springs Woods, Red Gate Woods, Sag Quarries, Sagawau Environmental Learning Center, Tampier Slough Woods, Waterfall Glen Forest Preserve

OTHER PLACES TO GO SLEDDING IN THE FOREST PRESERVES OF COOK COUNTY (FPCC) AND CHICAGO

FPCC-With Lighting: Caldwell Woods, Dan Ryan Woods (see page 30), Westchester Woods

FPCC-Without Lighting: Deer Grove, Pioneer Woods, Thaddeus Lechowicz Woods (see page 61), Schiller Woods East

Chicago Park District: Gompers Park, Horner Park, Humboldt Park, Montrose Harbor, Oz Park, Palmisano Park (see page 52), Soldier Field, Warren Park

WATERFALL GLEN FOREST PRESERVE

SOME OF THE MOST RUGGED TERRAIN IN DUPAGE COUNTY AND A BIODIVERSITY HOTSPOT

If you're looking for a vast, often-wild area (2,503 acres) to explore near Chicago, Waterfall Glen Forest Preserve is the perfect destination. This site is popular with hikers, runners, bicyclists, and other outdoor enthusiasts, but it is so large (and has so many trails) that it is easy to find peace and solitude. Waterfall Glen Forest Preserve—which surrounds Argonne National Laboratory—was my favorite south suburban hiking destination when I was in my 20s—when I had a lot more free time (i.e., before becoming a father, getting a real job and a boss who wasn't flexible about work hours). Here are a few things you can do at Waterfall Glen Forest Preserve:

See the waterfall. The preserve's popular tiered falls, which the Civilian Conservation Corps built in the 1930s, is located near the Rocky Glen waterfall parking lot. The Rocky Glen area, Old Oak Grove, and nearby Signal Hill (an area of limestone bluffs that overlooks the Des Plaines River in which the Illiniwek, Potawatomi, and, later, European fur trappers and traders lit signal fires to communicate across the area) were some of the first sections that were

© Andrew Morkes

> **Where:** Located in Darien, Illinois. There are three parking lots at Waterfall Glen. The main entrance is on Northgate Road. From I-55, take Cass Avenue 0.5 miles south to Northgate Road. Turn right on Northgate and go 400 feet to the lot. To reach the Rocky Glen waterfall parking lot, take Cass Avenue 1.5 miles south of Northgate Road to Bluff Road. Take Bluff Road 0.3 miles east to the lot. A third parking lot is on the east side of Lemont Road at 101st Street, one mile south of I-55.
>
> **Learn More:** Forest Preserve District of DuPage County (FPDDC), www.dupageforest.org/places-to-go/forest-preserves/waterfall-glen, www.openlands.org/2019/05/03/hyd-waterfall-glen
>
> **Hours:** Open daily from one hour after sunrise until one hour after sunset
>
> **Quick Review:** Waterfall Glen offers some of the most ecologically diverse open spaces in the FPDDC, 11 miles of trails, and wildlife and plant species in abundance. Dogs are allowed, but they must be on leashes under 10 feet long. (#62 on the map on page 12)
>
> **What You Can Do There:** Bicycling, Birdwatching, Cross-Country Skiing, Fishing, Hiking, Horseback Riding, Model Airplane Field (permit required), Orienteering Course, Photography, Picnicking, Running/Exercise, Snowshoeing, Youth Group Campground

acquired by the FPDDC in 1925. In 1973, the preserve received more than 2,200 acres of surplus land from the U.S. Bureau of Outdoor Recreation, and in that same year, the preserve was renamed Waterfall Glen Forest Preserve. There is excellent hiking in this area, especially near Sawmill Creek.

Enjoy a hike. There are more than 11 miles of trails through prairies, savannas, and forests. These include not only a 9.5-mile, crushed limestone loop trail and the 1.1-mile Tear-Thumb Trail (turf), but also plenty of unmarked side trails that you can use to explore the preserve. Just remember that not every side trail leads back to the main trail (i.e., keep your wits about you and consider using a GPS-enabled device!). Visit www.dupageforest.org/hubfs/Places-to-Go/Documents/Forest-Preserves/Waterfall-Glen-map-2020.pdf for a hiking map. In the northeast area of the park, the main trail connects to the Southern DuPage County Regional/Route 66 Trail (see the map at the aforementioned web link for details).

Climb the bluffs in the southwest corner of the preserve to enjoy stunning views of the Des Plaines River. The ancient dolomite that makes up these bluffs is three times older than the dinosaurs. These trails are steep, so take extra care when hiking.

Savor this biodiversity hotspot. Here are some impressive numbers. The preserve has 740 native plant species—75 percent of all the plants known to grow naturally in DuPage County. There are also more than 300 species of birds, fish, mammals, amphibians, and reptiles and another 300 invertebrates use the

> **DID YOU KNOW?**
>
> ✔ Waterfall Glen Forest Preserve is not named for its beautiful waterfall, but rather named in honor of Seymour "Bud" Waterfall, an early president of the district's board of commissioners.
>
> ✔ The area was once home to a federal launch site for Nike Zeus missiles.
>
> ✔ Argonne National Laboratory is a multidisciplinary science and engineering research center that is operated by the U.S. Department of Energy. Three of its scientists—Enrico Fermi, Maria Goeppert Mayer, and Alexei A. Abrikosov—have been awarded the Nobel Prize. The laboratory facilities are surrounded by 500 acres of woodlands, 330 acres of grassland and prairie, and 50 acres of wetlands and other habitats. You can learn more about touring the laboratory by visiting www.anl.gov/tour-the-lab.

forest preserve either year-round or during spring and fall migrations. Be sure to check out 773-acre Bluff Savanna, which covers the southern part of the preserve between Argonne National Laboratory and the Des Plaines River. The FPDDC says that it is "one of the highest ranked conservation areas in the county; the savanna contains 422 native plant species, including one state threatened and 36 of special concern. Individual black and white oaks, shagbark and bitternut hickories, and black walnuts range from 180 to 215 years old and are some of the oldest in the county." The forest preserve has also worked hard to restore 120-acre Poverty Prairie (which is located in the southwest corner of Waterfall Glen). It has more than 340 native plant species and resident animals.

Try your hand at orienteering, which is defined as finding your way in the woods or other locations with a map and compass. There is a permanently marked course in the preserve. Visit www.dupageforest.org/places-to-go/forest-preserves/waterfall-glen for a basic introduction to orienteering and beginner, intermediate, and advanced orienteering maps. This sounds like something fun to do with one's kids.

Enjoy challenging biking on hilly terrain. To protect the fragile ecosystems at Waterfall Glen, cyclists may only use the 9.5-mile loop limestone trail—which isn't anything to spin your wheels at.

Go fishing. Waterfall Glen is not known for its fishing, but some adventurous fishers hike down to the Des Plaines River, where they fish for northern pike, largemouth bass, rock bass, and other fish. Several old quarries in the park also provide opportunities for fishing.

NEARBY NATURE DESTINATIONS

Black Partridge Woods Nature Preserve, Cap Sauers Holding Nature Preserve, The Forge: Lemont Quarries, Keepataw Preserve, Red Gate Woods, Tampier Slough Woods

INDIANA

© Andrew Morkes

INDIANA DUNES NATIONAL PARK

ONE OF OUR NATION'S NEWEST NATIONAL PARKS AND A MIDWEST "BUCKET LIST" DESTINATION

Congress finally did something right! In 2019, Indiana Dunes National Lakeshore became Indiana Dunes National Park (IDNP), making it the country's 61st national park and the first in Indiana.

At 15,000-acres, Indiana Dunes National Park may be smaller than large national parks in the western U.S. such as Yellowstone, Glacier, or Yosemite, but it makes up for it in towering dunes, sandy beaches, and crashing surf; wetlands, rivers, prairies, swamps, bogs, marshes, and quiet forests; biodiversity (more than 350 bird species have been sighted at the park, and it features 1,100 native plants, which places it fourth in plant diversity among all NPS sites); and tons of history. Here are a variety of things you can do at the park:

Hike its 50 miles of trails on one or more 14 trail systems that will take you along Lake Michigan; along the Little Calumet River; through bogs, forests,

> **Where:** Indiana Dunes Visitor Center is located on Indiana State Road 49, between U.S. Highway 20 and Interstate 94 (1215 North State Road 49, Porter, IN 46304)
>
> **Learn More:** National Park Service, 219/395-1882, www.nps.gov/indu, www.facebook.com/IndianaDunesNPS
>
> **Hours:** General Hours: 6:00 a.m. to 11:00 p.m. (EST) (for day visitors)
>
> Nature Center: 9:30 a.m. to 4:30 p.m. (EST); closed on Thanksgiving Day, Christmas Day, and New Year's Day
>
> **Quick Review:** 15,000 acres of sandy beaches, dunes, wetlands, rivers, prairies, swamps, bogs, marshes, forests, and historical homesteads. 50 miles of trails. Amazing birdwatching and awe-inspiring biodiversity. Only 50 miles from downtown Chicago. (#63 on the map on page 14)
>
> **What You Can Do There:** Beach Fun, Bicycling, Birdwatching, Bookstore, Camping, Canoeing/Kayaking/Boating, Cross-Country Skiing, Dune Climbing, Educational and Self-Enrichment Opportunities and Classes. Fishing, Hiking, Horseback Riding, Local History, Nature Center, Photography, Picnicking, Running/Exercise, Snowshoeing, Swimming, Visitor Center

ravines, bur oak savanna, and wetlands; and to historic homesteads and other sites (including 1933 Chicago World's Fair Century of Progress Homes and The Bailly Homestead, a National Historic Landmark). Learn more: www.nps.gov/indu/planyourvisit/hiking.htm

View the fall colors by taking a hike on the Glenwood Dunes Trail System or on other trails.

Swim, build sandcastles, or simply relax on 15 miles of beaches.

Climb to the top of Mount Baldy and other famous dunes for beautiful views of Lake Michigan and perhaps even a glimpse of the Chicago skyline. (Note: The Mounty Baldy hike requires accompaniment by authorized staff.)

Enjoy one or more of 400 interpretive programs and ranger-led walks that are offered by the NPS at the park each year. Examples includes sunset hikes, campfire programs, and nature events for children.

Savor the wildflowers in the late spring, summer, and fall.

Visit the Paul H. Douglas Center for Environmental Education (www.nps.gov/indu/planyourvisit/deec.htm), which is open daily, except for federal holidays). You can take ranger-guided hikes, view live animals, try your hand at nature-based arts and crafts, and hike the Paul H. Douglas Trail through Miller Woods. There is also a Nature Play Zone at the center.

Check out the Visitor Center (www.nps.gov/indu/planyourvisit/idnlvc.htm), which is a good place to pick up brochures about the park and other area attractions, view short orientation videos, talk with rangers about destinations and activities at the park, and browse the center's bookstore.

Go birdwatching; more than 350 species have been identified as residing in or passing through the park during spring and fall migrations.

Visit historical sites. The NPS says that "there are over 60 historic structures including a National Historic Landmark, the Bailly Homestead. Other notable sites include Camp Good Fellow, the Chellberg Farm, and five houses from the 1933 Chicago World's Fair."

Participate in other outdoor activities such as fishing, boating, and horseback riding.

Attend the annual Indiana Dunes Outdoor Adventure Festival (www.dunesoutdoorfestival.com), which takes place throughout the Indiana Dunes region.

© Andrew Morkes

Camp at Dunewood Campground. There are 66 camp-sites (53 conventional drive-in sites and 13 walk/carry-in sites). Four sites (numbers 15, 30, 41, and 55) are wheelchair accessible. Learn more: www.nps.gov/indu/planyourvisit/campgrounds.htm.

Enjoy winter activities such as hiking, cross-country skiing, and snowshoeing.

Despite its small size, you will not be able to see and do everything that's available at the park in one visit. Check out www.nps.gov/indu/planyourvisit/itineraries.htm for tips on what to do if you have 1–2 hours, a half day, or an entire weekend to spend at the park.

MY HIKE

So, what did I do when I visited one of our nation's newest national parks? I took a fantastic, nearly five-mile hike on the Cowles Bog Trail System on a sunny, 90-degree day. According to the NPS, the Cowles Bog Trail, the park's "most rugged trail...highlights an area of such outstanding plant diversity that it was designated as a National Natural Landmark in 1965. This location, where Dr. Henry Cowles conducted much of his early work in plant ecology and succession in the early 1900s, remains an important focus for scientific study today." On this trail, which has moderate to very demanding sections, you'll see ponds, marshes, and black oak savannas, as well as enjoy stunning views of the lake from nearly 200-foot dunes.

> **WHO WAS DR. HENRY COWLES?**
>
> Dr. Henry Cowles was an American botanist and ecologist who published his doctoral dissertation on Lake Michigan dunes ecology in 1899. He was one of the first Americans to use the word "ecology," and he was an early advocate to protect the unique ecosystems and biodiversity of the Indiana Dunes.

This trail also features great views of spring wildflowers and fall colors.

It's important to remember that IDNP is an island of nature and biodiversity amidst industrial northeast Indiana. In some sections of the park, you'll hear the sounds of trains because the South Shore Line (www.mysouthshoreline.com) travels through much of the southern portion of the park. (The train line provides a great alternative for those who don't have their own vehicle who'd like to visit.) Some areas of the park border heavy industry, the Port of Indiana, and small, lakeside towns. On the western edge of the Cowles Bog Trail, you can see and hear U.S. Steel's monstrous manufacturing plant. As you walk on some areas of the beach, you'll see smokestacks in the distance. But this is the reality for many national parks or other NPS sites that are located in developed areas. The bright side of parks like these: at least some beautiful areas were saved. The dark side: why didn't far-thinking people a century or more ago seek to preserve more of these special places throughout the United States? However, the sights and sounds of industry and trains will be a temporary distraction as you enjoy Indiana Dunes National Park. Most of the trails at the park are situated in such a way that you will feel far removed from the modern world.

Beachwalkers   © Andrew Morkes

Pair a visit to IDNP with one to its neighbor Indiana Dunes State Park (IDSP; see page 227), which is located within the national park's boundaries. It features nearly 200-foot sand dunes rising above three miles of beautiful Lake Michigan beach, as well as black oak forests, bogs, creeks, marshes, and other natural wonders filled with rare plants and animals.

NEARBY NATURE DESTINATIONS

Coffee Creek Watershed Preserve, Indiana Dunes State Park, Moraine Nature Preserve

INDIANA DUNES STATE PARK

BEAUTIFUL BEACHES, PEACEFUL FORESTS, AND A BIODIVERSITY HOTSPOT

Less than an hour away from Chicago there is a wild and beautiful place that features towering sand dunes that rise above miles of Lake Michigan beach, as well as black oak forests, bogs, creeks, marshes, and other natural wonders filled with more than 1,000 plant and animal species. No, this is not Indiana Dunes National Park (one of our newest national parks and a wonderful place, too), but its neighbor Indiana Dunes State Park (see page 227). The park, which consists of 2,182 acres of wonderful, was established in 1925. You can do many things at IDSP, including:

✔ Visiting its Nature Center

✔ Having a picnic

✔ Going cross-country skiing (trails available, no ski rental) and snowshoeing

✔ Viewing the spring wildflowers or fall colors.

✔ Fishing (smelt only)

✔ Going birding. More than 300 species have been found in the park and, while birdwatching at Indiana Dunes is enjoyable in all seasons, spring and fall are wonderful times to visit to view the wide range of migrating birds.

Where: 1600 N. 25 E. Chesterton, IN 46304

Learn More: Indiana Department of Natural Resources, 219/926-1952, www.in.gov/dnr/parklake/2980.htm

Hours: Park: Sunrise to sunset (for day visitors)

Nature Center: 9:30 a.m. to 4:30 p.m. (EST)

Quick Review: A wild and beautiful place that features nearly 200-foot sand dunes rising above three miles of Lake Michigan shoreline, as well as black oak forests, bogs, creeks, marshes, and other natural wonders filled with more than 1,000 plant and animal species. Seven hiking trails (16 miles in all), and the 9.2-mile Calumet Trail travels along the park's southern edge. (#64 on the map on page 14)

What You Can Do There: Beach Fun, Bicycling, Birdwatching, Camping, Canoeing/Kayaking, Cross-Country Skiing, Educational and Self-Enrichment Opportunities and Classes, Fishing (smelt only), Hiking, Horseback Riding, Local History, Nature Center, Photography, Picnicking, Running/Exercise, Shipwreck, Snowshoeing, Swimming

View from the dunes © Andrew Morkes

✔ Visiting the J.D. Marshall Preserve, which is based around the *J.D. Marshall* shipwreck site; the ship sank on June 11, 1911

✔ Going camping at one of 147 campsites (including 134 with electrical hookups).

But on my most recent visit, I was there to hike and find solitude. And that is exactly what I found on a sunny, 90-degree day with a heat index of 104 degrees.

Indiana Dunes State Park has seven trails (16 miles in all) to choose from (additionally, the 9.2-mile Calumet Trail travels along its southern edge). There are easy, largely flat trails (Trail 2), moderate trails (Trails 3, 4, 7, and 10), and rugged trails (Trails 8 and 9). Visit www.in.gov/dnr/parklake/files/dunes_trail.pdf for more on the trails.

I chose Trail 9, which travels 3.75 miles through dense forests, wildflower-filled meadows, marshes, and tall dunes. The hike was both relaxing (the woods and the stunning lake vistas) and taxing (climbing the dunes and walking through the sand), but well worth it to anyone who is in relatively good health. (Note: You can also significantly shorten your hike by completing only a portion of each trail, so don't let the total distance of some of these trails deter you.)

Trail 9 does not take you to the beach (Trails 4, 7, 8, and 10 do), but there are several spots where you can follow a short path from the top of the dunes to the shore. That's what I did when I reached Furnessville Blowout. A blowout is an area in a sand dune ecosystem where wind has eroded bare areas of sand in a location that is otherwise covered by vegetation.

I headed from the cliff to the beach. I'd left a city of 2.7 million people not even 45 miles away the day before, and I quickly discovered that I was the only person on the beach, and it felt very good. Just the sound of the waves, the blue sky, the bright sun, the hot stones and sand underfoot, and the occasional gull and butterfly gliding overhead.

© Andrew Morkes

I sat on a log near the shore and had lunch. And when I finished, I spent an hour in the solitude.

I walked amongst the hot rocks and sand, occasionally cooling my feet in the water.

I searched for fossils, shells, and pleasantly shaped rocks.

I marveled at the various pieces of driftwood and wondered about their origin.

I waded again in the lake, and I saw what I thought was a pretty flower floating in the waves, but quickly realized that it was a downed butterfly. I gently scooped it out of the water. Its wings looked damaged, and I thought it was dead, but then it began moving in my hand. I placed it in a shady spot on the beach.

I sat back down on the log and gazed at the waves. The lake changed color—from blue, to light green, to grayish—as the clouds occasionally obscured its rays.

Fog kept building above the still-cold lake water and tried to work its way onto the shore. I knew Chicago was just across the lake, but I couldn't see it because of the haze—and that was fine with me.

The sun beat down relentlessly. Thunderheads formed above the water.

I looked around and instead of seeing and hearing people and cars and motorcycles and lawnmowers and jackhammers (a 6:30 a.m. treat

© Andrew Morkes

that was happening next door to my house every morning around the time I visited the park), I saw the area as it was for thousands of years. Rocks and driftwood, dunes and grass, the occasional bird and butterfly. And the only sounds I heard were the lapping of the waves on the shore and the occasional gull.

I thought of everything and then nothing as I soaked in the solitude.

I emptied my mind of troubles and just lived in the moment—the feel of the hot sand on my bare feet, a smooth rock in hand, the sound of the waves, the stunning dunes behind me.

Eventually, it was time to go. I checked on the butterfly but was surprised to see it was gone. I'd like to think that it did not become gull food, but rather that its wings were not as damaged as I thought. No matter. It was out of my control no matter what I desired.

A six-lined racrerunner lizard   © Andrew Morkes

I climbed to the top of the dunes and resumed my hike. Trail 9 provides excellent views of Lake Michigan. I eventually reached the Beach House Blowout, an area of stunning beauty. Six-lined racerunner lizards scampered away from me as I hiked along the trail.

Atop the dune, the wind was a blast furnace, so I took frequent water breaks. Several different species of dragonflies flew close by, then landed on plants and flowers near me. They seemed as curious about me as I did about them. They're so amazing to observe!

As I walked the narrow dune path, I saw the lake and the blowout on one side and the tops of the trees below on the other. It was a beautiful sight, and I was glad that I made the effort despite the blistering hot day.

The trail gradually descended into the forest, and the temperature felt 10 degrees cooler. I enjoyed the last mile or so of my hike, taking a portion of Trail 10 that ran past a beautiful marsh as a shortcut. It began to rain—just enough to cool me off and wet the trees and plants.

I finally reached my car and headed out of Indiana Dunes State Park. In just 40 minutes, I'd be in south suburban Chicago to pick up my son from grandma's house. A tent I'd ordered had been delivered there and was waiting to be assembled in her backyard. For our next camping trip—perhaps even to Indiana Dunes State Park.

NEARBY NATURE DESTINATIONS

Coffee Creek Watershed Preserve, Indiana Dunes National Park, Moraine Nature Preserve

© Andrew Morkes

JASPER-PULASKI FISH AND WILDLIFE AREA

THE PLACE TO SEE THE GREAT EASTERN SANDHILL CRANE MIGRATION EACH FALL AND SPRING

The sight of migrating birds in the sky has always moved me—even if it's just 20 or so geese flying in their familiar V-shaped formation. It's nice to know that some cycles of nature remain after human actions over the past 100+ years have caused nearly 500 animal species to become extinct as a result of overhunting, the destruction of prime natural habitat, and other factors. The migrating birds also help humans mark the passage of seasons. Seeing and hearing these beautiful birds tells us that change is in the air. Winter or spring is coming, and we better get ready. It makes me feel good to know that this time immemorial migration continues in the skies above America and other countries throughout the world.

Cranes are some of the most impressive and beautiful migratory birds. Some cranes—such as sandhill cranes—are numerous (although they're still vulnerable to habitat loss), while others, such as the whooping crane are endangered. The whooping crane, which only lives in North America, is our continent's tallest bird, with males approaching 5 feet when standing erect. In some cultures, cranes are symbols of happiness, good fortune, and eternal youth because of their fabled life span of a thousand years. Cranes don't live that long, of course, but they can live to more than 35 years old in the wild. It's kind of cool that cranes that passed over my head when I was in college still may be doing so this fall and spring. Way to go cranes!

> **Where:** 5822 Fish and Wildlife Lane, Medaryville, IN 47957 (about 83 miles southeast of downtown Chicago)
>
> **Learn More:** Indiana Department of Natural Resources, 219/843-4841, www.in.gov/dnr/fishwild/3091.htm
>
> **Hours:** Sunrise to sunset, year-round
>
> **Quick Review:** More than 8,140 acres of wetland, upland, and woodland habitat. A wonderful place to see the fall and spring eastern sandhill crane migration. At its peak in November and December, there are 10,000 to 30,000 cranes and other migrating birds on site per day. Hiking, fishing, hunting, and other outdoor activities are also available. (#65 on the map on page 14)
>
> **What You Can Do There:** Bicycling, Birdwatching, Cross-Country Skiing, Fishing, Hiking, Hunting, Photography, Picnicking, Running/Exercise, Snowshoeing

Heading to the Goose Pasture Viewing Area © Andrew Morkes

CRANE-WATCHING IN THE CHICAGOLAND AREA

You can see cranes in the lakes and wetlands throughout the Chicago area, but if you want to see thousands—if not tens of thousands—of cranes in one place, you should visit Jasper-Pulaski Fish and Wildlife Area as I did recently on a mid-November day. Jasper-Pulaski—which features 8,142 acres of wetland, upland, and woodland habitat—is located about 1 hour and 10 minutes from Chicago's far South Side.

Cranes and more than 325 other bird species make the round-trip each year along the Mississippi Flyway. They travel to and from their breeding grounds in Canada and northern Minnesota, Wisconsin, and Michigan to their wintering grounds along the Gulf of Mexico (primarily Georgia and Florida) and in Central and South America. (As the climate has warmed in recent years, some cranes and other birds are wintering in the Midwest.) The Indiana Department of Natural Resources reports that "sandhill cranes can be seen at Jasper-Pulaski from late September through December. Crane numbers peak in mid-November. Magnificent, noisy flocks are usually seen at the northern Indiana property from mid-October through mid-December." The cranes can be viewed at the Goose Pasture Viewing Area.

SANDHILL CRANE FACTS

Height: 3–4 feet

Weight: 6–12 pounds

Wingspan: 6–7 feet

Lifespan: 20–40 years

Flight speed and distance: 25–35 mph; cranes typically travel 200–300 miles in a day but can reach 500 miles with a good tail wind.

Source: Iain Nicolson Audubon Center at Rowe Sanctuary

MY QUEST TO SEE THE CRANES

I arrived at the parking lot of the Jasper-Pulaski crane viewing platform at around 4:20 p.m. (Eastern time). Sunset was at 5:30 p.m. I headed toward the crane viewing platform, which is short walk from the parking lot. Birdwatchers who have disabilities can use a separate entry to park next to the platform.

The viewing platform was filled with people gazing at the sky, cameras around their necks or tripods in hand. I headed to an area below the platform with a low wooden fence to grab a crane-viewing spot. Before me was a large green field surrounded in the distance by trees that had shed all of their leaves. The cranes forage for food in the wetlands and farm fields beyond the trees during the day and return to the area near the platform each night to socialize before heading to their night roosting spots. About 25 deer grazed in the field.

AND WE WAITED

The crowd buzzed with anticipation. A woman who was setting up a large tripod began telling stories to anyone who would listen about past visits to Jasper-Pulaski. Others played with their kids or dogs. One guy had an extended conversation with his dog: "I don't think you've ever seen so many deer…maybe two to three, but this is more than a dozen….Let's go read that sign to learn more about the cranes, although I'm not sure if you can read or not." Some people just sat in camp chairs and enjoyed the warm (65 degrees), but very windy, day. There were even a few foreign-language speakers in the crowd. I savored the musicality of Hindi and Dutch as I watched the sun gradually sink toward the horizon. It felt wonderful to soak in the warmth of the sun, watch the ever-changing clouds, and scan the sky for cranes.

AND THEN THEY ARRIVED

The cranes began arriving from the northeast. You first hear their distinctive throaty trill before you see them, and then you spot them in the sky. At any one time, there were up to 100 birds flying above us in beautiful formations. Some formations had an almost mathematical precision, while others were a little ragged. You could tell that the strong gusts were blowing them around a bit because some flocks would have to reorganize mid-air before resuming their journey. The cranes kept coming and coming. It was like a

© Andrew Morkes

© Andrew Morkes

bird highway. But we soon learned that there was no off ramp to our rest stop. From 4:30 to 5:30 p.m., the bird highway kept going, but only 10 or so cranes landed in the field below the viewing platform. There were more deer on the ground than cranes. Not the thousands I'd seen in the field in photographs and videos that you can view on YouTube. This was disappointing, but that's nature. Maybe the cranes were tired due to the 30- to 40-mile-per-hour winds and simply decided to head to their night roosting area. Who knows?

MAKING LEMONADE FROM LEMONS

My disappointment didn't last long. It was a great visit because I was able to take a short road trip. I like to drive through small towns, see farm animals (I saw an alpaca and a miniature horse at one farm), and otherwise see a bit of the Midwest. The 1,000+ cranes I saw were a beautiful and powerful reminder of nature's timeless cycles. The deer—including the one that bounded across the grass—were not too bad either. The weather was great, and it was fantastic to feel the sun and wind on my face. And the sunset, mixed with just the right amount of passing clouds—was picture-perfect.

NIGHTFALL

As it became clear that the birds would not be visiting the viewing platform field, the crowd began to disperse. But the sunset was stunning, the weather was nice (although windy), a few straggler cranes were still flying by, and I'd driven a little over an hour to get there, so I decided to stay. By 5:40 p.m., nearly everyone had drifted away as a crescent moon rose and the sky grew pinker. Soon, I was the last visitor on the platform and—regardless of the day's developments—it felt good to soak in the sunset (which reminded me of a Mark Rothko painting), the moonglow, and the solitude and darkness. As a city person, I'm always fascinated about how dark, still, and lonely the country gets at night. Eventually, I walked down the platform steps and took the trail through a small pine forest back to my car and the land of streetlights, houses, dinner plans, and my family.

FINAL THOUGHTS

You should head out to Jasper-Pulaski this fall or next spring to see this amazing crane migration. Your quest will allow you to experi-

© Andrew Morkes

ence the powerful cycles of nature. I'll be heading back to Jasper-Pulaski because, while I enjoyed my visit, I still want to see the cranes en-mass at the viewing platform. If you visit, I can't promise that you'll get the full crane experience or just the crane sky highway like I saw, but I can guarantee that if you love birds, you'll have an enjoyable time regardless.

TIPS BEFORE YOU GO

✔ Use this map (www.in.gov/dnr/fishwild/files/fw-jasper-pulaski.pdf) to help you to navigate Jasper-Pulaski. Note that there are multiple pull-off parking areas throughout the property, where you can park and explore.

✔ According to the IDNR, the best times of the day to see the cranes are: "Sunrise: Gigantic flocks rise and fly out of roosting marshes to Goose Pasture. The cranes socialize in the pasture for a while before flying out to feed in surrounding private land (agricultural fields). Sunset: Beginning about one hour before sunset, flocks of cranes kite into Goose Pasture from all directions. They gab and socialize again before returning to roosting marshes at dusk."

✔ Visit www.in.gov/dnr/fishwild/3109.htm to see a daily crane count and sign up for an email update on crane numbers.

✔ Bring binoculars, although there are a few viewing scopes at the viewing platform.

✔ Dress warmly, when necessary.

✔ Arrive at least one hour before sunrise and sunset to ensure a good viewing spot and so that you don't miss the cranes.

✔ Washrooms are available on site.

✔ In addition to crane watching, visitors to Jasper-Pulaski can also hike, fish (primary species include catfish, bluegill, and largemouth bass), and hunt (deer, quail, rabbit, squirrel, snipe, dove, sora rails, woodcock, waterfowl, and wild turkey are common).

NEARBY NATURE DESTINATIONS

Prairie Border Nature Preserve, Tippecanoe River State Park

OTHER CRANE-VIEWING SPOTS IN CHICAGOLAND

You can see cranes in smaller numbers at forest preserves, lakes, and other areas throughout Chicagoland, but these areas are known as popular resting spots for cranes as they migrate.

✔ Wolf Lake: https://hammondportauthority.com/wolf-lake

✔ Sand Ridge Nature Center: https://fpdcc.com/places/locations/sand-ridge-nature-center (see page 206)

✔ Little Red Schoolhouse Nature Center: https://fpdcc.com/places/locations/little-red-schoolhouse-nature-center (see page 175)

✔ Sagawau Canyon Nature Preserve: https://fpdcc.com/places/locations/sagawau-environmental-learning-center (see page 204)

KANKAKEE SANDS

BISON "HUNTING," WIDE OPEN SPACES, AND GREAT HIKING

There is nothing like hiking on a prairie or through a dense forest without seeing nearly another soul for more than four hours. And that is what I experienced during my last visit to Kankakee Sands on a sunny, humid day in the high-80s. This stunning natural area may be only 60–75 miles from Chicagoland and its 9.5 million residents, but it felt like a million miles away from city life.

Kankakee Sands is part of The Nature Conservancy's Efroymson Restoration, which the conservancy describes as "a biologically rich, diverse and healthy ecosystem of prairies and wetlands...[that is] one of the largest restorations east of the Mississippi River." More than 240 bird species live in or migrate through the Efroymson Restoration. The Restoration, when combined with the neighboring Willow Slough Fish and Wildlife Area, Beaver Lake Nature Preserve, and Conrad Savannah Nature Preserve, comprises more than 30,000 acres of protected natural habitat.

BISON QUEST

Bison were what first attracted me to Kankakee Sands. I'd seen bison in Yellowstone National Park, Theodore Roosevelt National Park, and in other places out west, but I really wanted to see our national mammal in its former range in the Midwest. At their peak in the mid-1800s, an estimated 30 to 60 million bison ranged from Canada to northern Mexico and from the Plains to Eastern forests. Indiscriminate killing of bison by white hunting parties nearly exterminated the bison. By about 1890, only 1,000 or so bison remained, including two dozen in Yellowstone. But ranchers, conservationists, and others stepped

> **Where:** Morocco, Indiana; Kankakee Sands is located in Northwest Indiana in Newton County, on either side of U.S. 41.
>
> **Learn More:** The Nature Conservancy, 219/285-2184, www.nature.org/en-us/get-involved/how-to-help/places-we-protect/kankakee-sands
>
> **Hours:** The Bison Viewing Area is open from 7 a.m. to dusk.
>
> **Quick Review:** A great place for bison and bird watching, hiking, and solitude. 8,400 acres of nature. More than 85 rare threatened and endangered species. My favorite hikes: Conrad Station Savannah Trail and especially the Grace Teninga Discovery Trail. (#66 on the map on page 14)
>
> **What You Can Do There:** Bicycling, Birdwatching, Hiking, Hunting, Photography, Picnicking, Running/Exercise, Snowshoeing

238   Nature in Chicagoland

© Andrew Morkes

in to save the last remaining animals. Today, there are approximately 150,000 bison in the United States, with nearly all found in the West.

But you don't need to go west to see bison. There are nearly 10 places in the Midwest where you can see bison, including Kankakee Sands, which has more than 70 bison. They are descendants of the Wind Cave National Park bison herd. You can find them on 1,100 acres of prairie that are located both north and south of the Kankakee Sands Office in the Bison Viewing Area. This acreage is surrounded by an electric fence that protects both the bison and visitors from potentially deadly encounters. You don't want to make a bison mad! They are massive creatures that can run up to 30–45 miles per hour.

Did I see any bison? Unfortunately not, despite visiting the Bison Viewing Area twice to try to catch a glimpse. The herd is hard to find at times in the vast grassland and savannah, but I enjoyed the "hunt," camera and zoom lens at the ready, and walking the fence line amidst the sunflowers, butterflies, and birds. I would've loved to see the bison, but sometimes the quest in itself is enough. Bison rangers are on duty at the Bison Viewing Area on the last Saturday of each month from 10 a.m. to 4 p.m. (EST) in case you want some extra help locating the bison.

HIKING AT KANKAKEE SANDS

There are several hiking trails at Kankakee Sands that you should check out. I hiked the 1.6-mile Conrad Station Savannah Trail and the two-mile Grace Teninga

Discovery Trail, which I'll discuss later in this story. Other trails include a Birding Overlook; the one-mile Wet Prairie Trail, which is open only when the bison are not in the north pasture; the 0.1-mile Monarch Trail, which features educational signs about monarchs and milkweeds; and the 0.3-mile Milkweed Trail at the Kankakee Sands Nursery, which features informational signs about milkweeds and pollinators. Visit www.nature.org/en-us/get-involved/how-to-help/places-we-protect/kankakee-sands for maps and other information about these trails. This link also provides information on a two-hour, self-driving tour you can take of this vast area. My advice: start your visit at the Kankakee Sands Office to get ranger advice and brochures. If the office is closed, there is an outdoor informational kiosk that will help you to learn about the area and help you to navigate this vast expanse.

Here is some information on the Conrad Station Savannah and Grace Teninga Discovery trails.

CONRAD STATION SAVANNAH TRAIL

On this trail, you will journey through sand dunes that have been populated by a dense forest of black oak savannah as well as a tallgrass prairie restoration. You'll also pass the ruins of the town of Conrad, which was platted in 1908 and founded by Jennie Conrad. A plaque, which is situated next to the ruins of the former hotel, tells the story of Jennie Conrad and her dreams of building a community. A June 27, 1990, story in the *Lowell Tribune* presents a much-harsher depiction of the town's founder, and her family's negative effects on the natural world in Indiana. I was fascinated by how quickly the town of Conrad returned to nature once it was abandoned in the early 1940s. Unfortunately, much of the damage that some members of the family inflicted on the environment in the 19th century remains today.

© Andrew Morkes

Here are the animals and plants that you might see at Conrad Station Savannah (courtesy of The Nature Conservancy):

✔ Birds: orchard oriole, barred owl, blue grosbeak, brown thrasher, vesper sparrow, field sparrow, lark sparrow, rose-breasted grosbeak, bobwhite quail, red-head-

© Andrew Morkes

ed woodpecker, scarlet tanager, rufous sided towhee, wild turkey

✔ Reptiles and Amphibians: blue racer, bull snake, Fowler's toad, grey tree frog, hognose snake, glass lizard, chorus frog, milk snake

✔ Insects: common green darter and ruby meadow hawk dragonflies, tiger swallowtail butterflies, great spangled fritillary butterflies, solitary wasps (nicknamed cicada killers)

✔ Plants: lead plant, smooth blue aster, Pennsylvania sedge, New Jersey tea, woodland sunflower, rough blazing star, wild blue lupine, downy phlox, purple milkwort, bracken fern, Carolina rose, sassafras, lanceleaf figwort, goat's rue, white oak, black oak, lance leaved violet

GRACE TENINGA DISCOVERY TRAIL

I enjoyed hiking through the dense forest and occasional prairies of the Conrad Station Savannah Trail, but I loved hiking the Grace Teninga Discovery Trail. This moderately strenuous loop trail takes you through a sand prairie ecosystem. You'll hike to the top of the dunes that once overlooked Beaver Lake, Indiana's largest lake at 7.5 miles long and 5 miles wide, which was drained in 1854 by Lemuel Milk, Jennie Conrad's father. (The destruction of Beaver Lake and all of its wildlife is a sad story of greed and selfishness that we unfortunately see being repeated more than 165 years later throughout the world.) I loved the Grace Teninga Discovery Trail because it allowed me to experience vast, wide open spaces where there were just a few black oak saplings, big blue skies, and beautiful scenery around every corner. I loved:

✔ Watching two butterflies dance together above the prairie

✔ Small armies of dragonflies engaging in aerial gymnastics amidst the backdrop of bright sun and blue sky; the one that flew into the back of my head at high speed later in my hike was not one of my favorites, but it certainly made me feel alive to the randomness of nature

✔ Seeing both a lizard and a plains pocket gopher scurry across the trail ahead of me

✔ Suddenly glimpsing a "herd" of prickly pear cactus atop one of the dunes—something I equate with the western united States, but that are also found in open sand and dry areas at Kankakee Sands, in the dunes along Lake Michigan, and at Powderhorn Marsh and Prairie (see page 58). Visit Kankakee Sands in July to see the cacti's beautiful yellow blooms.

✔ Seeing the vast array of currently blooming flowers and lamenting the one's I missed earlier in the year (I'm heading back in early summer to see them)

✔ The total absence of human voices, car horns, loud music being played from cars, and other "city noise."

Visitors planning a hike on the Grace Teninga Discovery should keep in mind that there is NO SHADE on the trail. Bring sunscreen and water, and wear a hat.

Here are the animals and plants that you might see at the Grace Teninga Discovery Trail (courtesy of The Nature Conservancy):

✔ Birds: field sparrow, grasshopper sparrow, lark sparrow, meadowlark, red-winged blackbird, red tail hawk, rough-legged hawk, turkey vulture, wild turkey

✔ Reptiles and Amphibians: chorus frog, eastern box turtle, legless lizard, leopard frog, milk snake

✔ Plants: lance-leaved coreopsis, showy tick trefoil, rattlesnake master, sweet everlasting, Western sunflower, round-headed bushclover, wild bergamot, prickly pear cactus, foxglove beardtongue, obedient plant, yellow coneflower, little bluestem, Indian grass

✔ Insects: ruby meadowhawk dragonfly, regal fritillary butterfly

TIPS FOR A SUCCESSFUL VISIT

✔ Bring plenty of water and sunscreen because many of the destinations at Kankakee Sands do not have a lot of shade.

✔ Pack mosquito repellent and be careful of ticks

✔ Be sure to visit the spots I cited in this story, but keep an eye out for small, pull-off parking areas throughout Kankakee Sands in which you can park and wander the prairies and savannahs.

✔ Dirt bikes, ATVs, horseback riding, and camping are prohibited.

✔ Be careful during hunting seasons and prescribed burns.

✔ Slow down, take a lot of photos (then put the camera away and create some memories that don't depend on technology), savor nature, and have some fun.

NEARBY NATURE DESTINATIONS

Iroquois County State Wildlife Area, LaSalle Fish & Wildlife Area, Willow Slough Fish and Wildlife Area

MICHIGAN

© Brittx, Shutterstock

GALIEN RIVER COUNTY PARK

**EXPLORE MARSHES, WETLANDS, AND WOODS VIA
A CHARMING BOARDWALK AND A 60-FOOT TOWER**

At Galien River County Park, an 86-acre preserve in Michigan's Harbor Country, you can explore marshlands and wetlands via a 600-foot-long boardwalk and enjoy river and marsh views during a 300-foot-long canopy walk that leads to a 60-foot-high overlook tower. There are also opportunities for fishing and wildlife viewing. More than 190 bird species have been recorded at the park according to Ebird.com, including yellow-throated warblers, cerulean warblers, Nashville warblers, blue-winged teals, red-bellied woodpeckers, northern flickers, red-

> **Where:** 17424 Red Arrow Highway, New Buffalo, MI 49117
>
> **Learn More:** Berrien County Parks Commission, https://berriencounty.org/1297/Galien-River-County-Park
>
> **Hours:** Sunrise to sunset, year-round
>
> **Quick Review:** A mix of upland and wetland habitats along the Galien River, with river and marsh views from an overlook tower and a boardwalk. All walkways are Americans With Disabilities Act-accessible. The park is closed in the winter. Dogs are allowed (on leashes). (#67 on the map on page 14)
>
> **What You Can Do There:** Birdwatching, Fishing, Hiking, Photography, Picnicking, Running/Exercise

breasted mergansers, sandhill cranes, Cooper's hawks, red-tailed hawks, and dark-eyed juncos. Visit https://ebird.org/hotspot/L2355891 for the complete list.

This is just the kind of small preserve that sometimes gets overlooked by tourists who are focused on nearby, big-name destinations such as Warren Dunes State Park or Indiana Dunes State or National Parks. But you should visit this park because it's beautiful (the fall colors are amazing), there's excellent birdwatching, it will be far less busy than the large state and national park properties in the area, and because kids love to have an adventure in the woods exploring boardwalks in the forest and climbing viewing platforms. Include a short visit to Galien River County Park as part of a day trip itinerary that features stopovers at larger preserves.

NEARBY NATURE DESTINATIONS

Chikaming Township Park & Preserve, Grand Mere State Park, Indiana Dunes National Park, Indiana Dunes State Park, Warren Dunes State Park, Warren Woods State Park

GRAND MERE STATE PARK

STUNNING BEACHES, MASSIVE SAND DUNES, AND ENJOYABLE HIKING TRAILS

Grand Mere State Park is not as popular as many other lakeside state parks in Michigan, Illinois, Indiana, and Wisconsin because it doesn't offer easy access to Lake Michigan (i.e., there is no parking lot next to or near the beach like at many other parks), it does not have camping facilities, and it only has one official trail. But the lack of these amenities makes Grand Mere attractive to people who do not want to visit a park filled with sunbathers, beachball boppers, and hordes of hikers. The type of people who visit this park are seeking solitude and the stunning natural beauty of beaches, dunes, blowouts, three lakes (North Lake, Middle Lake, and South Lake), and forests. There were once two additional lakes to the south of the park, but they succumbed to the various stages of ecological succession from water-based communities to terrestrial. The process continues at the remaining lakes, and you will find that areas that were once lake shoreline have been replaced by wetlands, bog forests, and dunes.

Many people visit Grand Mere State Park to hike. The 0.5-mile Nature Trail, which is paved (but needs some repairs), begins at the picnic shelter at South Lake and winds between the lake and the wooded dune areas of the park. At the end of the paved Nature Trail, you'll find a footpath that heads to the beach. There are approximately four miles of sandy, unmarked foot trails that travel through the dunes and to the beach. The MDNR does not offer a map of the sub trails, but you can visit MichiganTrailMaps.com to access a map. Hiking the trails is fun, but also demanding because of the loose sand (which gets intensely hot in the summer) and the steep paths that you'll need to climb to reach the tops of the dunes. The 100-foot climb to the crest of Baldtop Dune will provide a cardio challenge, but

Where: Thornton Drive, Stevensville, MI 49127; about 90 miles from downtown Chicago

Learn More: Michigan Department of Natural Resources (MDNR), 269/426-4013, www.michigan.org/property/grand-mere-state-park

Hours: Sunrise to sunset, year-round

Quick Review: Nearly 1,000 acres of beach, dunes, and woods. The park is rustic and has few amenities, but is perfect for those who like solitude. A Recreation Passport must be purchased in order to enter MDNR properties. Dogs are allowed, but they must be leashed. (#68 on the map on page 14)

What You Can Do There: Beach Fun, Birdwatching, Boat Launch (to Middle Lake), Cross-Country Skiing, Dune Climbing, Fishing, Hiking, Metal Detecting, Photography, Picnicking, Running/Exercise, Snowshoeing, Swimming

> **WHAT IS A BLOWOUT?**
>
> A blowout is an area in a sand dune ecosystem where wind has eroded bare areas of sand in a location that is otherwise covered by vegetation.

the views are amazing. Be sure to wear durable footwear, as well as pack drinking water, bug repellent, and sunscreen (because many trails do not offer much shade). The side trails can be confusing at times, so pay attention to your surroundings and be sure to tell someone about your hiking plans before heading out.

Birding is popular at the park—especially during the spring and fall migrations because Grand Mere lies on a major migration flyway. Nearly 250 species have been sighted at the park, including common loons; double-crested cormorants; great blue, green, and black-crowned night herons; yellow-rumpled, bay-breasted, chestnut-sided, and other types of warblers; eastern screech owls; hawks; egrets; and American bald eagles. A partial list of birds recorded at Grand Mere can be found at https://ebird.org/hotspot/L1116422. In addition to hiking and birding, you can have a picnic, fish, hunt, and explore a metal detecting area.

This is not a park for the casual beachgoer. If you're looking for that kind of destination, visit Warren Dunes State Park (also in Michigan), Indiana Dunes State Park, Indiana Dunes National Park, Illinois Beach State Park, and Kohler-Andrae State Park (in Wisconsin). All of these great destinations are covered in this book.

NEARBY NATURE DESTINATIONS

Chikaming Township Park & Preserve, Galien River County Park, Indiana Dunes National Park, Indiana Dunes State Park, Warren Dunes State Park, Warren Woods State Park

© Andrew Morkes

ISLE ROYALE NATIONAL PARK

SEE WOLVES AND MOOSE AND ENJOY WILDERNESS SOLITUDE

Isle Royale National Park is the farthest place from Chicago in this book. It's definitely in the "week-long (or more) getaway" category, but I included it because it's one of the most beautiful, wild, and interesting places I've ever visited in the Midwest. The park is 50 to 70 miles by boat or air from the "Copper Country" of Michigan's Upper Peninsula and 18 miles from its nearest point to Minnesota. Isle Royale National Park is 45 miles long and 9 miles wide at its widest point, encompassing 210 square miles. There are visitor centers and lodging facilities on

© Andrew Morkes

Where: A remote, pristine island in Lake Superior that is only accessible by passenger ferry, seaplane, or private boat

Learn More: National Park Service (NPS), 906/482-0984, www.nps.gov/isro, www.facebook.com/IsleRoyaleNPS

Hours: Open mid-April through the end of October

Quick Review: This is the place to go if you love solitude. The park had only 18,725 visits in 2019, according to the NPS. You'll need to take a ferry or seaplane to get to the island, and lodging accommodations are Spartan (or you can camp). But the payoff is worth it: rugged and stunning scenery; moose and wolves; the chance to see the Northern Lights; and as much hiking, kayaking, canoeing, camping, and scuba diving that you can fit into your schedule. Dogs, cats, and other pets are not allowed. (#69 on the map on page 14)

What You Can Do There: Backpacking, Birdwatching, Camping, Canoeing/Kayaking/Boating, Educational and Self-Enrichment Programs, Fishing, General Stores, Guided Boat Tours, Hiking, Lodges, Park Bookstore, Picnicking, Photography, Running/Exercise, Scuba Diving, Snowshoeing, Visitor Centers

the western (Windigo) and eastern (Rock Harbor) sides of the island. No cars are allowed on Isle Royale, so all your explorations must be made by foot or boat. You can take a day trip to the island, stay overnight in one of the two lodges that are located on opposite ends of the island, backpack across all or some of the island, or set up a basecamp that allows you to explore the island during the day and return to your campsite at night. Or you can dock your private boat at the island and sleep onboard. My advice: Stay at least two nights—but, ideally, more—because there are way too many things to do and see in just one day.

You probably have a lot of questions about visiting the park and what to do there. There are too many things to do to cover in a short article, but here are some answers to basic questions about visiting Isle Royale. The National Park Service provides a variety of resources that will address any unanswered questions. Each year, the park publishes a newspaper, *The Greenstone,* that covers everything that you need to know about the park. Visit www.nps.gov/isro/greenstone-newspaper.htm for the latest edition. The main IRNP website, www.nps.gov/isro, is another excellent resource. In the meanwhile, here are answers to some of your questions.

HOW DO I GET THERE?

My wife and I visited Isle Royale National Park more than 15 years ago, but every year I think about going back. We took the ferry to Rock Harbor from the pretty town of Copper Harbor, Michigan. The ferry trip takes a little more than three hours. Passenger ferries to Rock Harbor also depart from Houghton, Michigan, and Grand Portage, Minnesota. If you want to base yourself on the western side of the island (Windigo), there are two ferries that depart from Grand Portage, Minnesota. There are different fares and schedules, and be sure to make a reservation because ferry spots fill up quickly. You can also travel to the island via seaplane or private boat. Seaplanes depart daily to Rock Harbor and Windigo from Hancock, Michigan, and Grand Marais, Minnesota.

WHERE CAN I STAY?

During our visit, we stayed at the Rock Harbor Lodge, the island's only full-service lodging facility. The lodge complex has 60 basic rooms (all with Lake Superior views), 20 duplex cottages, a gift shop, dockside store (groceries, camping supplies, etc.), and two restaurants. Windigo (at the western edge of the island) has two rustic, one-room camper cabins; tent camping; and a store. There are 36 campsites located across the island, and they are accessible only by foot or watercraft.

WHAT CAN I DO?

That's a big question that depends on your interests and the duration of your visit, but here are some suggested activities.

Go hiking or backpacking. There are miles of trails that climb steep, rocky

The spectacular views at Isle Royale are worth the hard work of getting there.
© Andrew Morkes

ridges, travel through dense forests, descend into wetlands or bogs, or follow the shore of Lake Superior or inland lakes and creeks. This is wild and beautiful country; 99 percent of the park's land base is designated as wilderness. Most trails are demanding and require hikers to be in good physical condition. The NPS provides suggested hikes for day visitors and backpackers at www.nps.gov/isro.

View wildlife. Because of its remote location, only 18 species of mammals (including red fox, marten, Isle Royale red squirrel, otter, and beaver) are found on the island, compared to more than 40 on the surrounding mainland. But the relative dearth of mammals is made up for by the presence of gray wolves and moose, which make for stunning encounters (especially with moose) if you are lucky enough to see them. It's estimated that there were only 14 wolves on Isle Royale in 2019, down from 50 in 1980. The NPS is now in the process of reintroducing 20 to 30 additional wolves. As the number of wolves on the island has decreased, the number of moose has grown. There were an estimated 2,060 moose on Isle Royale in 2019, an increase of 1,160 moose since 2003. During our visit, we rounded a bend on one of our hikes and first saw a moose calf and then its towering mom looking on just off the trail. It was a wonderful and slightly scary moment. Scary because female moose can reach six to seven feet in height (at the shoulders) and weigh more than 900 pounds. We need not have worried. The moose and calf largely ignored us as we carefully passed.

More than 245 birds have been recorded as visiting or living on Isle Royale, including golden eagles, bald eagles, teals, snow geese, belted kingfishers, loons, sandhill cranes, cedar waxwings, indigo buntings, red-winged blackbirds, boreal chickadees, magnolia warblers, wrens, thrushes, vireos, great blue herons, black-crowned night herons, American white pelicans, woodpeckers, and owls.

You might also see frogs, eastern American toads, central newts, blue-spotted salamanders, western painted turtles, northern red-bellied snakes, and eastern garter snakes.

Visit www.nps.gov/isro/learn/nature/species-list.htm for a complete list of the mammals, amphibians, reptiles, birds, and fish you can see at Isle Royale.

Go kayaking or canoeing on Lake Superior or inland lakes. You can bring your own boat (ferry transportation services charge a fee for this service) and the Grand Portage-Isle Royale Transportation Line, which operates the Voyageur II and Seahunter III ferries, has a limited number of canoes for rent. You can also rent canoes and kayaks at Rock Harbor and Windigo.

Go fishing. Cast a line on Lake Superior or at the island's inland lakes via shoreline fishing or by boat, canoe, or kayak. You might catch lake sturgeon, northern pike, muskellunge, rock bass, walleye, lake whitefish, Coho salmon, chinook salmon, trout, or other fish.

Go scuba diving in Lake Superior to see underwater nature and the remains of more than 10 shipwrecks. Some noteworthy shipwrecks are the *Cumberland* (a passenger steamer that sunk in 1877), *Algoma* (a passenger steamer that went down in 1885), and the *Chester Congdon* (a bulk freighter that sunk in 1918). A diving charter service is available. You can also see shipwrecks along the shores of Pictured Rocks National Lakeshore (see page 250), as well as in the harbor of Munising, Michigan, via Glass Bottom Shipwreck Tours (https://shipwrecktours.com).

Take a ranger-led guided tour by boat or on foot. Visit www.nps.gov/isro/planyourvisit/guidedtours.htm for more information.

Island trail through a white birch forest
© Andrew Morkes

NEARBY NATURE DESTINATIONS

Nearby is a relative term because this is an island, but other interesting destinations in the Keweenaw Peninsula (a common departure area to Isle Royale, although you can also depart from Minnesota) include Baraga State Forest Area, Bête Grise Wetland Preserve, Brockway Mountain Wildlife Sanctuary, Estivant Pines Nature Sanctuary, and Keweenaw National Historical Park. The historic towns of Houghton and Hancock are excellent spots to base oneself out of during your Keweenaw Peninsula adventures.

PICTURED ROCKS NATIONAL LAKESHORE

WILDERNESS, WATERFALLS, GREAT HIKING AND CAMPING, AND MUCH MORE

Lake Superior © Andrew Morkes

If I had a second wife, she would be Pictured Rocks National Lakeshore, which is located in the Upper Peninsula of Michigan. I've hiked its beautiful trails, hunted agates and fossils and collected driftwood on its rocky shores, swam in its bone-chilling waters, kayaked its stunning lakes, and camped along its rivers and on its big bluffs since 1995. Pictured Rocks has served as my Fortress of Solitude ever since I first discovered it on a solo trip to the Upper Peninsula when I was in my mid-20s. I visit there frequently to recharge and disconnect from city life.

Where: Located about 380 miles northeast of downtown Chicago on the shores of Lake Superior in the wild and wonderful Upper Peninsula of Michigan

Learn More: National Park Service, www.nps.gov/piro

Hours: Open year-round, 24 hours a day, though many roads are closed by snow in the winter

Quick Review: Waterfalls, beautifully-colored cliffs, 42 miles of beach, camping, hiking, kayaking, and much more. Put this at the top of your nature "bucket list." Dogs (on a leash) are allowed in certain areas of the lakeshore. (#70 on the map on page 14)

What You Can Do There: Beach Fun, Bicycling, Birdwatching, Bookstore, Camping, Canoeing/Kayaking/Boating, Cross-Country Skiing, Dune Climbing, Educational and Self-Enrichment Opportunities, Fishing, Hiking, Horseback Riding, Local History, Lighthouse, Museum, Photography, Picnicking, Running/Exercise, Shipwrecks on the Beach and Near the Shore, Snowmobiling, Snowshoeing, Visitor Centers/Gift Shops

But I don't always travel alone to this National Park Service gem. More than 20 years ago, I shared this special place with my girlfriend (now wife), and I was also able to introduce one of my best friends and his 12-year-old son—along with my nine-year-old—to its wonders recently. The four of us camped for four days at 12-Mile Beach Campground, which overlooks Lake Superior—the largest freshwater lake in the world by surface area and the third-largest by volume. 12-Mile Beach (36 campsites) is my favorite Pictured Rocks campground, although you can camp at Hurricane River

Miners Castle © Andrew Morkes

(22 sites; also pretty special) and Little Beaver Lake (eight sites; I've never camped there) Campgrounds if you choose.

Many of the campsites at 12-Mile Beach Campground are situated on 200-foot, tree-lined bluffs that tower over the lake. I love this rustic campground (pit toilets, no showers, well water) because of its great views and easy access to the lake. As you sit by your campfire, you can gaze out at the ever-changing colors and composition of the lake and sky and watch mind-bogglingly stunning sunsets (the elevation and views of the beach and lake really makes them special). These sites are great because you can head down the bluff (via stairs) and reach the water's edge (or jump in the lake) in less than three minutes. The crashing of the waves will serenade you to sleep at night or provide a warm hello when you wake up in the morning. I'll trade the sounds of beeping car horns, the thunder of trucks, and cacophony of voices of Chicago for the sound of the waves, wind through the trees, and bird calls any day.

If you're not a camper there's plenty to do and see at Pictured Rocks. Here are some suggestions:

Check out visitor centers (www.nps.gov/piro/planyourvisit/visitorcenters.htm) that are located on the east and west ends of the 42-mile long lakeshore to get ideas for activities and view interpretative displays, as well as purchase useful nature guides, books about the history of the region, and nature-oriented toys and games.

Kayaking to Beaver Lake © Andrew Morkes

View 15 miles of awe-inspiring—and colorful—sandstone cliffs that rise 200 feet over Lake Superior, and check out the fascinating rock formations (such as Chapel Rock and Miners Castle) along the lake. Some are accessible via hiking trails, while others can be viewed by taking tours offered by Pictured Rocks Cruises (that launch from the City Dock at Bayshore Park in Munising, which is located at the western edge of the lakeshore).

Hike more than 100 miles of trails in Pictured Rocks' 73,000 acres. Visit www.nps.gov/piro/planyourvisit/upload/Day-Hikes-2017.pdf for some suggestions.

Enjoy an easy 1.5-mile hike from the Hurricane River Campground to the Au Sable Light Station (established in 1874), where you can visit a small museum, tour the lighthouse keepers' quarters (www.nps.gov/piro/planyourvisit/guided-tours.htm), learn about the isolated life of lightkeepers and their families (the lighthouse was staffed from 1874 to 1958), and tour the lighthouse (which involves carefully climbing the winding metal staircase to the top of the 85-foot lighthouse tower for stunning views of Au Sable Dunes and Lake Superior). On your return trip, head down to the lakeshore to view the remains of several shipwrecks (www.nps.gov/piro/learn/historyculture/upload/Shipwrecks.pdf) that lost the battle with the brown sandstone shelf that juts out into the lake in this area.

Take a guided tour or participate in other educational programs. Visit www.nps.gov/piro/planyourvisit/guided-tours.htm to learn more.

View some amazing waterfalls—most of which cascade into rivers, creeks, and the lake from a cliff of sandstone called the Munising Formation. Outside the lakeshore, check out waterfalls in the Munising area and the mother of all

NEARBY TOWNS

Grand Marais is a treasure of a small town located about three miles from the eastern edge of Pictured Rocks. When not camping, we stay in this picturesque village, which has a few good restaurants, a swimming beach, a lightkeeper museum, a rock and gem museum, gift shops, postal museum, Pickle Barrel House, and a few hotels. Groceries, gas, firewood, and outdoor supplies are also available.

Munising is a larger town that is located about 50 miles west of Pictured Rocks on the shores of Lake Superior. Things to do and see in Munising include waterfalls, Grand Island National Recreation Area, and boat tours of Pictured Rocks. There are many restaurants, grocery stores, gas stations, hotels, and gift shops.

UP waterfalls at Tahquamenon Falls State Park (which is about two hours east of Pictured Rocks; see page 262).

Hike to the top of the 300-foot-tall Grand Sable Dunes, the largest collection of perched sand dunes on Lake Superior. (Perched dunes are those that form on an existing coastal bluff.) These dunes, which feature stunning views of Lake Superior to the north and Grand Sable Lake to the south, contain some of the rarest plants in the Great Lakes (including orchids, Pitcher's thistle, Lake Huron tansy, and moonwort ferns). You might also see white-tailed deer, black bears, and bald eagles during your visit.

Enjoy the wide variety of animals throughout the lakeshore. This is black bear, wolf, and badger country. I've never seen a wolf at Pictured Rocks, once glimpsed a bear print on the beach early one morning on 12-Mile Beach, and had a harrowing encounter with an American badger as I read a book on the cliffs above Lake Superior. Other animals to look for include American marten, fishers, migrating songbirds, turtles, frogs,

Au Sable Light Station © Andrew Morkes

many types of fish, beaver, skunk, red squirrel, the occasional moose, and raptors (such as bald eagle, peregrine falcon, and barred owl). In all, the NPS reports that the national lakeshore contains nearly 300 native vertebrates, with 48 fish, 12 amphibian, five reptile, 182 bird, and 42 mammal species currently identified.

Depending on the season, go fishing, bicycling, snowshoeing, or cross-country skiing.

Enjoy a kayak or canoe trip on Little Beaver Lake, Beaver Lake, Grand Sable Lake, or Kingston Lake. During a recent trip, we paddled crystal clear Little Beaver and Beaver Lakes in the Beaver Basin Wilderness. The trip was peaceful and fun until we began hearing thunder in the distance despite a bright blue sky and few clouds. We got off the lake just a few minutes before the rain started. If you're an experienced kayaker with a sea kayak, consider a kayaking adventure on Lake Superior.

Savor the silence of a solitary walk on the beach, atop a dune, or in the forest.

Enjoy some of the best stargazing in the Midwest in the dark skies above Pictured Rocks.

RULES AND ADVICE

✔ The NPS Pictured Rocks website (www.nps.gov/piro) offers a wealth of information about visiting the lakeshore (much more than I could include in a book chapter). Visit this website for an official lakeshore map and for a variety of useful e-brochures.

✔ Camping is by reservation only at Recreation.gov. The online reservation system was implemented recently, and it's much easier than the old days when you simply had to show up and hope that a camping spot was available. Make your reservations ideally six months before your trip to ensure that you'll be able to reserve your desired campsite. If the campsites are full, check Recreation.gov frequently for cancellations. That's how I was able to book a recent four-night stay at 12-Mile Beach.

✔ Weather in the Upper Peninsula changes frequently—especially in areas near Lake Superior and Lake Michigan. During a recent early-August visit, the temperatures ranged from the low 70s in the daytime to the high 50s at night. We experienced one very rainy day, and the wind seemed to always be blowing at the lakeshore. Be sure to dress in layers and pack an extra blanket for cool evenings.

✔ Mosquitoes, ticks, and black flies can be annoying at various times of the year. Bring bug repellent.

✔ Be careful when walking along trails on the high cliffs above the lake. Trails and rocks can be slippery.

✔ There is no firewood for sale at the lakeshore, but you can use downed wood for campfires. Also, you can purchase firewood in the nearby towns of Grand Marais and Munising, as well as from entrepreneurial homeowners who sell firewood in self-service kiosks on their front lawns in these towns and on the roads near Pictured Rocks.

✔ Be careful when swimming in Lake Superior. Its average summer surface temperature is 59°F. Hypothermia can occur in as little as 10 minutes in the right conditions. With that said, our boys swam and played in the water for an hour or so at a time without experiencing any issues.

✔ Black bears live at Pictured Rocks, but I've only seen evidence of one in my 25 years of visits—a big footprint on the beach below our campsite. To stay safe from bears, you will need to take special precautions when you visit the lakeshore.

FINAL THOUGHTS

If 15,000-acre Indiana Dunes National Lakeshore, with its 15 miles of shoreline, can be upgraded to a national park, so should the much-larger (77,000 acres and 42 miles of shoreline) and equally, if not more, stunning Pictured Rocks National Lakeshore also receive this vaunted status. Pictured Rocks can easily be categorized with the great national parks of our country. But don't take my word for it, take a trip to this North Woods jewel yourself sometime this summer or fall.

NEARBY NATURE DESTINATIONS

Grand Island National Recreation Area, Muskallonge Lake State Park, Seney National Wildlife Refuge

© Andrew Morkes

© Andrew Morkes

SENEY NATIONAL WILDLIFE REFUGE

WILDERNESS, TOP-NOTCH BIRDWATCHING AND WILDLIFE VIEWING, AND RECREATIONAL ACTIVITIES

Seney National Wildlife Refuge is located in the eastern region of the Upper Peninsula of Michigan—which is one of my favorite places to vacation. Visiting the refuge is certainly not a day trip from Chicago. It will take you at least 6.5 hours from Chicago to reach this spectacular wildlife refuge. But the trip is worth it—especially if you pair it with a visit to Pictured Rocks National Lakeshore (which is about a half-hour away) and other adventures in the Upper Peninsula.

Seney National Wildlife Refuge is vast (more than 95,000 acres), and it will take many visits to see and do everything at this preserve that was established in 1935 to protect migratory birds and other wildlife. The wildest sections of the refuge are the 25,150-acre Seney Wilderness Area (the second-largest wilderness area in Michigan) and the Strangmoor Bog Natural Landmark (which is mainly wetland and features unusual plants such as the carnivorous pitcher plant). These areas are roadless and challenging to access. Here are a few things you can do at the refuge.

Check out the Visitor Center, which has maps, informational booklets, a bookstore, bird identification guides and binoculars for loan, and other resources.

> **Where:** 1674 Refuge Entrance Road, Seney, MI 49883 (located in the Upper Peninsula of Michigan about 415 miles from downtown Chicago)
>
> **Learn More:** U.S. Fish & Wildlife Service, 906/586-9851, www.fws.gov/refuge/Seney/visit/plan_your_visit.html
>
> **Hours:** Refuge: Dawn until dusk, daily
>
> Visitor Center: Open May 15 to October 20 from 9 a.m. to 5 p.m. daily including all federal holidays.
>
> Marshland Wildlife Drive: Open May 15 to October 20 during daylight hours including all federal holidays.
>
> Fishing Loop: Open May 15 to September 30 during daylight hours including all federal holidays.
>
> **Quick Review:** A beautiful nature area that includes forests, wetlands, marshes, swamps, bogs, creeks, human-made pools (to increase the number of migratory birds that use the refuge), and the Manistique and Driggs Rivers. There is hiking, biking, snowshoeing, and cross-country skiing trails and an auto tour. Dogs are allowed (on a leash). (#71 on the map on page 14)
>
> **What You Can Do There:** Birdwatching, Canoeing/Kayaking (only on the Manistique River), Cross-Country Skiing, Educational and Self-Enrichment Opportunities and Classes, Fishing, Gathering [wild edibles (mushrooms and berries), pine boughs, and deer antlers], Geocaching, Hiking, Hunting, Nature Center, Photography, Picnicking, Snowshoeing, Visitor Center

Go hiking. There are 10 miles of hiking trails at the refuge. They can be used in the spring, summer, and fall. In the winter, the trails are groomed for cross-country skiing. You can snowshoe and cross-country ski in nearly every area of the refuge. The Seney area receives approximately 145 inches of snow a year on average, so having enough snow to enjoy winter sports will be no problem. A trail list is available at www.fws.gov/refuge/Seney/visit/plan_your_visit.html.

Take the Marshland Wildlife Drive, a seven-mile, one-way auto tour, where you can pull off and view wildlife (especially migratory birds) from three observation decks and other locations. More than 200 species of birds have been recorded at the refuge, including common loons; ruffed grouse; ospreys; trumpeter swans; American woodcock, Wilson's snipes, and other sandpipers; bald eagles; downy and hairy woodpeckers; American kestrels, peregrine and other types of falcons; herons; American bitterns; egrets; more than 20 types of warblers; and sandhill cranes. The refuge has been designated as an "Important Bird Area" (www.audubon.org/important-bird-areas) because it is the home to an endangered or threatened species and it provides key habitat for birds. A birding checklist is available at www.fws.gov/refuge/Seney/visit/plan_your_

© Andrew Morkes

visit.html. During your visit, you also may see white-tailed deer, snowshoe hares, beavers, muskrats, otters, foxes, minks, and perhaps even a black bear, moose, or bobcat in wilder areas of the refuge.

Enjoy kayaking or canoeing on the Manistique River, which travels through the southern part of the refuge. You can bring your own boat or rent one from an outfitter in the nearby town of Germfask. No boating is allowed on the refuge's marshes or pools.

Go fishing on waterways that are located on the refuge's 3.5-mile Fishing Loop or in other approved areas. You might catch northern pike, brown and brook trout, yellow perch, bluegill, pumpkinseed, walleye, and smallmouth bass. You'll need a Michigan state fishing license.

Head 80 miles northeast to the refuge's Whitefish Point Unit on the shore of Lake Superior to see thousands of migrating birds in the spring and fall, including the Great Lakes piping plover (a federally endangered species that nests on its beach from April/May to August). More than 335 bird species have been documented at the unit. If you decide to visit the Whitefish Point Unit, be sure to stop at **Tahquamenon Falls State Park** (41382 W. M-123, Paradise, MI 49768) on your way. This nearly 50,000-acre park features some of the most beautiful and largest waterfalls in the Upper Peninsula. Its Upper Falls, one the largest waterfalls east of the Mississippi River, is more than 200 feet across and has a drop of nearly 50 feet. See page 262 for more information about this must-visit destination.

NEARBY NATURE DESTINATIONS

Fox River State Forest, Hiawatha State Forest, Newberry State Forest, Pictured Rocks National Lakeshore

South Manitou Island Lighthouse © Dennis Yockers, National Park Service

SLEEPING BEAR DUNES NATIONAL LAKESHORE

TOWERING SAND DUNES, WILDERNESS, AND STUNNING NATURAL BEAUTY

I broke the side-view mirror of our car pulling too quickly out of the driveway on the way to Sleeping Bear Dunes National Lakeshore. But it didn't ruin my trip. On the same vacation, we ran out of gas due to a faulty gas gauge, and even that did not ruin my trip. I received a speeding ticket from a Michigan state police officer (who, incidentally, I later learned had swum the challenging Straits of Mackinac), and that did not ruin our trip (although the costly ticket lightened my wallet). Why? Because this national lakeshore on the northwestern shore of Michigan's lower peninsula is a "bucket list" kind of place that created that "back from vacation" feeling we all get, but for much longer than the typical vacation. I maintained that wonderful vacation feeling because Sleeping Bear has rugged bluffs that reach as high as 450 feet above Lake Michigan, beautiful sandy beaches, jaw-dropping sunsets, beguiling scenery (woods, forests, wetlands, lakes, and creeks), amazing stargazing, and activities for almost every outdoor interest. Here are just a few of the great things you can do at the lakeshore:

Hike more than 100 miles of trails. There are paths for hikers at every skill

> **Where:** Near Empire, Michigan, along the shoreline of Lake Michigan, including North and South Manitou Island (about 335 miles from Chicago)
>
> **Learn More:** National Park Service (NPS), 231/326-4700, www.nps.gov/slbe
>
> **Hours:** Grounds: Open year-round, 24 hours a day, though some roads may be closed by snow in the winter
>
> Visitor centers, campgrounds, and other facilities have separate hours; contact the NPS for the latest information.
>
> **Quick Review:** More than 71,000 acres of beaches; bluffs; dunes; northern hardwood, pine, and boreal forests; wetlands; bogs; fens; 26 inland lakes; several rivers and streams; and historic buildings. Excellent wildlife viewing. An entrance fee is required. Pets allowed (on a leash). (#72 on the map on page 14)
>
> **What You Can Do There:** Beach Fun, Bicycling, Birdwatching, Bookstore, Camping, Canoeing/Kayaking/Boating, Cross-Country Skiing, Dune Climbing, Educational and Self-Enrichment Opportunities and Classes, Fishing, General Store, Guided Tours, Hiking, Horseback Riding, Hunting, Lighthouse, Local History, Museum, Photography, Picnicking, Running/Exercise, Scuba Diving, Snowshoeing, Swimming, Visitor Center

level. Fourteen trails are available, and you can learn more about them at www.nps.gov/slbe/planyourvisit/trails.htm. The 3.5-mile Dunes Trail to Lake Michigan is the most-challenging trail in the park because it travels through rolling dunes, which can be especially demanding on hot and sunny days. You can also use the four-mile Sleeping Bear Heritage Trail for hiking, biking, and cross-country skiing.

Relax on the beach. There are miles and miles of beaches where you can swim, sunbathe, toss a Frisbee, or have other types of fun. Visit www.nps.gov/slbe/planyourvisit/beaches.htm for a list of recommended beaches.

Climb the Dune. The Dune is located about five miles north of the town of Empire on M-109. At the base of the dune there is a picnic area and the Dune Center, which has modern restrooms and a bookstore. As a visitor who has climbed the Dune many times, I know that this popular activity is not for the fainthearted. It is a strenuous climb that will tax your muscles and endurance. But the payoff is worth it: You're king of the hill and the views are fantastic. But be sure to bring water and a map, wear shoes (or at least bring them in your backpack because the sand gets very hot), and stay on the trails to avoid getting lost and walking into sandy areas that may collapse (it happens) due to erosion or other factors.

Go camping. There are 179 modern sites at Platte River Campground, 88 campsites at the more rustic D.H. Day Campground, and backcountry camping at walk-in campgrounds at the lakeshore and on the Manitou islands.

Pierce Stocking Scenic Drive Observation Deck © Kerry Kelly, National Park Service

Visit North and South Manitou Islands. The islands are a part of the Sleeping Bear Dunes National Lakeshore, and 15,000 acres of North Manitou Island are (with the exception of the village area) managed as a wilderness area. You can hike and otherwise explore the islands as a day visitor or as an overnight camper. Regular ferry service to both islands for campers and day trips to South Manitou is provided by Manitou Island Transit (https://manitoutransit.com). For a fee, you can even bring your canoe or kayak on the ferry.

Take the Geology Auto Tour. A tour brochure and maps are available at the Philip A. Hart Visitor Center, and you can learn more at www.nps.gov/slbe/planyourvisit/geologytour.htm.

Visit the historic logging village of Glen Haven, where you can check out the Cannery Boathouse museum, Glen Haven General Store, and a fully restored 1920s blacksmith shop.

Enjoy winter activities. Sleeping Bear Dunes National Lakeshore receives about 120 inches of snow on average each year, and the flakes begin to fall as early as mid-November. As a result, winter sports such as cross-country skiing and snowshoeing are very popular at the lakeshore. There are approximately 50 miles of marked, but ungroomed, trails at the lakeshore, and portions of the Sleeping Bear Heritage Trail are groomed. There are also ranger-led snowshoe hikes.

NEARBY NATURE DESTINATIONS

Arcadia Dunes: The C.S. Mott Nature Preserve; Betsie River State Game Refuge; Manistee National Forest

Tahquamenon Falls—Upper Falls © Andrew Morkes

TAHQUAMENON FALLS STATE PARK

WONDERFUL WATERFALLS, GREAT HIKING TRAILS, AND MUCH MORE

Tahquamenon Falls State Park is a must-visit if you are planning a trip in the Upper Peninsula—especially to its eastern region. It is the second largest state park in Michigan. Tahquamenon Falls features some of the most beautiful and largest waterfalls in the Upper Peninsula. Its Upper Falls, one the largest waterfalls east of the Mississippi River, is more than 200 feet across and has a drop of nearly 50 feet. It has a maximum water flow of 50,000 gallons per second. The waterfalls are colorful (due to tannins that leach into the water from a cedar swamp upstream), loud (in an invigorating way), and awe-inspiring. Here are a few other reasons I love this park.

Great hiking. There are more than 40 miles of trails, so if you want to escape the waterfall-viewing crowds, you can hike into wilderness areas. At its website, the park offers trail suggestions for day visitors and those who plan to spend a few days at Tahquamenon Falls. To reach some of the waterfalls and visit other areas, you'll need to climb many steps (more than 115 steps to check out the Gorge View at the Upper Falls) and traverse hilly terrain. The park offers the following advice: "Our trails include hills, exposed roots, muddy spots, and occa-

Where: Located in Michigan's Upper Peninsula, about 450 miles from downtown Chicago

Upper Falls: Upper Falls Drive, Newberry, MI 49868

Lower Falls: 6999 N. Lower Campground Lane, Paradise, MI 49768

Rivermouth: 32130 W. South River Road, Paradise, MI 49768

Learn More: Michigan Department of Natural Resources (MDNR), 906/492-3415, www.michigan.org/property/tahquamenon-falls-state-park, www.michigansparadise.com

Hours: 8:00 a.m. to 10:00 p.m., year-round (day visitors)

Quick Review: This nearly 50,000-acre rugged and heavily forested park stretches more than 13 miles. It offers amazing waterfalls, 13 inland lakes, camping, hiking, kayaking, fishing, and much more. A Recreation Passport must be purchased in order to enter MDNR properties. Dogs are allowed, but they must be leashed. (#73 on the map on page 14)

What You Can Do There: Beach Fun (at Whitefish Bay), Bicycling, Birdwatching, Café/Restaurant, Camping, Canoeing/Kayaking/Boating (including rentals), Cross-Country Skiing, Educational and Self-Enrichment Opportunities, Fishing, Gift Shop, Hiking, Horseback Riding, Hunting, Photography, Picnicking, Restaurant/Brewpub, Running/Exercise, Shipwrecks (nearby at Whitefish Point), Snowmobiling, Snowshoeing, Swimming (only in Whitefish Bay)

signal down trees. Allow yourself extra time, wear sturdy footwear, and bring water on every hike." Additionally, cellphone service is limited within Tahquamenon Falls, so be sure to give someone your itinerary before heading out on the trails.

The North Country Trail (https://northcountrytrail.org) travels 16 miles within the park, including the trail between the Upper and Lower Falls.

Spectacular wildlife viewing. More than 125 species of nesting birds have been sighted at Tahquamenon Falls (including bald eagles, spruce grouse, pileated woodpeckers, and a variety of songbirds and waterfowl), plus black bears, moose (especially along M-123 between Paradise and the Lower Falls) wolves, coyote, fishers, otters, beavers, mink, deer, fox, and porcupine.

The option to participate in a variety of other activities, including:

✔ camping (there are three campgrounds and backcountry sites) or you can stay at the Tahquamenon Falls Lodge

✔ boating (you can rent canoes and rowboats at the Lower Falls concession from Memorial Day weekend to mid-October)

✔ fishing for brown trout, walleye, yellow perch, muskie, northern pike, smallmouth bass, and other fish

✔ picnicking, with picnic spots located throughout the park

✔ viewing fall colors

✔ cross-country skiing (there are four miles of regularly groomed, single-track trails, as well as opportunities for backcountry skiing)

✔ snowmobiling (only on designated trails)

✔ snowshoeing (there are nine miles of marked snowshoe trails at the Upper Falls and Lower Falls and day-use areas, as well as opportunities for backcountry snowshoeing).

NEARBY NATURE DESTINATIONS AND OTHER ATTRACTIONS

Great Lakes Shipwreck Museum, Muskallonge Lake State Park, Newberry State Forest Area, Pictured Rocks National Lakeshore, Seney National Wildlife Refuge (including its Whitefish Point Unit), Tahquamenon Brewery & Pub (at the park), Two Hearted River State Forest, Whitefish Point Bird Observatory, Whitefish Point Underwater Preserve

© Andrew Morkes

WARREN DUNES STATE PARK

STUNNING BEACHES, FUN IN THE DUNES, AND CAMPING

Warren Dunes State Park is a family friendly destination in southwestern Michigan that's very popular in the summer, but worth a visit in any season. It's one of the busier Michigan state parks, drawing visitors from Illinois, Indiana, and Michigan. Warren Dunes has three miles of Lake Michigan shoreline, and its rugged dunes loom up to 260 feet above the lakeshore. Many people visit the park to sunbathe and swim, but you can also rent stand-up paddleboards, kayaks, and paddleboats at the north end of beach parking lot 2 from mid-May through Labor Day. Here are a few other fun things to do at Warren Dunes:

Have a picnic. Five picnic areas are located along the main entrance road leading to the beach. You can pack your own lunch, or purchase food from one of six food trucks that are located at the beach parking lot from May through October.

Enjoy a hike. Trails journey through dunes and forests of oak, maple, cottonwood, and beech trees. They range from 0.33 miles to 1 mile, but you can combine several trails to create a longer hike. The Mt. Randal Trail involves challenging dune climbs, but it also offers great views of the lake, dunes, and forest. After you've conquered the dunes (Tower Hill is the most-popular climbing spot), run (or tumble) down to the lake and enjoy a refreshing dip.

Go camping. The Mt. Randal Campground has tent camping, cabins and lodges, modern restrooms, concessions, electrical hookups at all sites, and a playground, while the Hildebrandt Campground is more rustic, and no electrical service is available.

Where: 12032 Red Arrow Highway, Sawyer, MI 49125

Learn More: Michigan Department of Natural Resources (MDNR), 269/426-4013, www.michigan.org/property/warren-dunes-state-park

Hours: Sunrise to sunset, year-round

Quick Review: More than 1,950 acres of beach, dunes, wetlands, and woods—with a sand-bottom creek thrown in for good measure. An entrance fee is required. Dogs are allowed in a 2.5-mile dog beach north of the third beach parking lot but must be leashed. (#74 on the map on page 14)

What You Can Do There: Beach Fun, Bicycling (in parking areas only), Birdwatching, Camping, Cross-Country Skiing, Dog Beach, Dune Climbing, Educational and Self-Enrichment Opportunities and Classes, Hang Gliding (permit required), Hiking, Hunting, Kayaking, Local History, Metal Detecting, Photography, Picnicking, Running/Exercise, Swimming, Snowshoeing

© Anne Kitzman, Shutterstock

Participate in weekly nature programs that will help you to learn about dune ecosystems, Lake Michigan, and the variety of flora and fauna you can see at the park.

While you are in the area, check out **Galien River County Park,** which is about 10 miles southwest of Warren Dunes. At this 86-acre park you can explore marshland via a boardwalk and enjoy river and marsh views from an overlook tower. There are opportunities for fishing and wildlife viewing. The park is closed in the winter. Visit https://berriencounty.org/1297/Galien-River-County-Park for more information. Another option is **Grand Mere State Park,** which is located about nine miles northeast of Warren Dunes. This nearly 1,000-acre park has one mile of Lake Michigan beach, three lakes, hiking trails that travel through woods and dunes, a metal detecting area, and opportunities for hunting and fishing. Visit www.michigan.org/property/grand-mere-state-park to learn more.

NEARBY NATURE DESTINATIONS

Galien River County Park, Grand Mere State Park, Indiana Dunes National Park, Indiana Dunes State Park, Warren Woods State Park

---

GOOD ADVICE

The park is often busy on summer weekends, and there may be wait times for vehicles entering the property. The MDNR has created the daily Recreation Passport program so that visitors can purchase the passport in advance online at http://mdnr-elicense.com to avoid long lines at the park's entrance. The advance passport purchase option is offered seven days a week from mid-May through early September.

WISCONSIN

The view from Parnell Tower in the forest's North Unit. It is the highest point in the forest.
© Tony Savino, Shutterstock

KETTLE MORAINE STATE FOREST

HIKE, BIKE, PADDLE, SWIM, AND OTHERWISE ENJOY THE OUTDOORS IN A VAST GLACIER-CREATED WONDERLAND

The area we now know as Kettle Moraine State Forest was created more than 10,000 years ago when two glacial lobes collided, causing the creation of ridges, valleys, kettle lakes, eskers, kames, and other landforms. This topography makes for beautiful views, challenging (but rewarding) hikes and biking experiences, and a diverse range of ecosystems for plants and animals.

I wish I had 52,000 words to cover the 52,000 acres at Kettle Moraine State Forest, but that's not possible in this type of book. So, instead, let me present the big picture of what you can do at its main Northern and Southern Units, and then you can learn more about your favorite activities (fishing, biking, horseback riding, etc.).

The Northern Unit—which is the forest's largest unit—is a linear property spread over 22 miles between Glenbeulah and West Bend, Wisconsin. At this sprawling 30,000-acre property, you can:

> **Where:** Wisconsin. The forest's Southern Unit is about 100 miles northwest of downtown Chicago, while its Northern Unit is about 140 miles north of downtown.
>
> **Learn More:** Wisconsin Department of Natural Resources (WDNR), Southern Unit (262/594-6200, https://dnr.wisconsin.gov/topic/parks/kms), Northern Unit (https://dnr.wisconsin.gov/topic/parks/kmn)
>
> **Hours:** Grounds: 6 a.m. to 11 p.m., year-round (day visitors)
>
> Visitor centers, campgrounds, and other facilities have separate hours; contact the WDNR for the latest information.
>
> **Quick Review:** Approximately 52,000 acres of glacial hills, valleys, forests, kettle lakes, wetlands, rivers, ponds, and prairies. There are multiple units of this vast nature area. A portion of the 1,200-mile Ice Age Trail (www.iceagetrail.org) travels through the forest. A vehicle admission sticker is required (it can be purchased online or onsite). Pets must be on a leash, except in designated areas that allow them to be off leash. (#75 on the map on page 14)
>
> **What You Can Do There: Backpacking,** Bicycling, Birdwatching, Camping, Canoeing/Kayaking/Boating, Cross-Country Skiing, Educational and Self-Enrichment Opportunities and Classes, Environmental Learning Center, Fishing, Gift Shop, Hiking, Horseback Riding, Hunting, Local History, Natural History Museum, Photography, Picnicking, Running/Exercise, Snowshoeing, Swimming, Visitor Centers

✔ **Check out the Henry S. Reuss Ice Age Visitor Center,** where you can get maps and brochures, view exhibits and a movie about the area's glacial history, participate in educational programs, and peruse the wares in its gift shop.

✔ **Go camping.** The Northern Unit has approximately 370 campsites. There are four campgrounds: Mauthe Lake Campground, Long Lake Campground, Greenbush Group Campground (which offers sites for larger groups), and the New Prospect Horseriders Campground. Campground maps are available at https://dnr.wisconsin.gov/topic/parks/kmn/maps.

✔ **Hike on a variety of loop, linear, and nature trails.** Some can also be used for mountain biking, snowshoeing, and skiing. Visit https://dnr.wisconsin.gov/topic/parks/kmn/maps for a list of trails.

✔ **Enjoy a bike ride.** You can bike the 6.5-mile crushed limestone Lake-to-Lake Bike Trail. It connects the Mauthe and Long Lake Recreation Areas and is popular with families because it traverses gentle terrain.

✔ **Go swimming.** There are three swimming beaches—two at Long Lake and one at Mauthe Lake.

✔ **Enjoy wildlife viewing.** Some of the best spots to view wildlife are found at the Ice Age Visitor Center, Jersey Flats Prairie, Spruce Lake Bog State Natural Area, Mauthe Lake, and Haskell Noyes State Natural Area.

✔ **Participate in a variety of other activities,** including spring wildflower viewing, boating, fishing, horseback riding, hunting, picnicking, and fall color viewing.

The Southern Unit is 61 miles east of Madison, Wisconsin, and 37 miles southwest of Milwaukee. Here are a few things to do at its 22,000 acres:

✔ **Spend the day hiking.** There are hiking trails available on the Emma Carlin, John Muir, Scuppernong, and Nordic trails, as well as the Ice Age National Scenic Trail. Visit https://dnr.wisconsin.gov/topic/parks/kms/recreation/hiking for more information and self-guiding nature trail guides for six trails.

✔ **Pitch a tent.** There are several campgrounds. The Ottawa Lake Campground is the only year-round campground in the Southern Unit. It has 100 camp sites, including 65 electrical sites. There is also a cabin designed especially for people with disabilities. The Pinewoods Campground has 101 campsites but no sites with electrical hookups. It also has a playground and a 24-hour quiet zone loop (which prohibits pets, radios, and mechanical device noise). Camping at Pinewoods is available from mid-May through mid-October. The Whitewater Lake Campground is a primitive facility with 63 campsites. There are also group campgrounds, walk-in campsites, a campground for horseback riders, and three designated trail shelter sites along the Ice Age National Scenic Trail for backpackers. Visit https://dnr.wisconsin.gov/topic/parks/kms/recreation/camping for more information.

✔ **Visit the Natural History Museum** to learn about glaciers, plants and animals, and park facilities; pick up maps; take part in a ranger-led nature program; and check out the offerings at its Trading Post Gift Shop.

✔ **Enjoy many other activities,** including spring wildflower viewing, mountain biking, horseback riding, boating, fishing, kayaking, canoeing, swimming, hunting, fall leaf peeping, and winter sports.

NEARBY NATURE DESTINATIONS

Glacial Blue Hills Recreation Area, Huiras Lake State Natural Area, Kohler-Andrae State Park, Long Lake Recreation Area, Milwaukee River Tamarack Lowlands & Dundee Kame, Richard Bong State Recreation Area (near Kettle Moraine's South Unit)

KETTLE MORAINE SCENIC DRIVE

The Kettle Moraine Scenic Drive is a 115-mile auto tour that journeys through six Wisconsin counties and the Northern and Southern Units. The northern end of the drive begins near Elkhart Lake in Sheboygan County and the southern end begins at Whitewater Lake in Walworth County. You can stop to picnic or enjoy a short hike, go camping or stay in a hotel along the way, visit historic towns, shop, and otherwise enjoy the trip. Visit https://dnr.wisconsin.gov/topic/parks/kmscenicdrive for maps, a list of attractions, and other useful information.

KOHLER-ANDRAE STATE PARK

CAMPING, SURF AND SAND, AND MUCH MORE

Beachtime © Andrew Morkes

"Will that cool sandbar still be at the lake like last year? Do you think the raccoons will visit our campsite again? Can we make s'mores by the fire like last year?" These were just a few of the questions my seven-year-old peppered me with as we drove to Kohler-Andrae State Park, which is just two miles south of Sheboygan, Wisconsin. And the answer was "YES" to all three questions, although I kept my salty language about last year's marauding raccoons to myself as we drove.

There's a lot more to Kohler-Andrae than a great sandbar that provides the chance for water roughhousing, curious raccoons, and the opportunity to make s'mores over a crackling fire. I've camped at this beautiful state park during many summers, and here are some of my favorite things:

Camping. There are 137 camp sites to choose from—all within about a 10-minute walk to Lake Michigan. Visit https://dnr.wisconsin.gov/topic/parks/kohlerandrae/recreation/camping for a campsite map.

Where: 1020 Beach Park Lane Sheboygan, WI 53081

Learn More: Wisconsin Department of Natural Resources, 920/451-4080, https://dnr.wisconsin.gov/topic/parks/kohlerandrae

Hours: Open for visitors 6 a.m. to 11 p.m., year-round; open 24/7 for campers

Quick Review: A beautiful state park alongside Lake Michigan with dunes, beaches, hiking (trails range from 0.25 miles to 2.5 miles), camping, a nature center, more than 150 bird species, more than 400 known plant species (including 50+ tree species), and much more. (#76 on the map on page 14)

What You Can Do There: Beach Fun, Bicycling, Birdwatching, Camping, Canoeing/Kayaking/Boating, Cross-Country Skiing, Educational and Self-Enrichment Opportunities and Classes, Equestrian, Fishing, Gift Shop, Hiking, Hunting, Local History, Nature Center, Photography, Picnicking, Playground, Running/Exercise, Snowshoeing

© Andrew Morkes

A wealth of hiking trails through sand dunes, wetlands, river marsh, and pine and hardwood forest. I suggest the Creeping Juniper Nature Trail Loop; Kohler Dunes Cordwalk; Ancient Shores Trail; and Black River Marsh Boardwalk, although there are other trails, too. Trails range from 0.25 miles to 2.5 miles. Visit https://dnr.wisconsin.gov/topic/parks/kohlerandrae/recreation/hiking for more information.

The Sanderling Nature Center, which features live animals; nature films; a small gift shop; interpretive exhibits; presentations by naturalists, geologists, and other scientists; and a domed viewing area where you can survey the lakeshore. A perfect destination when your kids get bored of making s'mores and sandcastles.

Wildlife in abundance. During your stay, you might see white-tailed deer, red fox, muskrats, coyotes, frogs, toads, snapping turtles, chipmunks, and many other animals. More than 150 bird species (e.g., ducks, gulls, woodland warblers, bald eagles, vireos, sparrows, sandhill cranes, and herons) live in or migrate through Kohler-Andrae. Visit https://dnr.wi.gov/topic/parks/name/kohlerandrae/pdfs/kabirdlist.pdf for a list of commonly seen birds. More than 400 plant species are found in the park, including more than 50 different types of trees.

Great opportunities for biking on some trails and on the park's main roads.

Close proximity to Sheboygan, which has a pleasant marina, an up-and-coming downtown, a riverfront boardwalk [check out the Duke of Devon (739

Riverfront Drive, Sheboygan, WI 53081, 920/458 7900) for tasty beer and food], and other attractions. While at the lakefront, be sure to visit the wreck of the *Lottie Cooper,* a three-masted schooner that sunk in 1894, but was salvaged in 1992. It's now on display at Harbor Center Marina.

THINGS TO KNOW BEFORE YOU GO

✔ Reservations are accepted April through October. You can reserve a campsite at https://dnr.wisconsin.gov/topic/parks/camping or by calling 888/947-2757. I strongly suggest reserving your site a few months ahead of time because the park fills up quickly in warm weather.

✔ As in most state parks, the campsites are relatively close together. So, if you get the wrong neighbors, it can be hard to enjoy the solitude of nature. Tip: Before you go, spend some time reviewing the campsite map (https://dnr.wi.gov/topic/parks/name/kohlerandrae/pdfs/kacampmap.pdf) to determine which site best fits your needs. Park staff can also provide advice over the phone, and, when you visit the registration office, a three-ringed binder is available that provides details on all 125 sites (should you choose not to reserve a site in advance). Also, a strategically placed clothesline and/or a screen tent can create an extra level of privacy at your site.

The wreck of the *Lottie Cooper.*
© Andrew Morkes

✔ Don't expect a wide beach. High water-levels and beachfront erosion have reduced the size of the beaches at Kohler-Andrae in recent years. There is certainly plenty of beach and dunes to make your visit enjoyable, but if you're expecting wide, flat sandy beaches, you should head north for a daytrip to Deland Park (715 Broughton Drive, 53081) in Sheboygan.

✔ Amenities available at Kohler-Andrae include firewood and ice for sale, showers, modern bathrooms, and a picnic area that offers a playground, volleyball court, and baseball diamond.

NEARBY NATURE DESTINATIONS

Deland Park, Harrington Beach State Park, Kettle Moraine State Forest

RICHARD BONG STATE RECREATION AREA

MORE THAN 25 ACTIVITIES FOR OUTDOOR ENTHUSIASTS

What a difference a few days make. Richard Bong State Recreation Area was once slated to become a jet fighter base, but in 1959, the efforts of local citizens thwarted this plan three days before concrete was to be poured for a 12,500-foot runway. Their hard work—and restoration efforts—helped to create a beautiful multiuse destination that is easily reachable from both Milwaukee and Chicago. A wealth of activities are available at Richard Bong State Recreation Area. During your visit, you might see hikers, horseback riders, runners, fishermen (and women), model airplane flyers, kayakers, and hang gliders—or actually enjoy trying one or more of these activities yourself. Here are a few things that I like to do at this beautiful recreation area:

Hiking. There are more than 16 miles of hiking trails. There are eight hiking trails that range in length from the 0.7-mile Visitor Center Nature Trail (which is a great place to see migrating and resident waterfowl at Wolf Lake) to the 8.3-mile Red Trail (on its north end, you can see how the area's topography looked before the Air Force

> **Where:** 26313 Burlington Road, Kansasville, WI 53139 (located about 71 miles northwest of downtown Chicago)
>
> **Learn More:** Wisconsin Department of Natural Resources (WDNR), 262/878-5600, https://dnr.wisconsin.gov/topic/parks/richardbong, https://bongnaturalistassociation.org
>
> **Hours:** 6 a.m. to 11 p.m., year-round (day visitors)
>
> Visitor centers, campgrounds, and other facilities have separate hours; contact the WDNR for the latest information.
>
> **Quick Review:** Approximately 4,500 acres of wetlands, ponds, lakes, grasslands, and forests. There is something to do for visitors who have almost any outdoor interest—from hiking and biking; to snowshoeing and cross-country skiing; to kayaking, hang gliding, and fishing. A vehicle admission sticker is required. Pets must be on a leash, except in designated areas that allow them to be off leash. (#77 on the map on page 14)
>
> **What You Can Do There:** ATV/Off-Highway Motorcycle Trails, Beach Fun, Bicycling, Birdwatching, Camping, Canoeing/Kayaking/Boating, Cross-Country Skiing, Educational and Self-Enrichment Opportunities and Classes, Fishing, Gift Shop, Hiking, Horseback Riding, Hunting, Nature/Visitor Center, Photography, Picnicking, Playground, Running/Exercise, Snowshoeing, Special Use Zone (model airplanes, rockets, hang gliders, hot air balloons, etc.)

> **WHO WAS RICHARD BONG?**
>
> The recreation area is named after Major Richard I. Bong, a Wisconsin native who was the leading American fighter pilot during World War II. While piloting a P-38 fighter jet, Bong downed 40 enemy aircraft in the Pacific Theatre. He received the Congressional Medal of Honor and other accolades for his bravery and skill as a pilot. Tragically, Bong was killed test piloting the first Lockheed jet fighter plane—just six months after returning stateside. He was only 24 years old. A memorial was dedicated to Bong in his hometown of Poplar, Wisconsin. The **Richard I. Bong Veterans Historical Center** (305 E. 2nd Street, Superior, WI 54880) honors the memory of Major Bong and all World War II veterans. Visit https://bongcenter.org to learn more about Bong and the center (which features a fully restored P-38 Lighting, M-60 Tank, and other exhibits) and its hours of operation.

began altering the site). The WDNR touts the Blue Trail (4.2 miles) as one of the area's nicest trails. On this path, you'll trek through prairie and woodland, past wetlands, and around Wolf Lake. Visit https://dnr.wisconsin.gov/topic/parks/richardbong/recreation/hiking for detailed information about the trails.

Birdwatching. Bring your binoculars, camera, and bird identification guide because more than 230 bird species have been recorded at the recreation area. Some of the birds that you might see include eastern phoebes, blue-gray gnatcatchers, eastern bluebirds, eastern kingbirds, chickadees, nuthatches, yellow warblers, bobolinks, black terns, least bitterns, mute swans, ring-necked ducks, pied-billed grebes, American coots, Henslow's and savannah sparrows, Wilson's snipes, willow flycatchers, great egrets, sandhill cranes (large numbers in the fall), northern harriers, rough-legged hawks, short-eared owls, and northern shrikes.

Biking. Off-road biking trails are available on the paths north of Highway 142. Bike paths include the Gray Trail (1.7 miles), Yellow Trail (4.4 miles), Orange Trail (6.4 miles), and Red Trail (8.3 miles). Visit https://dnr.wisconsin.gov/topic/parks/richardbong/recreation/biking for detailed information about the trails. Note: Bicyclists 16 years of age and older must have a state trail pass.

Camping. There are two modern campgrounds with a total of 217 campsites, and 54 have electric hookups. A cabin designed specifically for people with disabilities is also available.

That's just the beginning of what you can do at this recreation area. Visit https://dnr.wisconsin.gov/topic/parks/richardbong for info about the other outdoor recreation opportunities that are available at this southern Wisconsin gem.

NEARBY NATURE DESTINATIONS

Case Eagle Park, Honey Creek Wildlife Area, Kenosha Silver Kettle Moraine State Forest-South Unit, Lake County Park, Peat Lake State Natural Area

NATURE ESSAYS

EIGHT REASONS WHY I LOVE THE OUTDOORS—AND YOU SHOULD, TOO

Ninety-five percent or more of my outdoor adventures have been wonderful and fulfilling—and some have even been life changing. But if you hike, camp, boat, and otherwise enjoy outdoor activities, there will be the occasional mishap, or two, or three. But these mishaps have never deterred me from heading outside. But...during my more than 30 years as an adult hiker, I've:

✔ Had my cornea scratched by a windblown tree branch as I hiked at Cap Sauer's Holding Nature Preserve (see page 149) in a southwest suburb of Chicago. I was supposed to go on my first date with my future wife the next day but had to cancel. Years later, she loves recounting my "excuse" and says that she still doesn't believe a word of it.

✔ Rode Lake Superior's version of the *Titanic* as my wife and I traveled to Isle Royale National Park (see page 246) from the Keweenaw Peninsula in Michigan. We left the harbor on a pretty summer morning with calm waters. Within an hour into the four-hour trip, the boat was tipped so far to the side due to rough winds and high waves that all we saw from the windows was blue sky. I spent most of the trip lying on the floor of the ship's washroom. The rest of the passengers were either sprawled on the floor or slumped in their seats. My wife was the ONLY person on the boat to not get sick.

✔ Been impaled by a jumping cholla cactus, which embedded itself in my arm as I hiked at Organ Pipe Cactus National Monument in southern Arizona. It was not fun pulling it out of my arm. Some call the jumping cholla the most feared and hated cacti in the desert because its hollow spines make it hard to extract from human skin. But I couldn't see getting back on an airplane to go home with a prickly piece of Arizona in my arm, so out it came.

✔ Developed serious cellulitis from a bug bite after visiting North Park Village Nature Center (see page 49) with my son in the "wilderness" of the Northwest Side of Chicago. Yes, urban nature centers are dangerous places!

✔ Was nearly bitten by a wolverine on the bluffs above Pictured Rocks National Lakeshore (see page 250) in the Upper Peninsula of Michigan, almost walked into a buffalo that was hanging out just on the other side of a trail on a hill I was ascending at Theodore Roosevelt National Park in North Dakota, and had several interactions with venomous snakes on the rivers and trails in several midwestern, western, and southwestern states.

✔ Almost developed hypothermia while on a solo hike in a drenching rain in the dense hilly forests at Pictured Rocks National Lakeshore. This story is ironic because it was summer, and 25 miles away back in town, my wife was enjoying (as she told me later) a relaxing 70-degree, rain free day by the lake with our toddler son. Even though Pictured Rocks is known for its microclimates, you would not believe this story unless you lived it. I shivered constantly as I walked, felt clumsy on my feet as the cold rain came down, and knew I'd have a real issue if I stopped moving and generating heat. Luckily, I'd packed a silver emergency heat-saving poncho, and donned it as I began my walk out of the woods—despite knowing that I probably looked like some sort of cheesy 1950s B-movie alien.

So, why do I keep hiking, camping, kayaking, snowshoeing, and what-not outside despite these challenges? There are many reasons, but here are eight reasons why I love the outdoors:

1. To escape urban life. If you live in a metropolitan area with millions and millions of people like I do, it's wonderful to escape miles of concrete, endless lines of rush-hour traffic, assorted noise issues, unhealthy air, and tons of people by visiting nature areas. If you visit the Palos Forest Preserves and other large forest preserves in Chicagoland and travel off the main trails, you may not see another person during your entire hike. If you live in a big city, when was the last time you could say you were out and about and didn't run into someone doing something? Being alone helps you to slow down, reset, and appreciate life.

2. Being outdoors gets you away from *Fortnite*, Facebook, and other f-ing technological diversions. Despite purporting to make us more connected, studies show that Facebook and other social media sites make many of us depressed. There have been documented cases of people dying from playing video games too much. Fresh air and sunlight can provide a free mental fix, and a good hike is a great cure for the modern world.

3. For the opportunity to see animals in their natural habitats. Sure, I almost was gored by a bison, but it was one of the most memorable moments I've had in the wild. It was exciting to suddenly be just feet from a massive bison and have to think quickly to extricate myself from the situation. (The bison also did his part by not charging me.) I've also had the chance to glimpse a grizzly bear just across a river in Yellowstone; view a pack of wild horses at Theodore Roosevelt National Park; watch hundreds of dragonflies hover above Visitation Prairie during the partial eclipse in Chicago in 2017; see a coyote emerge from its den as I crouched in a creek bed in a forest preserve in Cook County; see thousands of pollywogs churn the water into a frenzy as I walked along a stream; and view many other wild animals.

4. It keeps me aware of the fragility of nature and the need to protect it from further development. In addition to its beauty, nature provides many practical benefits to humans. Wetlands serve as reservoirs for rainwater that would otherwise floods our streets and homes. Trees produce oxygen and sequester carbon dioxide (an overabundance of carbon dioxide is worsening global climate change). Studies also show that trees increase the value of our homes, help us to fight stress, and reduce crime.

5. The great outdoors has not been Disneyfied. Unlike our often predictable, planned, and scheduled world, anything can happen when you hike. If you take precautions (e.g., extra water, cell phone, compass, bear spray, etc.), this feeling of unpredictability can be exhilarating.

6. There is something very Zen about not having a destination or plan, but just making a journey where your feet and eyes take you. When things get stressful, I often head to the woods with no expectations or plans, just a goal of wandering to see what new things I can discover. There is something joyful about making unexpected discoveries as you wander the natural world.

7. Nature helps build friendships and memories. I began a long and rewarding friendship with my friend Imad (who was working as a freelancer at my company at the time) because he saw a photo I had in my office of Edward Abbey, the author of *Desert Solitaire* and many other great books). Our shared love of nature led us to our first hike together at Cap Sauer's Holding. My good friend Dave and I, although living in different states, go camping together each year at Wisconsin's Kohler-Andrae State Park (see page 270), Lake Kegonsa State Park (https://dnr.wisconsin.gov/topic/parks/lakekegonsa), or Pictured Rocks National Lakeshore with our kids. Nature serves as a great meeting place to keep our 30+-year friendship going. Finally, my cousin Janet and I traveled together to Yellowstone National Park and had the time of our lives. We climbed Mount Washington, viewed mega- and micro-fauna, and simply marveled at the mind-blowing scenery. I'll always treasure this time we had together in our 30s before life got more complicated.

8. Provides me with the chance to spend time with my wife and son. My father took my brother and I hiking all the time, and I've enjoyed passing on the love of nature to my son. Forty years later, I still remember my first hikes with my dad, and 40 years from now, when I'm 91, I hope my son will have fond memories of all the times we spent outdoors. And I hope the cycle continues with his kids and grandkids.

I'm sure you have other reasons for enjoying the outdoors. Regardless of what gets you outside, the key is to get off the couch and savor the great destinations that in our area. The occasional misadventure is usually just a minor aspect of the wonderful memories that you've created for yourself and your family.

18 TIPS FOR CAMPING WITH KIDS

© Andrew Morkes

I went on my first camping trip at age 10. I've pitched a tent everywhere from Chaco Culture National Historical Park in New Mexico, to Sleeping Bear Dunes (see page 259) and Pictured Rocks (see page 250) National Lakeshores in Michigan. I've camped alone and with friends, but camping with children is a completely different experience. There's nothing worse than hearing "I'm bored" when you're miles from play dates, a library, or the comfort of one's Lego- and game-filled home. And the unfamiliar surroundings of nature (noisy crickets and other strange sounds, midnight visits from raccoons and opossums, the absolute darkness of the woods at night, etc.) can be scary or disconcerting at first to kids used to city life.

I took my now 11-year-old son camping for the first time when he was four, and we have visited Lake Kegonsa (https://dnr.wisconsin.gov/topic/parks/lakekegonsa) and Kohler-Andrae (see page 270) State Parks in Wisconsin and Pictured Rocks in Michigan. I treasure these trips with my son, my high school friend Dave, and his now 14-year-old son. It's wonderful to share my love of nature with my son, to continue a 30-year friendship with my friend, and let our sons build a friendship that will hopefully last past their dads' time on Earth. But camping with your kids can be challenging at times. Here are some tips that will help you to have a great camping trip with your children:

1. Conduct a test run. Pitch your tent and have a backyard campout to acclimate your children to the camping experience and troubleshoot issues with your tent, air mattresses or cots, and other camping equipment.

2. Choose your campsite wisely. Some parks allow you to reserve your site ahead of time. Since many parks fill up quickly, it's best to book at least six months before your stay. Additionally, take geographic location and nearby amenities into account when selecting a site. If you have young children, you'll want to choose a site that is near bathroom facilities and showers. My personal preferences are a campsite that is closest to trails and a lake or river (if there is a body of water where you are camping). Finally, carefully review campground layouts in order to select a campsite that is far from the main road as possible to reduce the risk of danger from cars and RVs.

3. Allow the kids to bring a favorite toy or two. This helps them to feel comfortable in their new surroundings. When he was younger, my son brought a favorite stuffed animal or two. My friend has brought his son's oversize Tonka trucks that both boys enjoyed playing with, and my son brought his bug-catching gun and viewing equipment—also a hit.

4. Be flexible and ready to do the unexpected. On our first night at Kohler-Andrae, our kids lobbied for a night swim in Lake Michigan. Out came the flashlights, and after a 10-minute hike, we jumped into the lake, the stars twinkling above us. This unplanned swimming sojourn turned out to be a lot of fun, and it was interesting to play in the lake at night. Of course, we stayed very close to shore given the dangers of swimming in a massive lake at any time of day.

© Andrew Morkes

5. Orient your kids. Point out major landmarks ("The washroom/showers are four campsites from our campsite by that large oak tree.") to help your children become comfortable with the campground and reduce their chances of getting lost.

6. Be safe. Give your child a whistle that he or she can blow if lost or in danger. Also, every child should have their own flashlight. Also, teach them your campsite number (and loop number, if applicable) so—if they become lost—they can give it to adults.

7. Let them try new things. Camping provides an excellent way to let your kids try out new things that they would never do in the city. Let your children experiment at an appropriate level for their age. A few years back, my friend and I let our eight- and 11-year-olds light the fire and bug deterrent candles under close supervision. We let them pound tent stakes, make s'mores, and throw wood into the fire. As they have gotten older, we've allowed them to cut firewood using saws and small axes.

8. Set up a play tent. Last year, our sons used my red screen tent as a police station. This year, it was a spy headquarters. Giving your kids a place of their own—a sort of camping clubhouse—allows them to have quality non-parent time. A screen or other type of tent also serves as a great group destination if it rains or if the campsite is buggy.

9. Become an expert. Okay, maybe not an expert, but a devotee of something in nature that you can teach your children about and expand their understanding of the world. I love astronomy and shared a little planet and star talk with Dave and the kids. Dave is an arachnid aficionado, and during one hike, he taught us about the web building and hunting habits of several types of spiders. The kids had a lot of fun catching ants and tossing them into spiders' webs, at which, depending on the spider, the ant would be wrapped up like a mummy in seconds or stung with immobilizing poison and left on the web like a steak in an icebox for a midnight snack. Additionally, many campsites have nature programs that are led by rangers and naturalists.

10. Let them get dirty. It's understandable to want to apply city rules to camping, but that's impractical. Let your children play in the sand and dirt, get a little messy after carrying firewood or making s'mores, or engage in other outdoor activities. Keeping clean is a losing battle when you camp. Hopefully, you'll camp in a place where there are showers that you can use at the end of the day, or where there's a lake everyone can jump into to wash away some of the dirt.

11. Be prepared for downtime. While you want your kids to be out hiking, swimming, fishing, boating, and doing other outdoor activities, they may get bored of these activities, not feel 100 percent, or just want to stay in camp sometimes. Due to some last-minute work at home, I was not as prepared as I would have liked for downtime during our last camping trip. And on the first morning of this recent trip, my friend and I paid dearly for our lack of preparation. We were forced to listen to a far-from-beautiful chorus of "I'm bored," "He doesn't want to do what I want to do," etc. from our kids. A quick trip to a local retailer helped us to acquire a book for my son (to replace the two we forgot), Legos, and a glow-in-the-dark cornhole game that became staples of camp downtime.

12. Head to town. Camping purists may shudder at this advice, but we actually left nature for a change-of-pace visit to Sheboygan when we camped at Kohler-Andrae. We had lunch at the Duke of Devon, walked the marina, checked out the catch of a group which had recently returned from a fishing trip on Lake Michigan, and simply enjoyed the amenities of this charming lake town for a few hours to give us all a break from the woods. In past years, we've headed to the vast beach at Deland Park in Sheboygan for a taste of city beachgoing and checked out the recovered portion of the *Lottie Cooper,* a schooner that capsized off Sheboygan in 1894.

13. Choose a camping area with a nature center. This is another built-in opportunity for nature education and time-killing on rainy or stifling-hot days.

14. Educate them about wildlife. In most instances, city kids are taught to fear or avoid wild animals. Camping is much different from city life because there are no hard walls to protect you from insects, birds, and mammals. It's important to teach your children that most animals want nothing to do with humans or, if they do, are largely harmless. Of course, bears, wolverines, wolves, and the megafauna that are largely found west of the Mississippi River or in the upper Midwest can be very dangerous.

During our trip, we saw hundreds of daddy-long-leg spiders in our campsite (and sometimes in our tent). They were whimsical and harmless. We also encountered a massive ant colony, beautiful herons, chipmunks, deer, a few bats that flew by our fire late one night, and raccoons that would not take no for an answer when they tried to repeatedly visit our campsite each night as Dave and I sat around late-night campfires. The boys also enjoyed discovering a variety of caterpillars on milkweed and other plants near our campsite. Their excitement at discovering these beautiful creatures is a nice memory now that we're back home.

15. Maintain bedtime and other routines. You don't need to do everything you do at home, but touchstones—reading a book, prayers, discussing favorite moments of the day, etc. before bedtime—will make your child feel comfortable in his or her new surroundings. If your children are still very young, keep them on their nap schedules. My son also took comfort in his morning and evening rituals of brushing his teeth and washing up.

16. Encourage them to make friends. Camping is a very family-friendly activity, and you will most likely end up camping near other families. Encourage your children to meet and play with kids in nearby campsites. This will help them become skilled at meeting new people, allow them to learn about new places (our last campsite neighbors lived in a small town in Wisconsin, which is much different than the life my son lives in a big city), and take a bit of the pressure off you as you make dinner and do other campground tasks. On the last morning of a recent camping trip, a nice lady in the next campsite took my son and her two daughters

Day trip to the harbor at Sheboygan, Wisconsin
© Andrew Morkes

Chopping wood at Pictured Rocks National Lakeshore © Andrew Morkes

on an impromptu nature hike as I rushed to pack up our camp under ominous skies. Her help allowed me to work without interruption, and I literally finished packing the car five minutes before monsoon rains arrived.

17. Let the kids lead. Giving your children autonomy will provide them with a sense of control and a low-risk introduction to life as an adult. You could let them lead the way on hikes, choose the day's activities, make dinner, gather firewood, put up the tent, etc. Camping should be fun, but it can also serve as a good way to build character and encourage an adventurous mindset that will help your children not only when camping, but in life in general.

18. Have a plan in the event of bad weather. Thunderstorms and heavy rains can quickly ruin a camping trip, and they can be very scary for children. Have board games, crafts, and other tabletop activities ready for rainy days. If dangerous weather is forecast, know the campground's protocols for this situation. And, if heavy storms persist, be ready with a backup plan—a night at a hotel in town, heading home a day early, etc. After all, your ultimate goal is to keep your children safe and to create positive camping memories so that they will be excited when you plan your next camping trip.

NIPPERSINK CREEK PROVIDES A GREAT KAYAKING OR CANOEING ADVENTURE JUST AN HOUR FROM CHICAGO

We came, we readied our 10-foot inflatable kayak, we floated placidly at times down the winding creek with the sun shining down on us, we were wowed by the wildlife and wildflowers, we paddled vigorously buffeted by high wind at other times, and we had a lot of fun and faced a few challenges, but ultimately completed a nearly seven-mile canoe trip on Nippersink Creek in Glacial Park (see page 104), McHenry County Conservation District's largest property at 3,439 acres.

With the heavy rains lately, Nippersink Creek was more like a small river than a creek at times when my nine-year-old son and I set out on our kayak trip from Keystone Road Landing on the western edge of Glacial Park to Pioneer Road Landing near its eastern edge.

This was my son's first-ever kayak trip, and my first boat trip in nearly 35 years. I don't count pleasure cruises or sitting on a pontoon boat drinking beer in the middle of a lake as an actual boat trip. If I could summarize our trip in a few words or phrases, they would be:

✔ Fun
✔ Peaceful
✔ Challenging and tiring at times
✔ Wildflowers and birds galore
✔ Wide-open spaces
✔ An adventure
✔ Special
✔ A great father-son experience.

Nippersink Creek, which is the largest tributary to the Fox River, is pretty, tree-lined, and narrow at Keystone Landing. But as we rounded bend after bend the creek widened, its banks grew higher and became crowned with six-foot-tall grasses and what seemed like a junior forest of wildflowers (such as purple coneflowers, sunflowers, and pretty pink Joe Pye Weed), the landscape grew more open, and it felt as if we were in the middle of a vast wilderness rather than only 55 miles from the third-largest city in the United States.

Birdsong accompanied us as we paddled, and occasionally floated, down the creek. We spotted herons, red-winged blackbirds, white egrets, and other birds, as well as the occasional turtle and fish in the water. We didn't see any beavers, river otters, bald eagles, or deer as some paddlers have reported seeing. But that didn't matter. The sky was a cerulean blue, the sun felt warm (but not too warm) on our

My son and I on Nippersink Creek
© Nature in Chicagoland Press LLC

backs, and we enjoyed watching wildlife and the puffy clouds as we drifted along

As we rounded bend after bend, we were wowed by several kames, which loomed over the largely flat terrain like massive brontosauri crouched over the lush landscape having lunch. (The kames at Glacial Park are large hills of sand and gravel that were deposited by glaciers about 10,000 to 12,000 years ago.) After being surrounded by skyscrapers and neighborhoods of bungalows and two-flats in Chicago, the green uncluttered expanse of Glacial Park was a welcome sight.

Our kayak trip was not without challenges. The water was fast at times, and the wind seemed to blow constantly. If you canoe or kayak on Nippersink Creek, take the time to check the water conditions (speed, depth, etc.) before you go. If you don't, the creek may be too shallow for an enjoyable experience or be challenging or unpassable if the water levels are too high. The U.S. Geological Survey provides handy real-time water speed (cubic feet per second, CFS) and depth measurements at its website, https://waterdata.usgs.gov/il/nwis/uv?05548280. According to the McHenry County Conservation District, "at least 100 CFS would allow for an enjoyable ride. When waters are moving above 300 CFS, it is considered fast. When levels are above 750 CFS, or 7 feet, all launches will be CLOSED due to lack of clearance under two bridges. All activities in this area are at the user's own risk."

At 11 a.m. or so when we started our trip, the river measured 510 CFS (and by 6 p.m. the CFS had dropped to 431). I knew that the water would be fast, but we had driven out from Chicago, we had lifejackets, and my son was lobbying hard for us to try out our new kayak. So, we decided to take the plunge. The water was fast in some areas, and meandering in others. The conditions largely depended on the creek's topography, the direction we were traveling, and the wind. I believe the wind created more of a challenge than the water speed. At times, we had to fight from being blown toward the creek bank, but it was not a terrible challenge. Our initial plan was to canoe a few miles from Keystone Landing and then turn around and return, but the high winds and fast-moving water in some areas forced us to change our plans and travel to Pioneer Landing.

I presented the change of plans to my son as an opportunity, rather than a problem. We didn't have a way (yet) to get from Pioneer Landing back to Keystone Landing and there was a lot of paddling remaining, but the creek and its surrounding countryside were beautiful, and we had plenty of food, water, and a cell phone in case we ran into trouble. I was impressed by how my son embraced the additional four or so miles of travel. In the course of several hours on the creek, his paddling skills had grown. Although I did most of the paddling, he asked to help out at times, including keeping the kayak straight when I was taking photos or reviewing the water trail map (https://www.mccdistrict.org/visit__explore/things_to_do/paddle.php). It was nice to know that I could trust my copilot.

The day remained sunny and beautiful, and we were rewarded with a stunning view of a group of oak and hickory trees towering above the grassy savannah, wildflowers, and families of geese and ducks that barely gave us a look as we glided by a few away from them.

By the time we reached Pioneer Landing, we were ready for dry land. We pulled the kayak out of the water and carried it up the embankment. My phone's connection was not working as well as expected (and its battery strength was only 50 or so percent), I asked my cousin to arrange an Uber pickup, which she kindly did. While we waited, we deflated and dried out the kayak, disassembled the oars and seats, tasted some terrible well-water (my son had pitched it to me as tasting "very good!"), had a snack of pretzels and brownie bars on the park bench, and watched other kayakers return from their trips and pack up their cars. Within an hour or so, our Uber arrived, and we headed back to our car 6.5 miles away. I had a great conversation with our driver, who'd left the Logan Square neighborhood in Chicago 30 years ago for the beautiful rolling hills of McHenry County when he got married. He extolled the virtues of Glacial Park and asked if we'd visited the nature center or hiked its vast system of trails. I said we hadn't yet, but we'd definitely return to experience more of this beautiful gem in McHenry County.

FACTS AND TIPS ABOUT BOATING ON NIPPERSINK CREEK.

✔ Paddlers can launch from four locations: Keystone Road Landing (6500 Keystone Road, Richmond), Pioneer Road Landing (7049 Pioneer Road, Richmond), Lyle C. Thomas Memorial Park (7816 Blivin Street, Spring Grove), and Nippersink Canoe Base (400 East US Highway 12, Spring Grove).

✔ The MCDD says that the "estimated travel time along the longest stretch from Keystone Road to Nippersink Canoe Base can be up to four hours, while other stretches are estimated as two-hour paddles. Canoeing is also permitted on the 22-acre Lake Atwood at the Hollows in Cary."

✔ If you use an inflatable kayak such as we did, be sure to bring the air pump and patching material with you on your trip in case you run into troubles. We loved our Intex Explorer K2 Kayak, which I purchased for about $70 on Amazon. It's a good buy for those who'd like to try out kayaking, but don't want to invest hundreds of dollars for a regular kayak. The kayak took about 10 minutes to inflate and deflate and folds up to a manageable storage size. (As I write this, it's sitting folded and bagged up on my bedroom floor, and it's hard to believe this pile of fabric and rubber was our water lifeline for about 4 hours.) We did not move through the water as fluidly as those with plastic kayaks, but our kayak worked fine on this small waterway.

✔ If you don't want to own a kayak or canoe, you can rent them from the following outfitters: Ed's Rental & Sales, McHenry, IL 815/385-3232, www.edsrental.com (canoes and kayaks); Main Street Outfitter, Wauconda, IL 847/526-7433, www.msopub.com (kayaks only); Scull and Oars, Wonder Lake, IL 815/ 814-5155, www.scullandoars.net; Tip-A-Canoe, Burlington, WI, 262/342-1012, www.tipacanoellc.com (canoes and kayaks). I notice that Scull and Oars also has a pickup service, which would have come in handy for us.

✔ Be sure to place your phone, wallet, lunch, etc. in waterproof bags that you secure to your kayak or canoe.

✔ Bring a battery backup for your phone. This would have helped me at the end of the trip, and now my battery travels with me on every hike I take.

✔ My nine-year-old described our trip as "fun, gross (mud), beautiful, longggggg, and exciting."

✔ Print out a map of the Nippersink Creek Trail at www.mccdistrict.org/visit___explore/things_to_do/paddle.php and place it in a plastic bag with cardboard backing, or laminate it, so that you reference it as you paddle. You can also access an interpretive float guide at the aforementioned website.

✔ Don't rush down the creek. Take the time, as we did, to pull off at the occasional sandbar or creek bank to enjoy nature, enjoy a snack, snap some photographs, and splash in the water.

✔ Tell someone where you're going before your trip and set up a check-in time (or times) so that you remain safe on the water.

✔ Be very cognizant of the weather forecast for the day of your trip.

✔ Wear sunscreen and bug repellent, as appropriate.

✔ Always wear a lifejacket. One couple who were fishing on the banks of the creek yelled out kudos to us about wearing our lifejackets. Many boaters we met did not wear them.

✔ Leave no trace. Keep Nippersink Creek beautiful by packing out all of your garbage.

A winter walk at North Park Village Nature Center. © Andrew Morkes

12 TIPS FOR A SUCCESSFUL WINTER HIKE

Winter hiking is the perfect antidote for a Saturday morning marathon of Netflix's *Nailed It* (substitute your streaming show obsession here). That's what I discovered recently as I managed, after several hours of finagling, to pull my eight-year-old son away from the amateur baking competition culinary-astrophe (just kidding; I actually like the show in small servings) to go for a hike in a snowstorm.

Yes, I also felt the pull of a warm comfortable house on a frigid day, but resisted the urge to spend another winter day indoors. So, we headed to North Park Village Nature Center on the northwest side of Chicago (see page 49 for more about this great nature spot). It consists of 46 acres of oak savannah, prairie, ponds, and wetlands. This was Chicago's first substantial snow in months, and it was exciting to be outdoors in the middle of a snowstorm.

When we arrived at North Park, we were pleased to find that its grounds were deserted. We hiked the trail toward the center's big hill. There were a surprising number of birds in the trees, and we heard ducks honking overhead but couldn't spot them in the overcast sky. Snow covered the ground like a comfy blanket, and I thought of the mice, voles, toads, snakes, and other wildlife slumbering underfoot as my son occasionally tossed snowballs at my head. The woods were serene as the snow fell and occasionally blew sideways. We didn't care because we were snugly wrapped in many layers of clothing.

At the top of the hill, we looked down at the boardwalk, which winds its way through beautiful wetlands that, in the summer, are populated by frogs, turtles, water beetles, and other creatures. We were pleased to discover that we were the first to walk the boardwalk and many of the trails that day. When you live in a metropolitan area of nearly 10 million people or so, it's really cool to see no footprints in front of you as you walk.

We walked further and my son became obsessed with finding a big rock or stick to break the ice in the pond next to the wetlands. Kids and sticks, the eternal obsession! He also was fascinated to see orange and red fall leaves that had become frozen beneath the ice. I became obsessed with not falling again on the hilly incline that led down to the frozen water's edge. One sudden fall straight backwards and a slide to the pond's icy edge was enough for me. My son laughing at me was one laugh too many, but I probably looked pretty stupid as I flailed away before falling.

My son encountered his own challenges as we walked. He was bundled up so tightly in his snow pants and layers that when he fell, he couldn't get back up in the deep snow. I was about 25 feet ahead of him, so engrossed in enjoying the snowfall, the bare trees, and novelty of being outside in nature during a snowstorm that he had to yell for me to come back and pick him up. "Dad of the year," that's me.

As we walked, we began to encounter more people who had the same idea as us. Everyone was in a good mood. I had pleasant conversations with several parents and grandparents about the snow and the nature center. A couple who were deep in conversation in a foreign language passed us several times on the circuitous trails. Actually, the man was doing all the talking and, at first, I couldn't decide if he was fascinating or annoying the young woman. My vote: fascinating. More hellos were exchanged as we met other happy winter hikers. It was as if the snow helped us all to shake off our Chicago indifference and desire for anonymity. It was great to see people making memories that would probably stick with them longer than who won *Nailed It*.

My son and I walked further into the woods, and there they were—eight or nine deer just hanging out in the woods by a fallen tree, some resting on the forest floor, others nibbling on grass or bark, and others just kind of zoning out and enjoying the snow. They were preternaturally calm as if hypnotized by the snow.

Seeing the deer was a perfect coda to a hike in a snowstorm, so we headed toward the nature center to warm up. We checked out the tables of animal bones, deer antlers, bird nests, and fossils in the center, then headed toward our car. We were surprised to spot a young buck in the front of the nature center. It was a wonderful surprise ending to our winter hike.

When snow starts falling in Chicagoland, I highly suggest that you get out and enjoy the white winter magic before it's just a fond memory on a sticky-hot, mid-summer day.

Here are some tips to keep in mind when you go winter hiking:

✔ **Don't overdo it on your first winter hike.** Hiking in the snow is much more physically taxing than a summer jaunt through the woods. Remember, if you hike a mile in the snow, you'll have a mile's return (unless you're hiking a circle trail).

✔ **Be prepared.** Whether you plan to hike for 15 minutes or a few hours, pack water, a lightweight emergency blanket, a lighter (to try to start a fire if you get stranded), small flashlight, basic first aid kit, whistle or other signaling device, and a fully-charged phone (and a charger, too). Many outdoor experts also suggest taking a compass and a GPS-enabled device (although you won't need one at a city nature center). Although you may be familiar with your hiking area, everything looks different in the winter. You could become lost, fall and break your leg, or face other challenges. Getting lost is not a problem at North Park, but forest preserves (such as Busse Woods, see page 131), state parks (I suggest Matthiessen (see page 177), Rock Cut (www2.illinois.gov/dnr/Parks/Pages/RockCut.aspx), Apple River Canyon State Park (www2.illinois.gov/dnr/Parks/Pages/AppleRiverCanyon.aspx), and Starved Rock (see page 212) state parks in Illinois, as well as Indiana Dunes State Park (see page 227), national parks such as Indiana Dunes National Park (see page 223), and other hiking destinations are much larger.

✔**Protect your water.** Don't put your water bottle in your backpack because it can freeze (if you're outdoors for a long time). Place it in an interior coat pocket, if possible.

✔ **Keep batteries warm.** Phone, flashlight, and other batteries can drain quickly in the cold and leave you in a tough spot should you need them. As a result, it's a good idea to keep them in a pocket close to your body.

✔ **Dress warmly, but in layers,** because you'll probably break a sweat if you hike for a while (or hike in hilly areas) and may need to take off a few outer layers as you go. Be sure to cover as much exposed skin as possible to avoid windburn and frostbite.

✔ **Watch your footing.** Be careful of what's under the snow: tree branches, rocks, and other objects that might make you trip, depending on the depth of the snow. Additionally, bridges, boardwalks, rocky areas, and other spots can be very slippery in the snow. Avoid walking on icy lakes, ponds, and rivers—unless you're sure that the water is completely frozen.

✔ **Give someone your itinerary.** Always tells someone that you're going hiking, where you are traveling to, and what time you'll be back.

✔ **Bring sunscreen and sunglasses.** This might be surprising to some people, but the ice and snow make perfect reflectors for the sun's rays.

✔ **Try snowshoeing.** Consider spicing up your hike by donning over-the-shoe traction devices or snowshoes. If you need some basic snowshoeing tips, check out my essay, "First-Time Snowshoer Tells All: 10 Tips for Success and My Son's Thank You" on page 290. "

✔ **Have an "Act II" ready for after your hike**—a visit to the indoor part of a nature center (North Park's is small, but interesting), coffee shop, brewpub, or other place that you can warm up and reward yourself from avoiding the potentially terminal medical diagnosis of IStayedInsideAndWatchedNailedItAllDay.

FIRST-TIME SNOWSHOER TELLS ALL: 10 TIPS FOR SUCCESS AND MY SON'S THANK YOU

I'm not a big fan of winter. I am a summer-loving, hike-in-the-woods, hit-the-pool/beach, sit-on-the-deck-and-embrace-the-heat kind of person. Although Chicago winters aren't what they used to be because of global climate change, they can still pack a punch. It's tempting to become a couch potato during Chicago winters. But a few years ago, I decided to embrace the cold. I vowed to participate in more activities—sledding, snowball fights, fort building, and ice skating—that would take me back to my youth. I also vowed to try something new. I decided to surprise my son with snowshoes for our annual trip to Galena, Illinois. The morning after we arrived in this beautiful and historic town where President Ulysses Grant once lived, my son discovered the snowshoes hidden in our hotel room. Pandemonium ensued at the prospect of this unexpected outdoor activity. We headed to the Faerie Circle and the heavily-wooded hills and bluffs behind our hotel, the Irish Cottage Boutique Hotel, which I highly recommend.

Once we had donned our snowshoes, we experimented with walking in the deep snow of the gradually sloping Faerie Circle. As I walked, my feet sunk a few inches into the 10+-inch snow, but it was far better than punching deep holes into the snow with each boot step—and getting stuck in the snow as you tried to walk. I felt much more stable than I did just wearing boots. I didn't quite glide across the snow, but as I gained experience, I began to walk comfortably across the snowy expanse.

My son and I decided to take the hilly trail that led into the forest. It was about 15 degrees, and as we snowshoed, the sun occasionally popped out of the clouds, a fuzzy yellow dot in the ashen sky. My son kept saying, "this is fun, can we climb the next hill?" So, we snowshoed up and down many hills, stopping a few times to adjust our snowshoes and savor the silence that was occasionally broken by birdsong and the howls of coyotes.

My son was a natural. In his shorter snowshoes, he could actually run down the trail. When he became tired, he'd suddenly plop down and make snow angels. I certainly did no running in my 32-inch-long snowshoes, but I began to become more comfortable. Our spirits were high, but, after a while, our first-time snowshoeing legs became tired and the tiny bit of exposed skin on my son's ski-mask-covered face became bright red from the cold, so we headed back to the hotel. And a few hours later, I rewarded myself with a Guinness in the Irish Cottage's beautiful and cozy bar.

The next day, we were at it again, snowshoeing further than we had the previous day. After our hike, we met some of my son's friends and their parents at the Faerie Circle, and the kids tried out the snowshoes. For the next two hours, we parents watched as our kids played with the snowshoes, built snow forts, and had snowball fights.

As parents, we spend our lives trying to make our children happy, but often our kind words and actions aren't acknowledged (they're kids, for heaven's sake). But one night during our trip, my son said to me, "I'm having a wonderful trip thanks to you getting the snowshoes." Words can't convey how this type of a comment makes a parent feel, so I won't try—other than to say that it was just wonderful to hear.

Snowshoeing—especially with my son—was a great experience, and I strongly suggest that you try it if you haven't already. Most forest preserve districts offer free snowshoeing and other winter events, so you don't need to purchase snowshoes. But, if you choose to, adult snowshoes can be bought for as little as $60 to $70, and children's versions for around $40. Used snowshoes are less expensive.

Snowshoeing in the hills of Galena, Illinois.
© Andrew Morkes

While I am by no means an expert, here are some tips to keep in mind before you go snowshoeing:

✔ Spend some time finding the right size snowshoe for your weight. I used the Sierra Trading Post's helpful guide (www.sierra.com/lp2/snowshoe-guide).

✔ Try putting the snowshoes on before you get out in the snow. This will allow you to discover how to use your model's specific locking/strapping system. I did this in our hotel room, but should have spent more time locking down the perfect fit because it was very hard to adjust the snowshoes in the cold and snow with half-frozen hands. Getting the fit right before you hit the trail is extremely

> **SNOW PRAYER**
>
> I know there's a prayer for lost causes, but is there a snow dance, mantra, or prayer that snow-lovers can say to bring snow? Someone has probably written one, but here's mine.
>
> *Dear snow gods,*
>
> *Bring us a whopper of a snowstorm. A school-cancelling, work-cancelling monster of a snowstorm that brings Chicagoland to a grinding halt. That softens the noise of this metropolis. That covers tired-looking winter lawns, bushes, cars, and roofs with a thick blanket of soft wintry white. That bends snow shovels; that causes the local broadcasters to break into their annual "if you don't have to go outside, don't" speech; that takes snow lovers to a winter nirvana. That stops time long enough for us to catch our breath in this crazy modern world. That makes it right for the snowshoers, snow fort builders, snow angel makers, snowman makers, ice skaters, snowball throwers, and other lovers of winter. Send the snow. Send the snow. Send the snow.*

important. I initially thought my snowshoes were tight enough, but quickly realized they weren't as snug as I thought. When the snowshoes are on tight (but not too tight, or you'll lose circulation), you'll feel like they are an extension of your feet.

✔ Don't overdo it on your first foray on snowshoes. Try them out on a flat, snowy surface before venturing into more challenging terrain. Remember, if you travel a mile on snowshoes, you'll have a mile's return (unless you're on a circle trail).

✔ Whether you plan to snowshoe for a few minutes or a few hours, pack water, a lightweight emergency blanket, a lighter (to try to start a fire if you get stranded), and a fully-charged phone (and a charger, too). Many outdoor experts also suggest taking a compass and a GPS-enabled device. Although you may be familiar with your snowshoeing area, everything looks different in the winter. You could become lost, fall and break your leg, or face other challenges.

✔ Dress warmly, but in layers, because you'll probably break a sweat as you snowshoe and may need to take off a few outer layers as you go.

✔ Be careful when backing-up. It's very hard to do in snowshoes—especially for adults. If you need to back up, it's better to circle around to change direction.

✔ Be careful of what's under the snow: tree branches, rocks, and other objects that might make you trip, depending on the depth of the snow.

✔ Avoid walking on icy lakes, ponds, and rivers—unless you are sure that the water is completely frozen.

✔ Always tells someone that you're going snowshoeing, where you are traveling to, and what time you'll be back.

ON THE JOYS OF CARRYING MY SON

The author and his son in Grand Marais, MI.
© Amy McKenna

My first view of my son was in the delivery room on the day he was born. I looked down at my wife lying on the hospital bed, and I saw the top of my son's head and a shock of his hair in the "delivery zone." Would he ever come out, I wondered? My wife pushed and pushed, and deep-breathed and deep-breathed, but nothing.

And then he came out—hurtling into the air like a crazy amniotic-fluid-covered football. I saw the look of surprise on the Dr.'s face and then her Super-Bowl-wide-receiver-quality hands juggling this squishy football for a moment until securing him firmly in her hands. Our doctor did not spike our baby or do a touchdown dance, thank God.

Within minutes, I was holding my little premature baby boy for what was the first of countless times. A 40-year-old man holding a baby he thought he'd never have. I held him for what seemed like forever, but it was probably only minutes.

When our son came home from the neonatal intensive care unit, he was as small as a little loaf of supermarket bread. And I walked the house, loaf of baby bread in my arm, with my other arm free to empty dishwashers, type at the computer, and eat dinner.

I must admit, it made me so proud to head into family parties, events with friends, and other activities with my baby son either nestled in the crook of my arm or up against my shoulder.

One year after my son was born, we traveled to the Upper Peninsula of Michigan (see the Michigan section of this book for some trip suggestions) with our young guy, so eager to share one of our favorite places—and get some time on the trails. We spent $250 on a child hiking backpack and although we only used it four or so times, it was worth every dollar because we were as free as we were before our son was born. We hiked miles through the woods to Au Sable Point in Pictured Rocks National Lakeshore (add this beautiful place to your bucket list; see page 250), up hilly trails so steep that my wife had to hover behind myself and my son nestled snugly in his backpack in case we started to fall; along the beach, steps from the crashing waves of Lake Superior; and anywhere else our steps took us. (My wife carried him, too.) My son loved riding in the backpack. He liked sticking his fingers in my ears, pulling and letting go of the backpack mirror on a retractable string, and kicking me as we walked. But I didn't care. We were free, and we were showing our favorite places to our son. I wanted him to fall in love with Lake Superior and all the inland lakes, the hardwood forests of maple, beech, and conifer; and the rock-strewn beaches of the Upper Peninsula as I had.

As my son grew older, I could still carry him with one arm for quite a while, but then I had to start battling curious arms, kicking legs, and throbbing muscles, but it was all fun. I loved walking the neighborhood with my boy slung over my shoulder or in the crook of my arm. He was mine—at least for a while, and I was going to enjoy every minute of my time with him.

Eventually, I needed two arms to pick up and manage this fast-growing little beastie. And this former loaf of bread became an uber-talkative 35-pound turkey. Yet, I still carried him all over when he got tired. There is something quite wonderful about being able to take your son with you on your adventures. Since I did not have the privilege to birth him, this is actually the closest I will ever get to carrying him like my wife did—even if it's just for 10 minutes at a time.

I would carry my son up the stairs when he was tired, the last three or four blocks during a long walk home, or any other time he grew tired. Sometimes, he'd ask me to run, and we'd barrel down the street with him holding tightly, my knees starting to ache, but my spirits high.

My son is now seven years old, 58 pounds, and almost as tall as my shoulder (I'm only 5'7), yet I still pick him up and carry him on occasion, but as I get older and creakier and he gets bigger, I carry him only briefly for play or if he's really, really tired. He asks me to pick him up and spin him, so I spin him around (and fight vertigo). I pick him up and carry him because I miss my loaf of bread and turkey.

This summer, I carried my son up a steep trail in the rolling hills above the Mississippi River at Effigy Mounds National Monument (see page 103) in Iowa. He did not want to hike one more step, but I did, so up we hiked together, my heart pounding, sweat dripping down my back. As I carried him, I felt like this might be the last time I ever did so for such a long and challenging distance (perhaps half a mile). He's now so big that I can only carry him in a certain spot slung over my shoulder (75 percent of his body hanging over my right shoulder) without discomfort for both of us, but I did it (fear of heart attack on a humid summer day notwithstanding). We will probably never be this physically close again as my little boy grows so big that he can't be carried, so big that dad and mom embarrass him, so big as he heads away from us to his first solo hikes, to his first date, to college, to his first job, to his wedding day, and so on.

And one day, this once little boy may carry his elderly dad from bed to chair and back again. But we're not there yet, and I much prefer to be the one carrying than the one being carried. So, I'll keep it up till I can't.

JOURNALS, NEWSLETTERS & BOOKS

JOURNALS & NEWSLETTERS

Journals and newsletters are available from forest preserve districts, state departments of natural resources, and other organizations). Some are free, while others are available at a low cost.

The Citizen! Newsletter (weekly, Forest Preserve District of Will County) www.reconnectwithnature.org/Citizen-Newsletter

Compass **newsletter** (bimonthly, Chicago Audubon Society) www.chicagoaudubon.org/publications-research

Conservationist (quarterly, Forest Preserve District of DuPage County) www.dupageforest.org/news/conservationist

Driftless Area Magazine (monthly, https://driftlessareamag.com)

Forest Way **newsletter** (monthly, Forest Preserve District of Cook County) https://fpdcc.com/about/forest-way-monthly-newsletter

Horizons (quarterly, Lake County Forest Preserves, www.lcfpd.org/news)

Landscapes (quarterly, McHenry County Conservation District) www.mccdistrict.org/about_us/news/landscapes_magazine.php

Nature's Notebook **newsletter** (quarterly, Forest Preserves of Winnebago County) https://winnebagoforest.org/natures-notebook

Outdoor Illinois Journal (monthly, Illinois Department of Natural Resources) https://outdoor.wildlifeillinois.org

Outdoor Indiana (bimonthly, Indiana Department of Natural Resources) https://www.in.gov/dnr/10545.htm

TreeLine **newsletter** (quarterly, Forest Preserve District of Kane County) https://kaneforest.com/the-treeline-newsletter

Wisconsin Natural Resources (quarterly, Wisconsin Department of Natural Resources): www.wnrmag.com

Woods of Wisdom **newsletter** (bi-monthly, Kankakee River Valley Forest Preserve District): www.krvfpd.org/about_us

BOOKS

The Art of Migration: Birds, Insects, and the Changing Seasons in Chicagoland, by Peggy Macnamara, John W. Fitzpatrick, et al.

Chasing Dragonflies: A Natural, Cultural, and Personal History, by Cindy Crosby

The Chicago River: A Natural and Unnatural History, by Libby Hill

Chicago Transit Hikes: A Guide to Getting Out in Nature Without a Car, by Lindsay Welbers

The Driftless Land: Spirit of Place in the Upper Mississippi Valley, by Kevin Koch

Force of Nature: George Fell, Founder of the Natural Areas Movement, by Arthur Melville Pearson

The Great Lakes: The Natural History of a Changing Region, by Wayne Grady

Illinois Wildlife Encyclopedia: An Illustrated Guide to Birds, Fish, Mammals, Reptiles, and Amphibians, by Scott Shupe

Kaufman Field Guide to Nature of the Midwest, by Kenn Kaufman, Kimberly Kaufman, et al.

My Journey Into the Wilds of Chicago: A Celebration of Chicagoland's Startling Natural Wonders, by Mike MacDonald

The Natural Heritage of Illinois: Essays on Its Lands, Waters, Flora, and Fauna, by John E. Schwegman

A Natural History of the Chicago Region, by Joel Greenberg

Peterson Field Guide to Animal Tracks, by Olaus J. Murie and Mark Elbroch

Of Prairie, Woods, and Water: Two Centuries of Chicago Nature Writing, edited by Joel Greenberg

Prairie Plants of Illinois: A Field Guide to the Wildflowers and Prairie Grasses of Illinois and the Midwest, by Steve W. Chadde

Tallgrass Conversations: In Search of the Prairie Spirit, by Cindy Crosby

The Tallgrass Prairie: An Introduction, by Cindy Crosby

Wading Right In: Discovering the Nature of Wetlands, by Catherine Owen Koning and Sharon M. Ashworth

Walking Chicago: 35 Tours of the Windy City's Dynamic Neighborhoods and Famous Lakeshore, by Robert Loerzel

Wildflowers of the Midwest: A Field Guide to Over 600 Wildflowers in the Region, by Don Kurz

NATURE ORGANIZATIONS, AGENCIES, AND PUBLIC TRANSPORTATION RESOURCES IN CHICAGOLAND

FOREST PRESERVE/CONSERVATION DISTRICTS IN THE CHICAGOLAND AREA

Boone County Conservation District: www.bccdil.org
Chicago Park District: www.chicagoparkdistrict.com
DeKalb County Forest Preserve District:
 https://dekalbcounty.org/departments/forest-preserve
Forest Preserve District of DuPage County: www.dupageforest.org
Forest Preserve District of Kane County: https://kaneforest.com
Forest Preserve District of Will County: www.reconnectwithnature.org
Forest Preserves of Cook County: https://fpdcc.com/about
Forest Preserves of Winnebago County: https://winnebagoforest.org
Kankakee River Valley Forest Preserve District: www.krvfpd.org
Illinois State Geological Survey: https://isgs.illinois.edu
Jo Daviess Conservation foundation: https://jdcf.org
Kendall County Forest Preserve District:
 www.co.kendall.il.us/departments/forest-preserve-district
Lake County Forest Preserves: www.lcfpd.org
McHenry County Conservation District: www.mccdistrict.org

STATE DEPARTMENTS OF NATURAL RESOURCES AND RELATED ORGANIZATIONS

Illinois Department of Natural Resources: www2.illinois.gov/dnr
Illinois Nature Preserves Commission: www2.illinois.gov/dnr/INPC
Indiana Department of Natural Resources: www.in.gov/dnr
Iowa Department of Natural Resources: www.iowadnr.gov
Michigan Department of Natural Resources: www.michigan.gov/dnr
Wisconsin Department of Natural Resources: https://dnr.wisconsin.gov

FEDERAL AGENCIES

National Park Service: www.nps.gov/findapark
Natural Resources Conservation Service: www.nrcs.usda.gov
U.S. Environmental Protection Agency: www.epa.gov
U.S. Fish and Wildlife Service: www.fws.gov
U.S. Forest Service: www.fs.usda.gov

NATIONAL CONSERVATION ORGANIZATIONS

Friends of the Earth: https://foe.org
Latino Outdoors: https://latinooutdoors.org
National Audubon Society: www.audubon.org
The Nature Conservancy: www.nature.org
Outdoor Afro: https://outdoorafro.com
Rails-to-Trails Conservancy: www.railstotrails.org
Sierra Club: www.sierraclub.org
Student Conservation Association: www.thesca.org
Trust for Public Land: www.tpl.org

LOCAL AND REGIONAL ENVIRONMENTAL ORGANIZATIONS AND HIKING/OUTDOOR CLUBS

Active Transportation Alliance: https://activetrans.org
Alliance for the Great Lakes: www.greatlakes.org
Audubon Great Lakes: https://gl.audubon.org
Center for Humans & Nature: www.humansandnature.org
Chicago Audubon Society: www.chicagoaudubon.org
Chicago Herpetological Society: https://chicagoherp.org
Chicago Ornithological Society: www.chicagobirder.org
Chicago Wilderness: www.chicagowilderness.org
Chicagoland Environmental Network: www.chicagoenvironment.org
Environmentalists of Color: www.eocnetwork.org
Forest Trails Hiking Club: www.foresttrailshc.com
Friends of the Chicago River: www.chicagoriver.org
Friends of the Forest Preserves: www.fotfp.org
Friends of the Parks: www.fotp.org
Great Rivers Chicago: http://greatriverschicago.com
Ice Age Trail Alliance: www.iceagetrail.org
Illinois Paddling Council: www.illinoispaddling.info
Openlands: www.openlands.org
Outdoor Afro: https://outdoorafro.com
Save the Dunes: https://savedunes.org
Sierra Club-Chicago Group: www.sierraclub.org/illinois/Chicago
Sierra Club-Illinois Chapter: www.sierraclub.org/Illinois
Thorn Creek Audubon Society: www.thorncreekaudubonsociety.org

PUBLIC TRANSPORTATION IN CHICAGOLAND

Amtrak (train): www.amtrak.com
Chicago Transit Authority (bus, train): www.transitchicago.com
Metra (train): https://metrarail.com
Northern Indiana Commuter Transportation District (train): www.mysouthshoreline.com
PACE (bus): www.pacebus.com

INDEX

A

A. Philip Randolph Pullman Porter Museum, 39
Adler Planetarium, 44
African American history, 32, 39, 96, 208
American bald eagle viewing, 38, 77, 78, 89, 98, 102, 148, 163, 170, 182, 201, 208, 245, 249, 254, 257, 263, 271, 283
Apple River Canyon State Park, 102
Apple River Fort State Historic Site, 101
Argonne National Laboratory, 222
Asian carp, 203

B

bald eagle (*see American bald eagle*)
Belmont Prairie, 81-84
Berrien County Parks Commission, 243
Beverly Hills/Morgan Park, 32
    Barney Callaghan's Pub, 33
    Beverly Arts Center, 33
    Beverly Bakery & Café, 33
    Bookie's New and Used Books, 33
    Calabria Imports, 33
    Dan Ryan Woods, 30-33
    Givins Castle, 32
    Heritage Gallery, 33
    Horse Thief Hollow Brewing, 33
    Irish Castle, 32
    Open Outcry Brewing Company, 33
    Original Rainbow Cone, 33
    Ridge Historical Society, 33
    Wild Blossom Meadery and Winery, 33
Big Marsh Park, 21-23
Bill Jarvis Migratory Bird Sanctuary, 43
bison viewing, 125, 144, 187, 191, 237
black bear viewing, 250, 255, 258, 263
Black Parttridge Woods, 141-143
Blue Island Ridge, 30
Bluebell Festival, 184
Bong, Richard, 274
Bong State Recreation Area, 273-274
Buehler Preserve, 98
Buffalo Rock State Park, 144-146
Burnham Prairie Nature Preserve, 147-148
Busse Woods, 131-132

C

camping with kids, 278
Cap Sauers Holding Nature Preserve, 149-155, 275
Casper Bluff Land & Water Reserve, 98
Centennial Trail/Veterans Memorial Trail, 162
cherry blossoms, 34
Chicago Academy of Sciences, 56
Chicago Architecture Center, 28
Chicago Botanic Garden, 66-69
Chicago destinations, 21-64
Chicago Great Western Railway Depot Museum, 101
Chicago Park District, 21, 34, 37, 41, 46, 49, 52, 63
Chicago River, 24
Chicago Riverwalk, 24-29
    Architecture, 27, 28
    Public art, 28
Chicagoland North destinations, 65-80
Chicagoland Northwest, West, and Beyond destinations, 81-140
Chicagoland South and Beyond destinations, 141-222
Civilian Conservation Corps, 31, 109, 216, 218, 220
Clean Water Act of 1972, 25

Coral Woods Conservation Area, 85-86
Cowles, Henry, 225, 226
Crabtree Nature Center, 87-89
Cranberry Slough Nature Preserve, 156-157

D

Dan Ryan Woods, 30-33
Des Plaines River Trail, 72, 80
Des Plaines River, 71, 72, 77, 108, 142, 143, 161, 163, 164, 181, 182, 202, 203, 220, 221
Dick Young Forest Preserve, 90-93
digital adventure games, 159
Driftless Area (see Driftless Region)
Driftless Region, 97, 115, 295, 296
Dubuque (Iowa), 102
Durant House Museum, 112

E

Eastland Disaster, 26
Edward L. Ryerson Conservation Area, 70-72
Effigy Mounds National Monument, 103, 294
Effigy mounds, 103, 144
Effigy tumuli, 144
Efroymson Restoration, 237
Elizabeth (Illinois), 101
Elizabeth's Grand Antique Company, 101
elk viewing, 131

F

Farnsworth House, 211
Field Museum, 44
Ford Calumet Environmental Center, 23
Forest Preserve District of DuPage County, 94, 220
Forest Preserve District of Kane County, 90, 109, 112, 135,

Forest Preserve District of Will County, 161, 164, 171, 181, 183, 195, 201
Forest Preserves of Cook County, 30, 58, 61, 66, 77, 86, 107, 131, 142, 147, 149, 156, 175, 192, 197, 204, 206, 218
Forge: Lemont Quarries, 158-160
Fox River Trail, 117, 136
Fox River, 135, 136
Frederick's Grove, 181
Fullersburg Woods Forest Preserve, 94-96
Fullersburg Woods Nature Education Center, 94-96

G

Galena (Illinois), 97-103
Galena Gateway Park, 98
Galena River Trail, 98
Galien River County Park, 242-243, 266
Garden of the Phoenix, 34-36
Glacial Park, 104-106
Grand Marais (Michigan), 253
Grand Mere State Park, 244-245, 266
Graue Mill and Museum, 96
Great Lakes Phragmites Collaborative, 21
Great Western Trail, 113
Green Bay Trail, 64

H

Hal Tyrrell Trailside Museum of Natural History, 107-108
Hanover Bluff Nature Preserve, 102
Heron Rookery Nature Preserve, 170
Horseshoe Mound, 99

I

Ice Age National Scenic Trail, 269
Illinois and Michigan Canal, 162, 181, 198
Illinois Beach State Park, 73-74

Index 301

Illinois Department of Natural Resources, 73, 115, 138, 144, 177, 210, 212
Illinois Nature Preserves, 75, 114, 147
Illinois River, 144, 146, 177, 212, 214, 215, 216
Indian Ridge Marsh Park, 37-40
Indiana Department of Natural Resources, 227, 231
Indiana Destinations, 223-241
Indiana Dunes National Park, 223-226
Indiana Dunes State Park, 227-230
invasive species, 45, 62, 75, 152, 203
Iowa
    Backbone State Park, 103
    Broken Kettle Grasslands Preserve, 191
    Crystal Lake Cave, 103
    Dubuque Museum of Art, 103
    Dubuque, 102
    E.B. Lyons Interpretive and Nature Center, 103
    Effigy Mounds National Monument, 103
    Maquoketa Caves State Park, 103
    Mines of Spain Recreation Area, 103
    National Mississippi River Museum and Aquarium, 102
Isle a la Cache Preserve and Museum, 161-163
Isle Royale National Park, 246-249, 275

J

Jackson Park, 34
Jasper-Pulaski Fish and Wildlife Area, 231-236
Jo Daviess Conservation Foundation, 98
Johnson's Mound Forest Preserve, 109-111

K

Kankakee Sands, 237-241
Keepataw Preserve, 164-166

Keweenaw Peninsula, 249
Kerry Sheridan Grove, 181
Kettle Moraine Scenic Drive, 269
Kettle Moraine State Forest, 267-269
Kohler-Andrae State Park, 270-272

L

Lake Calumet, 21
Lake County Forest Preserves, 70
Lake Defiance, 117
Lake Katherine Nature Center and Botanic Gardens, 167-169
Lake Michigan, 41-45, 46, 56, 73, 75, 223, 227, 244, 259, 265, 270
Lake Renwick Preserve, 170-174
Lake Superior, 246, 250, 256, 262
laser tag, 159
Leatherleaf Bog, 117
Lemont (Illinois), 43, 158
Leroy Oakes Forest Preserve, 112-114
lighthouses, 41, 252, 260
Lincoln Park Conservatory, 43
Lincoln Park Zoo, 43
Little Red Schoolhouse Nature Center, 175-176

M

Maggie Daley Park, 45
Major Taylor Trail, 31, 32
Manhattan Project, 197
Matthiessen State Park, 177-180
McCormack Bridgehouse and Chicago River Museum, 28
McCormick Place Bird Sanctuary, 44
McHenry County Conservation District, 85, 104, 117, 133,
McKinley Woods, 181-182
Messenger Woods Nature Preserve, 183-186

302   Nature in Chicagoland

Metropolitan Water Reclamation District of Greater Chicago, 25
Michigan Department of Natural Resources, 244, 263, 265
Michigan Destinations, 242-266
Midewin National Tallgrass Prairie, 187-191
Millennium Park, 45
Mississippi Flyway, 38, 232
Mississippi Palisades State Park, 102, 115-116
Mitchell Museum of the American Indian, 163
Montrose Beach Dunes Natural Area, 46
Montrose Beach, 43, 46
Montrose Birding Blog, 47
Montrose Point Bird Sanctuary, 46-48
moose viewing, 246, 248, 250, 254, 258, 263
Moraine Hills State Park, 117-119
Morgan Park (*see Beverly Hills*)
Morton Arboretum, 120-124
Munising (Michigan), 253

N

Nachusa Grasslands, 125-130
National Mississippi River Museum and Aquarium, 102
National Park Service, 103, 223, 246, 250, 259
National Trust for Historic Preservation, 211
nature books, 295
Nature Conservancy, 125, 237
nature journals, 295
nature newsletters, 295
nature Organizations and agencies, 297
Ned Brown Preserve, 131-132
Nelson Lake Marsh Preserve, 92

Nippersink Creek Canoe Trail, 286
Nippersink Creek, 104, 283
North Branch Trail System, 62, 64
North Country Trail, 263
North Manitou Island, 260
North Park Village Nature Center, 49-50, 275, 287
Northerly Island, 44

O

Ogle County Nachusa Bison/John Deere Loop Bike Trail, 129
Openlands Lakeshore Preserve, 75
Openlands, 75-76, 192
Original Rainbow Cone, 33
Orland Grassland, 192-194
Outerbelt Trail, 51

P

Palmisano Park, 52-55
Palos Trail System, 176
Peggy Notebaert Nature Museum, 43, 56-57
Pictured Rocks National Lakeshore, 250-255, 275, 293
Ping Tom Memorial Park, 26, 27, 53
Pioneer Sholes School, 112
piping plover viewing, 47, 48, 258
Pleasant Valley Conservation Area, 133-134
Plush Horse, 169
Powderhorn Prairie, Marsh, and Lake, 58-60
Promontory Point, 44
public art, 28, 63, 76, 144
public transportation resources, 296, 297
Pullman National Monument, 39

Q

quaking bog, 138

R

Raccoon Grove Nature Preserve, 195-196
Rall Woods State Natural Area, 102
Red Gate Woods, 197-200
Resurrection Mary, 200
Richard Bong State Recreation Area, 273-274
River Trail Nature Center, 77-80
Rock Run Rookery Preserve, 201-203
Ryerson Woods, 70-72

S

S.S. *Eastland*, 26
Sagawau Environmental Learning Center, 204-205
Sand Ridge Nature Center, 206-209
Schurmeier Teaching Forest, 100
Seney National Wildlife Refuge, 256-258
Sheboygan (Wisconsin), 271, 280
Shedd Aquarium, 44
shipwrecks, 17, 227, 228, 249, 250, 253, 263, 272
Silver Springs State Fish & Wildlife Area, 210-211
Skokie Valley Bikeway, 64
sledding, 30, 45, 55, 110, 119, 211, 218, 219
Sleeping Bear Dunes National Lakeshore, 259-261
snow prayer, 292
snowshoeing advice, 290
Soldier Field Sledding Hill, 45
South Manitou Island, 260
South Shore Natural Area, 44
St. James at Sag Bridge, 198
Starved Rock State Park, 212-217
Strangmoor Bog Natural Landmark, 257
Swallow Cliff Woods, 218-219

T

Tahquamenon Falls State Park, 262-264
Tapley Woods Conservation Area, 102
Tekakwitha Woods Forest Preserve, 135-137
Thaddeus S. "Ted" Lechowicz Woods, 61-62
This Week in Birding (blog), 47
Trailside Museum of Natural History, 107

U

U.S. Fish & Wildlife Service, 257
Underground Railroad, 96
Upper Peninsula (Michigan), 250, 256, 262, 293
USDA Forest Service, 187

V

Valley of Eden Bird Sanctuary, 100
Vietnam Veteran's Memorial Plaza, 28
Visitation Prairie, 149
Volo Auto Museum, 140
Volo Bog State Natural Area, 138-140

W

Wapello Land & Water Reserve, 100
Warren Dunes State Park, 265-266
Waterfall Glen Forest Preserve, 220-222
waterfalls, 34, 52, 77, 97, 167, 169, 177, 212, 214, 215, 220, 250, 253, 258, 262
West Ridge Nature Preserve, 63-64
Wisconsin Department of Natural Resources, 268, 270, 273
Wisconsin destinations, 267-274
Witkowsky State Wildlife Area, 101
wolf viewing, 246, 263
Wonderland Express (train exhibit), 67
World's Columbian Exposition, 34

Z

ziplining, 158

ACKNOWLEDGMENTS

I want to thank all of the nature center, forest preserve, and state and national park staff and volunteers who work so hard to allow people to enjoy nature spots throughout Chicagoland and beyond. Their hard work and dedication help to improve and protect these special places. They are often underappreciated and underpaid. I would also like to thank the staff at these places who have provided me with information and answered my questions about birds, hiking trails, and other features. This information was extremely useful as I wrote the book.

The beautiful cover of *Nature in Chicagoland* and the book's detailed maps were created by Ted Glasoe, an old friend who is a talented graphic designer and nature photographer. Visit www.tedglasoe.com to learn how you can purchase his beautiful prints of Lake Michigan and other destinations in Chicagoland, order a copy of his annual Lake Michigan calendar, and read his *Lake Lover* blog. I also want to thank his wife, Maureen Glasoe (www.virgowords.com)—a good friend and a skilled writer and editor—who provided very helpful "big picture" advice during the planning process for the book. Thanks to both of you for your expertise, patience, and friendship.

Kudos are sent to Mika Jin (the owner of Midnight Oil Editing, www.midnightoilediting.com) for her help proofreading some of the articles in this book. You can be certain that any errors that you find in the book are mine, and not hers. Mika, thank you for all of your hard work on a tight deadline!

I want to thank my wife Amy for her patience (as she "held down the fort" at home as I was gone sometimes 12 hours at a time to conduct research for this book), for her company on some of these hikes, and for her love and support for more than 20 years. Finally, I want to thank my son for joining me on many of my nature excursions. It has been the joy of a lifetime to be a father, as well as to teach my son to love, appreciate, and protect the natural world. I hope that he someday passes on these lessons to his children and grandchildren.

Photo Credits Cover:

Front: All Copyright Andrew Morkes, except for top far left (bison), U.S. Fish & Wildlife Service; top far right (kids with toad), Andrew Morkes & Fode Family; and bottom center (family hiking), Shutterstock

Back: All Copyright Andrew Morkes, except for top far left (family hiking), Shutterstock; top far right (kids exploring), Andrew Morkes & Fode Family; and bottom center (kids at campground), Andrew Morkes & Fode Family